CAPITAL AS MONEY

Brian McGrath
L. Dwayne Barney

You see things, and you say; "Why?" But I dream things that never were, and I say; "Why not?"

George Bernard Shaw

This book and its ideas grew out of discussion amongst the authors, beginning on a trip into Idaho's mountains during October 2008 and continuing since then. The authors, both economists, have been faculty members at various universities and one of them has been a partner in an investment management firm and an institutional bond manager for a number of years. Obviously, the opinions and viewpoints expressed in this book are their own and do not necessarily reflect and are not necessarily supported by any of the employers, clients, or institutions the authors are or have been associated with. Helpful comments and suggestions in support and development of this manuscript were obtained from Christopher McGrath, Tristan McGrath, Neill McGrath, Cody Barney, Andy Wood, Jim Tidwell, Susan McGrath, Sue Ellis, Molly Haberl, and Eamonn Harter among others.

Insight and assistance from Colin McGrath, in particular, has been invaluable and deserves special mention. Without his advice, support, and effort, this book would not have been published. The authors, of course, are solely responsible for any errors and omissions.

Table of Contents

INTRODUCTION

As you may have guessed from the title of this book, we have a dream. Our vision is of a new, simpler, and more logical system of trade and valuation; a new "money" to replace the sorry and convoluted anachronism of a central-bank-controlled fiat currency. The destabilizing combination of fiat money and fractional-reserve banking has nearly destroyed the U.S. economy at least twice during the past 100 years, and has led to economic volatility and cycles in inflation many other times. Europe too is struggling with the volatility and uncertainty created by fiat currency. Bank runs happen over and over again, causing dramatic fluctuations in the money supply and sharp economic downturns. Given fiat money's pathetic track record, we believe the time for a change is now.

We hasten to assure the anxious reader that the idea offered here is not yet another re-heated, tired polemic advocating a return to commodity-based money such as the gold standard. If we have an unapologetic bias it is tilted toward an appreciation of and a faith in private property, unfettered markets, and individual freedom. Ultimately, we believe free people trading in the market, and not the government, should decide what is best for "money."

For some of you the path followed by this book in suggesting a new kind of money may seem a peculiar one. The book describes serious macroeconomic issues through a fictional story focused on the inhabitants of a rapidly-evolving island. An island economy is used in our descriptions in order to concentrate on the key characteristics of money that are present in any society. Also, using a fictional story allows us to condense hundreds of years of real-world history into a few short generations. Our ultimate goal is to sketch the historical evolution of a system of money and banking in a way that is clear and, hopefully, even mildly entertaining. If the book takes you on a journey that is enjoyable, and you end up

1

understanding more about the economy that surrounds you, then we will have succeeded in our objective.

Monetarist economists spend a great deal of time justifying the existence of a monetary or transactions good, which is "money," by explaining how money evolves in a trading economy. The motivation for money begins with the universal need to simplify and make manageable what would otherwise be complex barter exchanges. An agreed upon unit of exchange allows individuals to acquire their desired consumption bundles by breaking up complex trades into simple, single exchanges. Once a monetary good is universally accepted, individuals can specialize and produce a single good or service. They can then trade the good or service they produced for money, which in turn can be used to purchase the diverse multitude of things they choose to consume.

Money should embody certain characteristics: it must be easy for traders to recognize and readily acceptable by all to accomplish transactions, it must be a stable store of value over time, and it must be customarily used as the good in which the trading values of other goods and services are typically measured. In its role as the benchmark unit in which all other goods and services are priced, money is called the "numeraire."

Money is defined by what it does and not by what it is. For the U.S. economy the obvious unit of money is a dollar, whether it is in our hands, in cyberspace, or in our bank account. In simplifying exchange and generating efficiencies relative to barter, money contributes to the production of real goods and services in the economy. In a market economy, monetary exchange naturally arises because it makes the economy more efficient and productive. When compared to barter, money saves time and energy in production and trade.

When describing money, economists' sophistry continues to the point of discussing the evolution of the monetary good from commodity-based monies such as gold and silver to "fiat" monies. The term "fiat" money refers to money produced by the central bank or the printing presses of government that is backed by nothing at all, other than a habitual acceptance by traders to use it in exchange. People hold and use money based upon a faith in reasonably responsible supply behavior on behalf of the governments who print it. This is where economists' explanations get strange and mystical, and those listening are justified in growing increasingly uncomfortable. In the case of fiat money (e.g., federal reserve notes in the United States), monetarists sagely explain that the fiat money will function well as an exchange good and unit of value (unless the government or central bank is tempted to print too much of it). Monetarists point out that, in theory, an intelligently and prudently managed fiat money is, in fact, superior to commodity money. After all, the supply of a fiat currency can be rationally adjusted to match the growth rate of the real economy—thereby resulting in the nirvana of approximate average price stability.

Although we are self-proclaimed monetarists, when it comes to the optimality of fiat currency we must make a confession, a deep and lingering doubt must be revealed: we really don't buy it. Throughout history governments have repeatedly demonstrated the urge to print too much money. The result is accelerating inflation, which is referred to as a "tax" because it represents the declining value of the units of currency individuals hold. When money can be freely printed, real wealth is transferred from those who hold money to those who are able to print it. If the inflation tax imposed on holders of money (dollars) clearly exceeds money's value in facilitating exchange and production, then, at that point, the opportunity cost of holding money balances becomes intolerable. The fiat currency will burn out, and money will evolve to some other good embodying a more stable store of value.

When it comes to fiat currency, we share the same instinctive discomfort as our readers. We have seen too much history and too much abuse and confusion in the control of the supply of money. In the evolution of the money and credit system of the United States, and that of other countries, there are simply too many moving parts, too much accidental history rather than optimal

3

design, and too many anachronisms that live on into the present based upon tradition and embedded institutions rather than logic. Too many damaging, unintended consequences have resulted from our system of money, credit and banking. At its worst, the intelligent evolution of our monetary system has been brought to a halt by institutional regulation and rigidity—resulting in an unnatural monopoly that imposes an inferior and unstable money, banking, and credit system upon all of us perpetually. To complicate matters, the supply of money in our system is not just due to the central bank printing or lending fiat money, but also due to bankers lending out a large portion (a legal limit of 90 percent) of demand deposits (checking accounts) at their institutions. Banks make loans, sometimes poorly-underwritten, for the purpose of generating profits for their banks and not necessarily for any benefit to their depositors. Since it is up to commercial banks to determine how much money to loan out, the Federal Reserve is not able to control the money supply with any degree of precision. The Federal Reserve is able to control the monetary base, but the linkage between the monetary base and the total money supply is a loose one. At times overzealous bankers go on a lending frenzy, and the Federal Reserve is forced to bail out the banks that have made too many poor loans. At other times, such as the present (Spring 2012), commercial banks are reluctant to make loans and the Federal Reserve is somewhat thwarted in its attempt to stimulate the economy by expanding the money supply.

During the monetary history of the United States, the combination of a central-bank fiat currency, a fractional-reserve banking system, and aggressive loan underwriting by banks has proven to be a tiresome recipe for financial instability, general economic volatility and disaster, over and over again. We have experienced a sad and volatile money, banking and credit history during the last hundred years following the creation of the Federal Reserve. The monetary system appears to have evolved somewhat by accident. Problems or logical fallacies that have arisen within it, or because of it, have tended to be addressed with the band-aids of further regulation and constraint. As a society, we have too rarely stepped back and asked whether the money, banking and credit system in its entirety represents the best we could do in accomplishing the efficient allocation of loanable funds and exchange in our high-tech market economy. The reason is obvious and a sad but familiar commentary on human nature. A regulated, entrenched structure spawns its own constituencies and beneficiaries, and is therefore unlikely to critically examine and, if necessary, end itself.

The book begins by briefly describing what money is and what it does. We then point out and highlight the predictable problems and disasters that a money, credit and banking system such as ours has produced up to and including the most recent "credit crisis." We explain those features of the present system that have led to volatility and economic collapse, and suggest that information and communication technology has achieved a level where the benefits of a fiat money and a traditional, fractional-reserve banking system can be deeply questioned. A more rational and stabilizing alternative for exchange and valuation is proposed (shares of the broad capital market), and the benefits of such an alternative in terms of financial and output market stability and real economic productivity and sustained real consumption is presented.

In writing this book, we could have gone into a detailed description of past and recent U.S. economic history and attempted to produce a complete historical narrative. We chose not to do this, because our goal is the development of basic economic and monetary ideas, not to produce another detailed economic history. Others have done the historical analysis far better than we could in any case, for example, consider Milton Friedman's and Anna Schwartz's exhaustive and deservedly famous <u>Monetary History of the United States</u>. Instead we chose the time-honored approach of developing a fictitious monetary history or parable in the context of an "island" economy.

"Why did you resort to the vehicle of an island economy, especially when so much chaos in money and banking is happening right before our noses in the real world?" a reader might ask. It is a fair question. Use of this and other similar simplifying parables has a long tradition in economic discourses. The unifying

5

goal is that they are employed in order to focus primarily and simply upon a few key ideas or concepts on a stage that is intended to exclude everything else—as free of distractions and unnecessary complexity as possible. An early master of using parables to teach economic principles was Frederic Bastiat, a 19th century economist who was devoted to the principles of free trade. Through the use of parables—often combined with exaggeration—Bastiat was able to strip away minutiae and focus on a problem's most essential characteristics. For example, during Bastiat's time the French politicians and bureaucrats were quite concerned with the trade deficit France had with its trading partners, and were seeking to erect barriers to "improve" the imbalance. Bastiat did not see the trade imbalance as something that was harmful to the citizens of France, and argued that the nation actually benefits from an excess of imports compared to exports. To make his point Bastiat used an abstraction: "Assume, if it amuses you, that foreigners flood our shores with all kinds of useful goods, without asking anything from us; even if our imports are *infinite* and our exports are *nothing*, I defy you to prove to me that we should be the poorer for it."[1] In the area of monetary theory, in an early edition of their popular Money and Banking textbook Lawrence Ritter and William Silber use the tale of "An Island Paradise" to describe how a primitive economy operating with a commodity currency can develop through time into an economy with a fiat currency, which works out just fine so long as the islanders "trust" the currency.[2]

It is in this tradition that we will continue to return to an island economy to illustrate important ideas, even in the very last (optional) portion of the book where the mathematics get a bit sophisticated. By explaining concepts with a simplified, fictional economy one is able to educate, clarify, and cut to the simple heart of the matter. It also allows the authors the conceit of telescoping

---

[1] Economic Sophisms, by Frederic Bastiat, published by The Foundation for Economic Education, 1964, Irvington-on-Hudson, New York.
[2] See the tale "An Island Paradise," found in Principles of Money, Banking, and Financial Markets: 6th Edition, by Lawrence S. Ritter and William L. Silber, 189, Basic Books, New York, New York. .

centuries of money, banking and technological history into a conveniently few short generations. We hope readers will imaginatively see and understand the purpose of the authors in collapsing so much history into such a short period on the "island." We also hope that the island economy narrative makes the reader's journey up the monetary theory learning curve more fun. To proceed otherwise carries the risk of context turning the discussion into a pure historical track and risks losing the forest for the trees. The authors would hasten to add that any resemblance of the fictional island economy to certain modern individuals, situations, institutions, and economies, living or dead, is, of course, purely intentional.

There are several suggested alternative approaches to reading this book, based upon the individual reader's skill set, preferences and objectives. For the reader who wishes to digest the main intuition of the arguments presented at an intuitive or qualitative level, chapters 1 through 6 are sufficient—omitting chapter 7. For readers comfortable with math notation, graphs and basic calculus, chapter 7 can and should be included. Those readers who prefer to follow through the entire "island" narrative uninterrupted can read chapters 1-6 or 1-7, omitting chapter 2 until later. In either case, most readers will want to eventually read chapter 2 (in order or not), as it provides the linkage of the island parable to the last 100 years or so of U.S. monetary economic history. In particular, at the time of this writing it is the intention of the authors to draw attention to the strong parallels between the credit market collapse of the Great Depression (1929-1940) and the current one in order to show what we have learned about the effective practice of money, banking, and credit policy during the interim—practically nothing.

A brief road map of the journey followed in this book is as follows:

Chapter 1 The Evolution of Money, Credit and Banking— An Island Tale

We begin with the familiar motivation of what a monetary good is and what it accomplishes within an island economy. The story begins on an island economy characterized by barter. The island economy context is a useful and clear way to illustrate the basic logic and value of money in exchange, valuation, lending, saving and investing. It also provides a good stage for illustrating the evolution of a simple banking system, and for motivating the desire of banks to loan out "excess deposits"—thereby creating a de facto fractional-reserve banking system. In chapter 1 we follow the narrative of first generation bankers in their self-serving rationalizations for loaning out otherwise "idle" deposit funds. The discussion between Jim and Bob Jr. would be amusing if it were not so tragically parallel to the development of our own money and banking system. By the end of chapter 1 the island economy has a commodity-backed monetary system (silver) and a fractional- reserve banking system. By accident and greed we can see the table has been laid for the introduction of an overseeing central bank, fiat money without limit, and a banking system that unfortunately, while in its infant state, resembles our own.

Chapter 2 A Brief Review of Money, Credit and Banking in the United States

Chapter 2 is a brief historical discussion intended to relate the money and banking system from chapter 1's fictional island economy to the past history and present circumstances of the U.S. monetary system. The discussion focuses on how money and banking in the United States evolved to its present state from the 19th century commodity-based private banking system. Basic concepts of the money supply and its theoretical and historical relationship to nominal and real GDP are presented and analyzed using a minimal amount of mathematics. It is shown in chapter 2 that fractional-reserve banking is a fraudulent and destabilizing activity. It is fraudulent because investors who open checking accounts, also called demand-deposit accounts, are promised that their funds are available "upon demand," when in actuality a large portion of their money has typically been loaned out to someone else. Should too many depositors simultaneously decide to withdraw their money the bank runs out of vault cash and the fraud is exposed. People are not foolish, and most depositors are keenly aware of the dangers associated with banks maintenance of only fractional reserves—a fact which has led to many banking panics past and present and further regulatory devices such as the Federal Deposit Insurance Corporation. The last part of chapter 2 briefly addresses the obvious issues of the current "Euro-zone" crisis and explains that, while it may or may not be serious, its permanent resolution is hopeless.

Chapter 3   The Dinner

Here we conveniently skip forward over time in our island economy to a dinner between Bob Jr. and his now grown daughter Roberta—currently president of the island's Economic Club. It is a skeptical discussion and debate (on Roberta's part) questioning the efficacy of a fiat money, a fractional-reserve banking system, and the central bank. Have exchange and accounting technology and velocity increased to the point where a fractional-reserve banking system is not only unnecessary, but also undesirable? The contradiction at the heart of the fractional-banking system is an uncompensated transfer of property rights that banks hope will be validated by the law of large numbers. An analogy would be, noting that you're on vacation, your neighbor takes the risk without your direct knowledge of renting your house for his profit, knowing that at any point he may need to evict the renters, clean up, and restore your house to you should you unexpectedly return to demand residence. As the dinner conversation progresses it will be seen that Roberta's dad—now President of the Confederation of Islands Central Bank—sees an intelligent central bank and the enlightened policies of its board of governors as the stabilizer and savior of the island's economy. In contrast, Roberta sees the central bank as a main architect of economic volatility, credit market collapse, and recessions. Its current policies, in her eyes, represent ironic reactions to unwitting disasters of its own past design. At the end of the chapter, in a telling interchange between Roberta and her dad, she discovers that, as a result of the recent the credit crisis, banks are virtually unwilling or incapable of lending. They just continue to accumulate excess reserves. Thus, the money multiplier due to fractional-reserve banking is effectively not operating at all in increasing the supply of money—a situation on the island interestingly parallel to the one we currently see in the U.S. economy. She observes to her dad that there may never be a better opportunity to scrap the fractional-reserve banking system.

A fictional compression of time allows the island economy to have attained a level of technological capability similar to our own. In particular, two critical features allow the vision of a "capital-as-money" exchange and valuation system: (1) the possibility of the velocity and recording of exchanges increasing effectively without bound and (2) the evolution of an effective composite capital good (broad index shares) which could be used for valuation and trade.

Chapter 4   Edward's Vision – Movement toward Capital as Money

In chapter 4 we are introduced to Edward, an intelligent economist and an active member of the island's Economics Club. Edward's view of consumption and savings comes from a neoclassical perspective. One of Edward's favorite themes is how excessive leverage, poor loan-underwriting and intermediation by lending agents, and the fractional-reserve banking system have led to a misallocation between savings and consumption. The result is too little capital investment and a less than "golden-rule" capital intensity. It is Edward's contention that mispricing of current consumption relative to future consumption has led to a significant cost to the economy of sustained aggregate under-consumption—

an irrational trade-off—and is the result of an institutionalized, regulated, irrational money, banking and credit system. He ends his speech by introducing the logical alternative of capital as money. The view is advanced that technological advances and the evolution of the economy, as well as logic, now favor this alternative. Edward discusses how a capital-based exchange and valuation good could emerge, be practicable, and discusses the advantages of it in producing a more transparent and simpler system of money, banking and lending. In particular, the merits and transparency of direct lending are expounded.

(Edward's arguments tempt us to wonder, will museums of the future feature eager stuffed bank lending officers caught in mid-stride in ill-fitting vested suits gazing fearlessly but somewhat uncomprehendingly into the distance, aggressively making loans in a futile attempt to attain that which ultimately cannot be attained—aggregate consumption and investment in excess of current production? One could almost visualize the museum plaque below them, "Bankerus Americanus Dullardus.—IQ range typically 95 to 107, this species was frequently observed at civic booster club meetings and buffets of all types. They are best identified by the presence of sauce stains on vest or clothing.")

Chapter 5   Continuation of Edward's Speech

Edward's presentation continues in chapter 5 as he intends on bolstering his arguments in favor of capital as money using the original Solow neoclassical growth model. Edward claims that the island's achievement of the long-run, consumption-maximizing capital intensity is thwarted by the institutionally-imposed and controlled system of money, banking and lending the island presently finds itself saddled with. He also extends the intuition of the neoclassical model through the introduction of money and a government budget constraint. However, as the reader will see, Edward is unconvinced that conventional money really even belongs in a neoclassical growth model. The last part of Edward's presentation is a qualitative summary of the full quantitative paper that follows as the chapter 7 appendix at the end of the book.

Chapter 5 concludes with a discussion of the inevitable demise of fiat money and central bank policy as the technology of exchange increases in efficiency. Velocity and the level of money balances required to facilitate exchange become notional variables—driven by the collective intentions and desires of all of us—rather than being limiting constraints. You should be forewarned that there are several graphs in chapter 5 (and also in chapter 7), but as most of you know only too well, the only sure way to finally separate economists from their graphs is to "pry them from their cold dead fingers."

Chapter 6   Epilogue—Ten Years Later

In chapter 6 we once again move forward in time another ten years. Roberta, formerly an outspoken critic of the Island Confederation Central Bank, is now its chairman. With her assistance the island economy has successfully transitioned to a capital-based money system. Roberta is the honored guest at the end-of-year meeting of the Economics Club, and she is answering questions surrounding the changeover to capital as money. Unlike fiat currency, capital cannot be recklessly printed by an aggressive central bank or government—rather it grows slowly over time in concert with the economy's overall productive capacity. Thus, when shares of the economy's capital stock are used as money overall inflation is eliminated. Stock market fluctuations are also nonexistent, since capital prices are no longer measured using a volatile and illusory fiat currency. In a capital-based-money economy, all individual prices are measured using shares of a broad equity market index fund as the numeraire. By definition of the new monetary unit, a single share in the index fund has a value of "one," and all other prices are expressed relative to the numeraire. Thus, it is impossible for the broad stock market's value to fluctuate; the price of index shares remains constant at one.

Prices of individual consumption items fluctuate relative to the numeraire, as do the prices of shares of stock in individual companies. On average, there is no upward tendency in overall prices; all prices are held in check since they are now expressed relative to and balanced by the value of the ownership of real, productive capital. Since the island economy chose to define a unit of money as a constant proportion of ownership of a growing aggregate capital stock, the equilibrium price of the average consumption good is steadily declining over time. The lending market has become streamlined, transparent and efficient—the role of "bricks and mortar" banks has become largely an irrelevant anachronism and the direct lending market is on the rise. Significantly, when capital is used as money it becomes more widely recognized as the one and only fundamental true store of wealth. And, as it is more widely held, Edward and Roberta argue the proposition that the economy has trended closer to a consumption-maximizing level of investment and capital.

Chapter 7   Mathematical Appendix—Edward's Paper

Chapter 7 is the quantitative foundation for Edward's remarks and conclusions presented in chapter 5. It is optional reading, and is presented for those of you who enjoy a more formal mathematical presentation of economic ideas. Economists already familiar with the neoclassical model will have no difficulty following the arguments presented in chapter 7. Readers with a calculus background, but having no familiarity with the Solow model, may also want to develop a deeper understanding by reading chapter 7.

A final thought for the reader before you begin. A case can be made that the study of economies and economic policy aggregated to the country level—or "Macroeconomics"—began with J.M. Keynes and his publication of The General Theory of Employment, Interest and Money in 1936. Since that time the debate about what, if anything, governments can or should do has been fast and furious. We are inclined to follow the lead of Milton Friedman in believing that government expenditure and taxation policies intended to either "stimulate" or "slow" the overall economy exert little, if any, short-run impact. This is because the effect of a change in government expenditure, combined with how it is paid for, is likely close to zero in altering aggregate spending. The disappointing results of recent "stimulus" packages applied to the U.S. economy, in particular, seem to validate this view. This is not to say that the long-term effects of government spending and taxation policies are not important and real. Who pays and who gets has profound effects on the nature, efficiency, and growth of any economy during the long-term. It is an appropriate socioeconomic policy question for all economies and their constituents to grapple with. However, the application (or, more accurately, the misapplication) of central bank monetary policy combined with banking and credit market behavior does exert real short-run effects upon the economy. Unfortunately, these are often unanticipated, harmful, and destabilizing. Offering a view of how they and the apparatus that is responsible for them might be eliminated is the primary purpose of this book. Ironically, doing that by means of a simpler, transparent, market-driven system of trading and valuation may put "Macroeconomics" as a short-run policy or stabilization tool back to bed again.

CHAPTER 1

THE EVOLUTION OF MONEY, CREDIT AND BANKING—AN ISLAND TALE

The best way to understand the essence of any idea is to simplify it to its most basic elements. Money is best understood in this way. Use your imagination to consider a simple island economy— perhaps in the South Pacific or the Caribbean. Suppose this economy is initially what economists call an "autarky," which is an economy that is self-sufficient and trades with no other economy. Autarkies seem unrealistic in today's world but they are not unknown. (One example of an autarky is the earth itself, since trade with extra-terrestrials is probably nonexistent.) The population of this small idyllic island has achieved specialization in production of, say, ten goods. These goods might include foods, fish, some basic tools, clothing, furniture and shelter. Services are minimal and, in our primitive economy, there are no CPAs (as yet).

The inhabitants of our island understand how to trade and they specialize in production. Some of the first innovations they make involve improving the ease and efficiency of trading for the goods they desire. When they begin to trade islanders would quickly discover that wandering around with a bundle of goods they produced, for example a bundle of firewood, in the hopes of finding another individual who wants to trade for firewood is not optimal. Our firewood trader—let us call him Herb—and his fellow firewood producers realize that a trading center would be sensible. Everyone on the island would know where the trading center is, and the islanders can trade firewood there for any other of the nine goods the island economy produces. Through the magic of trading, exchange ratios based upon supply and demand would emerge for trading sticks of firewood for any of the other goods on the island. Now Herb can assemble, with greater ease, the amounts of all ten goods he would like to consume at current exchange ratios by trading a portion of his firewood in the firewood trading center. At one trading post in the Center Herb trades firewood for salmon; the ratio might be ten sticks of firewood per fish. At another booth he trades firewood for coconuts at, say, two sticks of firewood per coconut, and so forth. In order to trade firewood for each of the other nine items on the island, the Center would require a total of nine trading posts—each with a specified, market-determined exchange ratio.

Let's say that Herb has a smart friend, Jim. Jim contemplates the island trading system and notes that there is a trading center not only for firewood, but also for the other nine goods on the island. Even if all trading centers are combined at one location, there will still be a lot of trading posts and exchange ratios required for all the possible barters. In fact, the number of trading posts and exchange ratios will be 9+8+7+6+5+4+3+2+1= 45. That's quite a lot of trading posts for a lazy island economy producing only ten goods, and it represents a large number of barter exchange ratios for each islander to keep track of. Being bright, Jim realizes that if one good could be customarily used by islanders to accomplish all transactions then trading becomes much simpler—there would be only nine trading ratios or "prices" to keep track of in the marketplace.

On this island economy the universally accepted trading good that evolves will be one of the island's ten goods. It could be a good that has value in consumption as well as exchange, or it could be something that is only used for trading. Whatever good ultimately evolves into "money" will be useful in facilitating trade and thereby making the economy more efficient and productive. Let us suppose in our island economy that silver coins evolve into the generally accepted trading good. Silver has some nice attributes as a trading good that become obvious to the islanders. It is fairly portable and easily divisible, it doesn't spoil or wear out, and it is pretty easy to recognize.

Eventually by custom and agreement silver becomes universally acceptable as a trading good by all the islanders. The island economy has now evolved to include its first "money." Silver or money accomplishes some great advantages for the islanders. Herb now can bring his firewood to market and exchange it immediately for silver coins. Then he can exchange a portion of his silver for each of the other goods he desires at the market determined prices stated in terms of silver. In this way Herb much more easily secures his desired consumption bundle. Moreover, he can defer trades and store value over time. If the fish, for example, are not to his liking today, then he can take that portion of his silver home and bring it in again tomorrow, for fresher fish.

Because it simplifies trade for all of the islanders, the use of silver as a monetary good is a productivity-enhancing innovation. By promoting efficiency and saving time spent in exchange, the use of silver coins raises the total production of the island economy. Economists would say, therefore, that money belongs in the production function. Productivity increases when barter economies adopt a monetary exchange system.

"Money" is defined by what it does, not by what specific good it is. In any economy the monetary good is whatever is universally accepted for trades, is a good long-term store of value between trades, and is the customary unit of value in which prices of all goods and services is stated. In all times and in all economies, monetary goods have arisen. The motivation to adopt "money" in our simple island economy is multiplied for economies with thousands of goods and services.

In our island economy, when compared to barter, the adoption of a commodity-based money (silver) leads to great gains in exchange and production. But, the story doesn't stop here—further development of the monetary system is inevitable. Enterprising Jim notices that islanders are complaining about hauling their silver around with them for trades. And, they are also worried about stockpiling silver in their huts for fear of being robbed.

Jim decides to offer a service to the other islanders. He owns a cave he can use to provide a secure location for islanders to store their silver. In addition, he will keep track of the silver in each islander's "account" and the results of transactions that change ownership of the silver he stores. Jim will prepare a monthly statement of trading activity and net balance to each islander. For simplicity, Jim also can issue the islanders notes or pieces of paper that reflect their ownership of stored silver—and then place that silver in what he calls the bank's "common reserve". The depositors can then carry about and exchange these notes for trades as needed or, whenever they wish, redeem them at any time to withdraw the silver they represent. Jim does all this for a small fee charged to each islander based upon the size of average balances he tracks for them. Thus, Jim's service begins to resemble a crude sort of bank.

With the passage of time the convenience and safety of Jim's "bank" becomes a great success; it is almost universally used by the islanders for storing their silver. In fact, it is so successful that little silver actually circulates outside Jim's vault and the attractive banknotes, denoting ownership of and redeemable for a fixed amount of silver, become the "money" of the island economy. However some of the elderly islanders insist on silver transactions, as they believe there is a very human temptation for Jim to overdo it a bit in issuing his silver notes. By printing up too many notes and issuing them to himself, Jim could siphon off a small stream of real output from the island economy. If he printed up notes and purchased products himself, he would be stealing. However, Jim is honest and all turns out well. Occasionally there are rumors that the bank does not have enough silver in its vault, and brief runs occur. But, whenever depositors want to convert their notes back into silver there is always enough in the vault, and Jim develops a reputation for honesty amongst the islanders.

After years of satisfactory exchange in this system, Jim realizes that his cave is not large enough for continued silver deposits. He knows there is a larger and more secure cave for storing the silver on the other side of the Great Lagoon. So one day he carefully loads the entire stock of bank silver onto a great barge. With his young and trusted associate Bob Jr., he sails off across the lagoon to his new vault.

Jim pauses in his paddling and stares at Bob Jr. with some wonderment. The kid, Bob Jr. worked his tail off to build the raft. In his eagerness and hard work he was not unlike his fisherman father. Jim's thoughts wandered back to his first discussions with "Big Tuna" Bob Sr. about his son.

"My son has me at the end of my rope!" the senior Bob lamented. "He seems really smart in a book-learning sort of way—but he doesn't have enough common sense to find his way out of a paper bag with a ten man scouting party. The kid can't fish worth a shit. What's more, disaster seems to plague any fishing boat or crew he is a part of and he always seems to be at the center of it. He loves philosophizing about trade and business and banking, and he's good with numbers—so I thought maybe he might fit into your world better than mine. I was hoping you could take him under your wing as an assistant. He will work hard, I promise you that."

At the time, warning lights went off and Jim thought wryly to himself that he would rather have a few hours of root-canal work than to take on the apparently ham-handed Bob Jr. as a young assistant to be mentored. However, there was no denying that "Big Tuna" Bob was the most successful fisherman on the island, and his business and goodwill played no small role in Jim's own prosperity. Further, Big Tuna was a stereotypical island fisherman. He was brusque and outspoken, and Jim was intimidated by his demeanor as well as his overall physical size and strength. Jim's eyes wandered involuntarily to Big Tuna's hands with their thick, strong fingers covered with calluses and fishing line scars. To Jim, telling Big Tuna "no" was not an option to be taken lightly. Thus he replied, "I will be delighted to let him work with me at the bank. Send him on over. By the way, don't forget our annual bank dinner meeting next week—as an important customer and advisor we will be delighted to see you. Don't let the social stuff put you off, with a gourmet dinner it will be quite the gala affair."

"Oh dealing with your frou-frou guests and the social niceties doesn't bother me at all. I take to that high society stuff like a duck to water," Big Tuna boomed confidently. Here he had leaned back in his seat and paused as he opened his mouth widely and inserted a couple of scaly fingers on an exploratory expedition. Evidently encountering success, he withdrew them, triumphantly holding up a small shard of offending crab shell plucked from the roof of his mouth. Big Tuna regarded it thoughtfully for a few seconds before flicking it over his shoulder and continuing, "It's just that those meetings are so damn boring."

That had been almost two years ago and the boy had proved true to his father's words. He was an eager and hard worker and, by and large, had turned into a valued associate. He had learned the business fast and almost instinctively, but there had nonetheless been something slightly disturbing about him. He was opinionated and hard-headed to a fault and he was always trying to change things. Sometimes he was right, but by no means always—and when he was wrong, his stubborn, single-minded pursuit of ideas could be disastrous. He had made several attempts at simplifying the accounting systems at the bank that dangerously antagonized some clients as well as the bank's other workers. But, on balance, there was no denying he had made himself valuable by being a hard worker willing to take on any enterprise and by being able to keep confidences, as bankers must.

As Jim and Bob Jr. are transporting the silver across the lagoon to the new, larger cave, a horrible thing happens. About halfway across the lagoon, while Jim is dozing after a considerable lunch, Bob Jr. in a way not unfamiliar to romantic adolescents, allows his attention to wander…

"What a day!" Bob Jr. thinks to himself. "What place could be more beautiful? Look at the clouds—that big one looks exactly like a crouching tiger! Look at all the blues and greens of the waves and how they roar as they crash upon the reef, exploding into white spray. I can see how it would be cool to be a fisherman like my dad. I could do this stuff all day long, and I'm pretty good at it, too. Jim would never have been able to build this raft without me. And look how the wind is making us drift. I don't even have to row. We are going to end up at precisely the right place if the wind and current keep on pushing us toward the cliffs and cave. Look at the size of that yellow bird circling over us! Wha-a-at…"

At this point, the young Bob Jr.'s reverie is rudely interrupted. A large wave—perhaps a "sneaker" or a tsunami—who knows?—suddenly hits the raft at an odd, sideways angle. Perhaps if Bob Jr. had been paying attention he could have steered into the wave and surmounted it with a different outcome, but, alas, it starts tipping the raft rapidly to one side. Sadly, Jim and Bob Jr. are better as bankers than as sailors because the tipping is rapidly worsened as their inexpert lashings fail allowing all the crates of silver coins to suddenly shift toward the side of the raft opposite the wave. The raft flips as suddenly and neatly as a flapjack. Both Bob Jr. and Jim are rudely submerged and almost the entire stock of islanders' silver coins flitter delicately down like some kind of perverse, glinting, underwater butterflies—down through the seawater until they disappear from sight in one of the deepest portions of the Great Lagoon. Jim, who had been soundly asleep after a stomach filling and excellent lunch of wine and crab salad, emerges to the surface bug-eyed and sputtering. After taking on a fair amount of seawater, he struggles for air and retches as Bob Jr. grabs him and starts towing him toward the closest stretch of white sand beach.

"What the hell have you done this time?" Jim wetly hisses, still gasping like a beached flounder. "I can't even sleep for a few moments without you causing a disaster!"

Cut to the quick because, in common with many emerging adolescents, he had experienced a number of recent episodes where he had apparently fallen short of his mentor's expectations, Bob Jr. drags Jim none too gently up onto the beach and sits still catching his own breath. The magnitude of their misfortune fully strikes Jim as he rocks back and forth in despair continuing to howl, moan, and retch—tossing up his stomach's few remaining oddments of the crab salad picnic he and Bob Jr. had earlier enjoyed. The depth of his despair is further fueled by the realization that recovering the silver from the depths of the Great Lagoon is hopelessly beyond his capability or the islanders' technology.

"It was a really big wave," Bob Jr. defensively replies. "I couldn't have done anything to avoid it. I was paying attention—it came out of nowhere. But I guess that you might as well just go on with your histrionics because we really are screwed this time!"

It is Bob Jr., a bit more imaginative (some would say devious) than Jim, who finally arrives at a solution to their dilemma. He points out to the deeply melancholic Jim that it has been years since there has been any run by depositors on the bank for vault silver. In fact, each month there is typically a net inflow of new silver deposits in the bank—the reason they needed the larger cave vault to begin with. Bob Jr. explains that with a little luck, no one need know that they have lost the islanders' silver at the bottom of the lagoon. And, he argues, soon there will be enough new silver deposits to more than meet the occasional demand to cash in banknotes for silver.

Understandably, Jim is initially reluctant to take any advice from Bob Jr. But after some appropriately violent protests, necessity being the mother of invention, Jim finally acquiesces to his young associate's arguments and accepts the idea of prudent silence about the accident.

Surprisingly, the scheme actually works. The island economy and its monetary exchange system continue to function without a hiccup. Bob Jr., with the enthusiasm of youth, continues to argue with Jim that, in this new world, what would be the harm in being a bit more aggressive in printing new notes. After all, there is no reason to slavishly adhere to a supply discipline when the majority of the silver backing is a fiction in islanders' minds. Bob Jr. couches his arguments in new terms, suggesting that a little bit of ease in the supply of silver notes could only be helpful in stimulating the level of production and trade in the island economy—thereby raising the prosperity of the average islander. Noticeably missing in his argument is any reference to the benefit to himself in supplying new notes at little or no cost in exchange for real goods and services from the economy. Jim senses that this plan would be a slippery slope and, moreover, he has recently been the victim of a recurring nightmare involving what would happen if the periodic runs of old returned. What the two have actually unwittingly accomplished is, in fact, a version of a "fiat" money economy. In this type of economy the "money" is backed by nothing at all other than the general faith that it will continue to be a stable store of value and a universally accepted medium of exchange. Perception is more important than reality.

Bob Jr., however, is nothing if not enterprising. Without being named such he is an early version of a macroeconomist (heaven forbid). He has made a somewhat self-serving study of the island economy and its rudimentary monetary system. One day he makes a formal presentation of his conclusions to Jim.

"Let's call the stock of silver in circulation outside the bank and the stock of banknotes representing ownership of the bank's vault silver, as well as the silver at the bottom of the lagoon, the stock of money, "M", he states. Jim shifts uncomfortably at the mention of the lagoon.

Jim interrupts, "I was meaning to ask you about that. Of course, we are still following the prudent banking practice of destroying a bank note whenever an equivalent amount of silver is withdrawn, are we not, as well as *only* issuing a new banknote when an equivalent amount of new silver is deposited at the bank? After all, to do anything else would be tantamount to stealing from our depositors—we would be little better than counterfeiters."

Bob Jr. reddens and looks uncomfortable. "In a general sense, that is exactly what we aim to do, but it is very complex and who can say that the exact number of notes to correspond with daily deposits and withdrawals is, in fact, created and destroyed. But anyway... oh, what the heck! Come off of it Jim and quit living in

23

the past. You know how silly you sound don't you?" (Now, Bob Jr. was an ambitious but respectful young fellow who typically would not have spoken to his boss in such a fashion. Alas after the lagoon incident—a necessarily shared secret between them—a sad aspect of human nature had predictably manifested itself. It showed in his increased assertiveness with his employer). "Nowadays we simply record a deposit of silver notes by an individual as a deposit to their account and a withdrawal of silver notes out of the bank as a withdrawal. Fortunately for us, most depositors don't actually want to take out physical silver for their notes. Moreover we let them enjoy the convenience of changing ownership of their account assets to represent a trade by notifying us by means of a 'check' rather than by the ponderous and risky process of actually withdrawing and carrying around stacks of silver notes or, even worse, silver. Clients love this convenience.

"Our job is as it always has been—to keep fastidious records of each client's account balances after deposits, withdrawals and/or trades of which we are notified by check. In any case, as you are well aware Jim, these notes are very expensive to print. So rather than destroy them, we actually simply pull them from circulation and then use them later as needed."

"As needed!" Jim interjects. "You can only do that if they are needed for new deposits, but not if they are needed for bank expenses or your own personal expenses."

Bob Jr. bristles at this statement. "May I remind you that most of the silver that backs this whole system is only imaginary since it rests at the bottom of the lagoon. What the depositors don't know doesn't seem to hurt them."

"And may I *remind* you," Jim retorts, "that the silver was only lost in the lagoon because of your lapse of attention at a critical moment. And, may I also point out that much of the silver that is at the bottom of the lagoon belonged to your dad. "

"We can argue all day about the past," Bob Jr. responds, "but the purpose of this meeting is for you to understand my model."

Bob Jr. grabs a note pad and goes on to present a model that many would recognize as the classical quantity equation of money. Summarized succinctly, let

M = the stock of silver and silver notes in circulation outside the bank in the island economy,

V = the "velocity," or the average number of times per year a unit of silver or a silver note is actually employed in a trade,

P = an expenditure-weighted index of the prices of all the goods or services on the island (think of it as an average price for an average chunk of island output),

Y = the total amount of island output produced and sold during the year.

As Bob Jr. goes on to explain, if all transactions are accomplished by swapping money (silver or silver notes) for goods or services, then the following logical identity must hold for the island economy,

$$(M)(V) = (P)(Y)$$

That is, the island stock of money (M) held outside the bank, when multiplied by the average number of times a unit of money changes hands per year (V) is equal to the average price of a unit of output (P) multiplied by the number of physical units of output sold per year (Y).

Like most individuals with some conception of economics, Jim recognizes the equation and recalls that the relationship is referred to as the equation of exchange. Nevertheless, Bob Jr. decides to further explain the equation to Jim by providing a concrete example with numbers. "So Jim, to illustrate the equation, consider the following example: Suppose the money in circulation consisted of only 100 silver notes, so $M = 100$. And, suppose that the only good the island produced and sold were coconuts, and let's say 40 of them were sold. Then, $Y = 40$. Given that the price of a coconut is five silver certificates, $P = 5$, then it is a simple matter to conclude that each silver certificate on average was turned over two times. So, $V = 2$."

So far Bob Jr.'s model is simple enough. But, Jim is a banker, and he has not had a lot of training in mathematics. He grows somewhat uncomfortable as he suspects that Bob Jr. is going to push forward with more.

"Now," Bob Jr. continues, "the math people tell me that I can rearrange this equation in an equivalent, but slightly different form. As math guys regularly do, letting ' Δ ' represent 'change in,' the equation of exchange can be rearranged as

$$\frac{\Delta M}{M} + \frac{\Delta V}{V} = \frac{\Delta P}{P} + \frac{\Delta Y}{Y}$$

"Now, I'm done with equations for the time being," Bob Jr. says. "But what this new equation tells us is that the rate of growth of our money supply plus the rate of change in the velocity of money equals the rate of average price growth, which is inflation, plus the rate of growth of overall output on our island."

"Thank God we're done with the equations!" Jim interjects. "What is the point of all this, justification for some scam or other to defraud the depositors, I suppose?"

Bob Jr. stiffens at the indignity of such an accusation. "I am just going to lay some simple facts before you to suggest that our bank has a special responsibility to do better with island monetary policy."

He continues by explaining that the stock of island silver and silver notes held by the public, M, has hardly grown at all during recent years. At the same time output, Y, has grown at an average rate of about three percent per year during the same period because of people having children as well as inventions that have made the production of almost all goods and services more efficient. The velocity of money has increased only slightly during the same period as the speed of all transactions has been limited by travel time and/or the handwritten changes in account balances recorded in the bank's ledger. Therefore, he concludes, all the action has been on the right-hand side of the equation of exchange. Since the left-hand side of the equation has not changed, the growth in output, Y, has necessarily resulted in an average decline in prices, P, and the island has experienced deflation.

It is the island's deflation that Bob Jr. emphasizes. "It is no surprise that while the average rate of output growth has been three percent, the average rate of inflation has been *minus* three percent. Now this negative rate of price change is unfortunate because it is a real drag on the morale of the islanders. Much of the exchange of goods and services is contracted forward and it is really hard for businesses to lower the prices they expect to receive in the future and especially hard to explain to employees why the wages they receive for their labor services must continue to decline."

Knowing where Bob Jr. is heading, Jim interrupts. "However, we both know that what you are really driving at is the new lending market that has arisen that you are so eager to make the bank a part of!"

"Well since you mention it," Bob Jr. continues, "it is a drag on the lending market to deal with a negative rate of average price change. Individuals like my dad, who is always catching more fish than he needs for his own current consumption, always sells the extra and routinely finds himself with excess money balances. He lends his savings to other businesses on the island, and he usually demands that he be paid back about two percent more than he lends—as interest."

Jim looks at Bob Jr. quizzically and interrupts. "What's wrong with that? Your dad, and anyone else who wants to, is free to loan out their savings as they see fit. I don't see that this has anything to do with us at the bank. We provide a service, that service being the storage of silver, and we do it for a fee. I don't get why you always want to mix up a storage business with a lending business."

"Well," Bob Jr. answers, "the problem of the island's lending market is that it is too small—the pool of available savings from the very few savers out there is paltry. Think about it. Prices are falling on our island at about three percent per year. That means a saver can simply hold money balances and not lend at all. By simply clinging to his silver notes he will be able to buy three percent more stuff next year, since prices will be three percent lower then! So, some savers won't even consider making a loan in such a circumstance. There is a lot of evidence that this is why our pool of loanable funds is so small. Instead of making loans, some of the islanders with excess money simply hoard it in order to earn a real rate of return of three percent, thereby helping to stagnate the island's investment and future economic growth."

Bob Jr. continues with his justification, "And, since you brought it up, yes I am arguing that our bank is a very natural and needed participant in this new, embryonic lending market. It is our duty to do what we can to stimulate the growth and prosperity of our island's economy! At the very least, we should print enough new money certificates and loan them out to keep pace with the average rate of growth of the island's economy so that we do not have to suffer deflation—so that we can have stable prices and wages. For that matter, even if we don't make loans, but instead we print up some new silver notes and use them to buy stuff for ourselves it would benefit everyone by helping to stabilize prices." Bob Jr. stopped to let the last sentence sink in, as he wanted to make sure Jim understood any such action would be for the general welfare.

After an uneasy pause Bob Jr. continues, "By printing out more silver notes and providing more money for exchange to the island, we would be providing a very valuable service worthy of some form of compensation. If we printed just enough money to match the island's average rate of growth of real output, it would stabilize prices. But, since printing of money is a useful service benefiting all islanders, we could experiment with the capture of some of that value by printing money at a high enough rate to produce a little inflation—you can call it an 'inflation-tax' if you like—so that the islander's are properly compensating us for our service. I argue that if there is no inflation, we are under-compensated for the service we provide and—excuse the expression—we are leaving money on the table. By printing more money, we will be stimulating lending and economic activity; and the islanders would thank us for that."

"And for cheapening their money and diluting their silver stock," Jim wryly says, "while unavoidably enriching ourselves in the process of doing our 'duty' for the economy. As for your 'inflation-tax' scheme, it just seems like a simple rationalization for stealing. Moreover, I don't see how simply creating more borrowing and lending can generate more prosperity and output than is currently available with everybody working as hard as they prefer to on our island. You have not explained how our stealing output from others by printing more money can actually create a larger and more prosperous economy than what is. You haven't dealt with the paradox of what is!"

"Well," replies Bob Jr., "it depends on what your definition of 'is' is. Should we be worried about what is or what can be?" (Bob Jr. had recently taken an unfortunate, irrational detour in the direction of Keynesian economic theory.) "Many of us in the Economics Club believe that our island economy has persistent structurally unemployed productive resources. We can attain a higher level of island prosperity and welfare if only those of us with superior intellect and foresight take the lead in managing the economy to the higher level of employment and output, that it deserves and which it can achieve. That is why I believe that it is our duty to print more money—because the result will be increased welfare and prosperity for the entire population of our island. Moreover, how could we dilute the value of a stock of silver that, as you and I well know, is largely psychic anyway, as it exists only in the minds of the islanders."

"That is why my main fear is that we will have, once again, one of the old runs on the bank," his boss wearily acknowledges. "I suppose it hasn't escaped your attention that whether your palaver about increases in output and using unemployed inputs is correct or not, we must necessarily transport real output to ourselves in either case by printing more money."

"But I'm not just interested in printing more money," Bob Jr. responds, "I have other ideas too. It is so hard for those with excess money balances to find good borrowers to put them to work—sadly they often just let these excess balances fester in their bank account with us. These excess balances should be put to work, and what is a more natural location for the suppliers and demanders of loanable funds to find one another than our bank, itself? We could loan out the excess balances in bank accounts that no one is using. Who would be more expert at ferreting out idle money balances and employing them than us? We could even create a new class of accounts called 'savings' accounts where depositors who intend to lend could be matched up with borrowers willing to pay and borrowers that we have vetted for quality. We could make the whole island lending market and economy more efficient by being knowledgeable brokers in the market for loans."

"We would do all this for free, I suppose?" Jim asks with a knowing smirk.

"Of course not," Bob Jr. quickly responds. "For the new 'savings' accounts I propose, we would simply perform the community service of matching good lenders with good borrowers. We would pass through the interest on the loans to the savings account holders from which they originate. Of course, it is only reasonable that we would deduct a small portion of the interest flows, call it a spread if you wish, to cover our own expenses and needs. However, the best part is our standard and traditional money storage accounts, for which we now charge fees. On these

30

accounts we can see the excess money balances that lie around, practically forever. These idle balances we can loan out with nobody being any the wiser for a positive interest return that would flow to the bank."

Jim interrupts, "It appears to me that would be little different than stealing. Our traditional money storage accounts are called 'demand deposits' for a reason: Our depositors are told that their silver is available upon demand. What happens if these depositors suddenly show up one morning wishing to withdraw these 'excess funds' that we have loaned out?"

"That almost never happens," answers his young associate. "Moreover, if it did then there would be a bigger fish in the frying pan when they discovered that most of the silver they thought we held for them was at the bottom of the lagoon. I suppose we could give those people with demand deposits some of the interest we earn on the loans as well—but I suggest that we simply allow them to keep their money deposits with us for no fee. Most of them would be happy as clams with that."

"Useful fools! How generous of you," Jim exclaims.

"I find your acid tone sad and the way you are throwing the word 'stealing' around unjustified. You are a major proponent of the free market economy and, as such, you should realize that individuals have voluntarily opened and maintained accounts with us. If they don't like our fees and policies as a bank they are, as always, free to withdraw their accounts and go elsewhere or lug their own silver around."

Jim interrupts, "It's you who's forgetting this time that if they all try to do that, we don't have enough silver to give them."

"Good point," continues Bob Jr., apparently unconcerned. "And it's a good point in more ways than you think. My whole plan of optimizing the island's economic prosperity and growth through forward thinking monetary policy doesn't really make sense if there are a number of banks pursuing it without appropriate supervision. A coherent national money and banking policy is one broth that clearly would be spoiled by too many cooks. That is why I am thinking of going to the Island Council and proposing that we be chartered as a sort of super bank—the only one allowed to practice monetary policy for the economy as a whole and to regulate the other competing banks that will inevitably arise as our economy grows. We must set uniform fees, interest rates, reserve requirements and such—this work is simply too critical to be left to chance or the haphazard workings of the marketplace. We would then be a permanent natural monopoly with the blessing of and the exclusive charter from the government. It's only logical."

"Stop! Does your arrogance and ambition know no bounds? You're making my head spin," shouts Jim.

"And we at the Economics Club," Bob Jr. continues, unfazed by the sarcasm, "are concerned about another barbaric custom we follow on our island. The loan default bondage system is cruel and archaic and it must end. If the bank got involved in lending, it would free up credit and help do away with this pitiless practice." (The island has had a system of dealing with loan defaults by placing the debtor into the forced employment of the creditor, at subsistence wages, until the debtor earns enough to retire the loan obligation). "Moreover, what you call compound interest, which is the interest-on-interest provision on loans, is outrageous, and in many cases makes the working off of loan balances far more onerous."

"Why?" cuts in Jim, hotly. (He has made a number of personal loans and has a number of bonded debtors working off delinquent balances.) "When you borrow from another islander, you have borrowed somebody else's current or future consumption. If you fail to repay the obligation, you have literally stolen the food from the lender's mouth. I have never understood why the uncompensated taking of a person's property in the present is called 'stealing,' but taking a lender's property over the future is somehow a lesser wrong. Defaulting on a debt cannot be given a pass. Paying for borrowed consumption is a sacred trust. And, I know your dad feels the same way I do. Why should your dad's fish be given to someone else for nothing in return?"

"That's just more of your old-fashioned thinking. If you can grow the economy faster by lending more freely and with less dire consequences to those who must delay repayment of their loans, then there is more food for everyone's mouth. You just don't get it. When you loan to so-called 'weak' borrowers, the resulting expansion of our whole island economy creates a prosperity that allows them to rise to easily meet their debt obligations."

"Well, I knew that our prosperity would not come without costs," the older banker retorts. "The luxury produced on the backs of my generation has allowed you young drones to idle away your hours in activities like the Economics Club, where you produce no useful output but do grow a bumper crop of half-baked and dangerous ideas. If the bank gets involved in lending and follows your route of easy lending and irresponsible borrowing, the result will simply be a pyramid of overvalued debt claims hanging over an economy with a given amount of real output. Owners of the debt, as well as borrowers, will have an inflated image of their own wealth. Eventually the pyramid will implode as the real wealth of the island is unable to exceed the output and property that actually exists. It will bring down our island economy and our bank along with it. Following your scheme of printing more money and producing more debt can only transfer claims on output, it cannot magically create more output. This, again, is what I call the paradox of what is! In fact, the crime of an inefficient lending market would be that it would actually hobble our island's future economic growth by allowing scarce and precious savings to be steered away from its best and highest use in productive investment, toward frivolous uses and unwarranted consumption. However, I do agree with you that the productive resources of this island are not presently as fully employed as they might be. Let us begin with the drones that inhabit your Economics Club. They should stop producing gas and start producing real output."

CHAPTER 2

A BRIEF REVIEW OF MONEY, CREDIT AND BANKING IN THE UNITED STATES

At this point we will temporarily depart from the island economy. The purpose of the first chapter was to allow the reader with only a rudimentary economic background to gain a clear understanding of the essential principles of money, banking and lending in a simple, and hopefully painless, context. Also, we wanted to compress history in explaining the basics of why and how fiat money systems tend to develop. As we trace through the development of the U.S. economy to its current state and current problems, it is our opinion that the ideas developed in the previous chapter readily extend to the U.S. monetary system and will be useful in understanding the forest as well as the trees. The parallels between the island economy and the U.S. history of money and banking are intentional. What the reader already knows of the functions of money, banking and lending will clarify the exposition throughout the remainder of the book. Our thumbnail sketch here is necessarily brief and broad. The interested reader wishing for more detail is urged to start with the incomparable work <u>A Monetary History of the United States, 1867-1960</u> by Milton Friedman and Anna Schwartz.

Commodity money, silver and gold, first arose in antiquity for the same reasons and motivations portrayed in our island community. Economies primitive and advanced need an agreed upon medium of exchange, a store of value, and a unit of pricing. Kings and governments quickly saw the value in controlling and monopolizing money, controlling its supply, and debasing it for the profit of their treasuries and their personal profit.

Similar to Bob Jr.'s undertaking, private banks arose wanting to be large or exclusive participants in the lucrative lending market. They cast a greedy eye on what they viewed as excess and idle balances of deposited funds. It is important to realize that in loaning out these "excess" reserves, while at the same time guaranteeing individual depositors that their funds are available on demand at any time, banks are playing a potentially dangerous, fraudulent game. This fraud injects a potential element of instability into the banking system and the economy, and is based upon an uncompensated transfer of property rights. In a voluntary exchange economy, *stealing* is not too strong a word to be used in describing such an uncompensated exchange. Put simply, it is an economic practice that is based on a pyramid of claims that exceed the original property rights represented by deposits. As such, it is as inherently fraudulent and destabilizing as chain-letters, pyramid schemes, and other appropriately illegal economic activities.

The 19th century in the United States was characterized by long periods of stable prices and deflation interrupted by occasional episodes of price inflation coupled with the major gold and silver discoveries in the West and in Alaska. Unsurprisingly, the era was also characterized by periodic runs on banks by skeptical depositors. Banks themselves were largely unregulated or only limited in their behavior by rational banking practices in the interest of long-term survival. A prudent or conservative bank might choose to lend very little of its excess reserves of vault cash, resulting in a low probability of stress or failure due to withdrawals by depositors. However, an aggressive or opportunistic bank might loan out almost all of its available vault cash, especially in a region of the country that enjoyed strong economic growth and high loan demand—gambling that it could probably meet the demands of current depositors by continued growth in new deposits. In doing so, a particularly opportunistic lending bank incurred the risk of runs by depositors and failure. Usually the runs on banks were regional in nature and could be, and were, stabilized by an inter-bank loan market of excess reserves (the precursor to today's federal funds market). Thus, this market in excess reserves allowed short-term loans between banks that had plenty of reserves on hand to those banks that were stressed and in need of currency to meet the short-term withdrawal demands of their depositors.

36

Of the periodic runs on banks, the Banking Panic of 1907 was the worst. It was so broad it almost brought down the entire private U.S. banking and monetary system. Unlike the earlier, regional banking panics occurring during the 19th century, the Banking Panic of 1907 was large and pervasive enough to be described as "national." No doubt it caused major stress and self-examination within the entire private U.S. banking system. There is also no doubt that, following the panic, most reasonably astute bankers understood very clearly the potential instability and peril of a fractional-reserve banking system. That is one in which the typical bank held vault reserves equal to much less than 100 percent of the claims of its depositors.

In the aftermath of the Panic of 1907, bankers dreamed of a government sponsored "super bank" that could create loanable reserves of currency without limit, when needed, in order to stabilize the banking sector and the economy, avoid banking panics, and to allow banks to aggressively lend their "excess" deposits for profit. Such a bank would inoculate the system against banking panics while at the same time allowing individual private banks to continue to pursue profits by loaning excess reserves. Congressional lobbying by banking interests following the near disaster in 1907 led directly to the creation of the U.S. central bank in 1913 and the following fiat currency—Federal Reserve Notes. Of course, the creation of the first U.S. central bank and the Federal Reserve System was intended by private banks to simply provide federal validation and insurance for their lending policies, certainly not to regulate them or to restrict their access to profit. The name "Federal Reserve" telegraphs exactly what bankers intended the central bank's primary function to be, a reserve creator and lender of last resort.

The Basic Monetary Propositions

To have insight into the arguments presented in the rest of this book, the reader needs to understand some basic propositions that follow from the logic of money and exchange in a growing economy. Recall the equation of exchange Bob Jr. presented to

Jim back in chapter 1. If the velocity of money remains constant, then the rate of average or broad index inflation in an economy with a fiat-money-printing central bank will be positively related to the sustained rate of growth of the money supply. Mathematically, the relationship can be expressed simply as follows:

(2-1) Inflation Rate = Rate of Money Growth – Rate of Growth in Real Output.

Equation (2-1) tends to hold in economies where the velocity has adjusted to a stable level determined by technological constraints covering the speed of exchange and/or the volume of desired trades. To see how the equation works at a very simple level it is instructive to put in some numbers and consider three separate cases.

Case I: Rate of Money Growth = Rate of Growth in Real Output

When money and real output are growing at the same rate, the right-hand side of equation (2-1) will be zero, and the result is no sustained inflation. Not every price of individual goods or services will remain constant, but there will be stability for the overall or average price level of the economy. For example, a broad price index such as the CPI will remain stable. Of course, individual prices making up a price index will go up or down in response to changes in demand and supply in individual markets. But, when money grows at the same rate as real output, there is no broad upward pressure on all prices over time. This is the basis for the famous Friedman rule: The central bank should expand the money supply at a rate equal to the rate of real growth of the economy in order to maintain overall price stability. Put simply, if the annual growth rate of real output in the United States averages about 3 percent per year, then price stability is consistent with an expansion of the money supply of about 3 percent.

Case II: Rate of Money Growth > Rate of Growth in Real Output

Unfortunately, this is the typical case in most economies as the result of the behavior of most central banks. The situation is often described as "too much money chasing too few goods." Because of too much money printing, practically all fiat-money economies usually experience positive rates of sustained inflation. Again, refer to equation (2-1), and suppose that the central bank is increasing the stock of money at an annual growth rate of, say, 10 percent, while the average growth rate of real output is only 3 percent. Then the sustained rate of inflation will be the difference between the two, which is 7 percent.

Case III: Rate of Money Growth < Rate of Growth in Real Output

If the rate of growth in the money supply is too low, the result is deflation. This is the case that Bob Jr. put forth at the end of chapter 1 in order to rationalize his argument that the island bank should print more money than was warranted by the static supply of silver. To provide a simple numerical example, let us suppose that the rate of growth of the economy's real output is averaging about 3 percent per year, while the central bank is not increasing the money supply at all. Referring to Equation (2-1), the result would be a negative rate of inflation—that is, deflation or prices falling at a rate of 3 percent per year.

These monetary propositions are intuitively appealing and in a broad sense tend to be followed by all economies over sustained time periods—there is no escaping them. Moreover, most observers realize that Case II is typical for the U.S. economy and may well ask, "What's the harm?" The economy could in theory adapt to any constant rate of positive inflation that individuals and markets expect by simply embedding the anticipated inflation rate into all forward-looking price or wage contracts. If, for example, inflation is expected to be 2 percent, then build a 2 percent rate of increase into nominal wage rates and everything will work out fine.

There is some truth to the argument that a steady, predictable rate of modest inflation is in and of itself not a big problem. However, the printing of fiat money at a positive rate also gives its issuer (typically governments or central banks) a power to "steal" a portion of the real output of the economy when the notes are injected into circulation. In the U.S. economy, new fiat money created by the Fed enters into circulation as the central bank buys government bonds previously issued to finance federal government expenditure.

The U.S. government frequently runs enormous budget deficits. Since tax receipts fall far short of spending, the government borrows the difference by selling bonds to the public. The Federal Reserve can enter into the secondary market and buy these previously-issued bonds, paying for the bonds by creating new fiat currency. When the government bonds mature, the U.S. government then owes the Federal Reserve. However, by law, all excess Federal Reserve profits must be promptly returned to the U.S. Treasury. So, after the money is handed back and forth, the end result is precisely the same as if the government was able to finance its expenditures by printing money itself.

A big problem does occur in the U.S. (or any other) economy whenever the rate of inflation deviates from the rate that is generally anticipated. When there is an unexpected change in the rate of money growth by the money-printing central bank it will surprise the marketplace and produce a shock to the economy. The shock is an unexpected increase in the rate of inflation if the rate of money growth is unexpectedly increased. A recessionary shock (declining output growth and rising unemployment) occurs if the rate of money growth is unexpectedly decreased. This is because forward-looking wage and price contracts in the declining money growth case will have set wages and prices "too high" resulting in reduced demand and unemployment. If the Fed slows money growth unexpectedly when the U.S. economy is particularly vulnerable due to overvalued and structurally delicate markets such as the equity market (1929) and the real estate market (2008), then the recession/depression generated is severe and long.

A second issue is instability in money growth, independent of Federal Reserve fiat money growth policy, caused by the structural vulnerability of a fractional-reserve banking system. Later in this chapter we will show that, under a fractional-reserve banking system, the Fed is unable to accurately predict and control the rate of growth in the money supply. Unexpected swings in the money supply occur when depositors en masse move money from their checking accounts to cash. In such a case, monetary contraction occurs, and prices unexpectedly fall, again resulting in a recessionary shock.

The unfortunate and chaotic history of booms and busts in the U.S. economy during the past 100 years or so is largely attributable to unexpected increases or decreases in fiat money growth initiated by Fed monetary policy and often exacerbated by the convoluted and unstable structure of our money and banking system. It is analogous to an inexperienced driver on an icy road creating a destabilizing feedback cycle by stepping first on the brake and then on the accelerator in quick succession until disaster finally strikes. In our fractional-reserve banking system, the problem is worsened by the fact that the fiat-money printing Fed does not have direct control over all components of the money supply. In particular, the Fed, who sets a minimum reserve requirement for banks of 10 percent of demand deposits, actually cannot control the portion of reserves banks ultimately choose to lend out. Nor can it precisely control the amount of currency individuals actually choose to deposit in banks. For example, during the current period (2008 – 2012) the Fed has been very aggressive in expanding bank reserves (the monetary base), but banks, more stringently regulated and gun-shy due to recent loan defaults, have responded by cautiously accumulating excess reserves rather than lending them out. The cumulative result has been high growth in bank reserves but

41

disappointingly slow growth in the broader money supply. The potential uncertainty and instability of this system is staggering. It revises the car on ice analogy above. The correct analogy is more nearly a car driven on ice by a panicking driver (banks) with an also panicking Fed sitting in the back seat shouting instructions.

Ironically, rather than the supreme stabilization tool envisioned by early 20th century bankers, it is arguable that the Federal Reserve's monetary policies during the period leading up to the Great Depression actually helped add to volatility in the U.S. money supply and its rate of growth. The Fed-created volatility was largely responsible for deepening and lengthening the Great Depression, 1929-1941. This was certainly the hypothesis first presented by Friedman and Schwartz. Intended to foster money and banking stability, the Fed instead became a major source of instability to the money and banking system. Moreover, as for lobbying for a powerful federal super bank, bankers should have been careful for what they wished. What they actually got, to their probable dismay, was a robust new source of banking regulation and oversight.

Following World War I, the 1920s was a period of remarkable economic expansion in the U.S. economy. The expansion of the U.S. equity market, in particular, during this period seemed to exhibit increasingly bubble-like vulnerability to sober observers. Large and small investors were enthusiastic participants in the stock market and yet, by many modern metrics, it could also be argued that the U.S. equity market was not then necessarily overvalued. However, what definitely was true was that there was an enormous volume of bank lending that was created to support the expansion of ownership of U.S. stocks. Brokerage firms of the period had extended a large volume of margin debt to speculative investors. This margin debt, in turn, was based upon loans, or credit lines, from banks to the brokerage firms. The collateral backing these margin loans to investors was largely the value of the stock they purchased. Moreover, a large volume of this debt was issued at as much as 90 percent margin. This meant that the loan extended to purchase a given quantity of stock was as much as

90 percent of the current value of the stock purchased. Individual investors with such loans in place had as little as 10 percent net equity in a stock purchase they made, while 90 percent of the purchase was debt-financed with the value of the stock as collateral. Everything was fine in such a pyramid of leverage if equity prices continued to rise, as they did during most of the 1920s. However, the system was top-heavy and catastrophically vulnerable to even a modest decline in stock prices. Moreover, although most discussions of the Great Depression focus mainly on stock prices it can be argued that other asset markets, such as real estate, were vulnerable and overvalued as well. Sound familiar?

Given a very vulnerable economy, the initial spark that lit the powder keg was likely a tightening of monetary policy by the Fed initiated during the spring and summer of 1929. A policy shift toward slower money growth pushed short-term interest rates upward and started to push financial asset prices downward. A stock price decline commenced during the summer of 1929 and worsened during September and October. Though the initial monetary tightening was modest, it was akin to skiing across a slope that was more than ready to avalanche. Many investors faced margin calls as stock market prices went down to where the value of the stock purchased fell below the valuation necessary to repay the loan. Since, in the case of a 90 percent margin loan, the loan could not be repaid by selling even all of the stock to generate funds, brokers expected investors to provide a payment in cash to make up the difference. At the time an "uncovered speculator" was an investor who could not cover his potential losses or margin calls—in other words, an investor who might have to default on his margin loans. In 1929 there were hundreds of thousands of these uncovered speculators. The result was a cascading and accelerating decline in stock prices in response to a growing wave of sellers. Given the rapid decline in equity prices during the fall of 1929, margin loan defaults to brokers and loan defaults to banks soared.

There were many culprits in the collapse of the stock market, the credit market, and the banking system that produced the death-spiral known as the Great Depression. We could blame irresponsible borrowers, irresponsible bankers, and irresponsible brokers. We could also blame the Federal Reserve at the time for not recognizing the powder-keg of an over-valued, over-leveraged equity market. The effect of higher interest rates on equity prices and lending was not unexpected. What the Fed evidently didn't expect were the disastrous effects of this policy in causing the implosion of over-extended equity and credit markets. (Interestingly, by substituting the housing market and "uncovered" mortgage-debt for the equity market and "uncovered" margin-loan market of 1929, we could just as easily be describing the conditions that led to the collapse of the U.S. credit market during 2007-2009).

It can be argued that the inherent structural instability of the banking and credit markets during 1929, and the Federal Reserve's policy responses, led to the inception and worsening of the Great Depression. Ironically, Friedman and Schwartz make the point that if the Federal Reserve had not been created, a private banking system, along the lines of that existing in 1907, might have had a better chance of stabilizing the economy without producing a depression. Theirs is probably the original argument questioning the existence of the Fed.

The linkage between the early stages of the Great Depression and the failure of much of the banking sector and the credit market is painfully obvious. As loan defaults ballooned, banks came under pressure. In a fractional-reserve banking system, whenever bank assets decline significantly in value, it is reasonable and rational for depositors to become concerned and to wish to withdraw their deposited funds. This they did, creating three major rounds of banking panics in the United States. By the end of the period 1929-1933, more than 4,000 banks had failed and the stock of monetary aggregate M1 had declined by nearly 50 percent as a result. The internal collapse of the private banking system as depositors attempted to withdraw their funds produced the bulk of this monetary contraction. This was a catastrophic secondary collapse in money growth that was outside the direct control of the

44

Federal Reserve. It was directly due to the nature of our fractional-reserve banking system. Such a system can expand the money supply when deposits of cash are made and disastrously contract the money supply when deposits are withdrawn—all outside the direct control of the Fed.

By the trough of the Great Depression in 1933, real economic output had dropped by approximately one-third and an estimated 25 percent of the U.S. labor force was unemployed. Deflation was roaring as prices were falling at an astounding annualized rate of 19 percent. Dysfunctional equity and bond markets could not begin to match the risk-adjusted return that could be obtained by simply holding money balances—as long as your money balances were held outside a bank. Not surprisingly, the most sensible investment around was simply hoarding money, under the mattress or under the floor boards. To criticize the hoarding of cash during the Great Depression as naïve or unpatriotic was absurd. Where else could one obtain a risk-free rate of return of 19 percent during that period?

To understand the mechanics of such a staggering contraction in the money supply of the United States as occurred during the Great Depression it is worthwhile to reproduce a little algebra employed in the Friedman and Schwartz' description. Let us define the following terms:

M = the stock of money as contained in monetary aggregate M1.
C = the stock of currency held by the public (outside of commercial banks).
D = the current funds held by the public in checking accounts or demand deposits.
R = the stock of commercial bank reserves, which are currency held in the vaults of commercial banks combined with commercial bank deposits at the Fed.
H = the stock of high-powered money (commercial bank reserves plus currency held by the non-bank public).

Then,

(2-2) $M = C + D$

and,

(2-3) $H = C + R$

After some algebraic manipulation of these two equations (not reproduced here), it is possible to obtain:

(2-4) $$M = \frac{H(D/R)(1 + D/C)}{(D/R + D/C)}$$

The lowest allowable value of R, bank reserves, depends upon the level of a bank's demand deposits D and is set by Federal Reserve policy. The minimum allowable ratio (R/D) is called the "required reserve ratio" and in the United States it is currently 10 percent. That is, a bank must hold reserves in an amount at least equal to 10 percent of its demand deposits. Thus, the value of the ratio (D/R) occurring when banks loan out all their excess reserves is 10. This maximum ratio of (D/R) that can be attained, which is the reciprocal of the required reserve ratio, is often called the "money multiplier." The idea is that an increase in bank's reserves of, say, $1 billion, can result in an eventual increase in the money supply of $10 billion, all as a consequence of fractional reserve banking and banks industriously lending out all their allowable excess reserves.

The stock of high-powered money, H, is determined by the amount of total fiat money the Federal Reserve injects into the economy—either by means of open-market purchases of bonds or by lending reserves directly to banks. The deposit to currency ratio, (D/C), is determined entirely by the public's preference about how to best hold money balances. Do people want to hold crisp green dollar bills in their wallet (C) or would they prefer to carry less cash and keep more in their checking account (D)? It is important to realize

46

that neither banks nor the Fed have any direct control over this decision—but it has important implications for the size of the money supply.

The supply of high-powered money, H, is independent of public preferences about whether to hold money as printed currency or as checking account balances. That is, the form taken by high-powered money can change, depending on whether individuals choose to hold printed currency or demand deposits, but the total remains constant. For example, suppose a person has been keeping a stack of 20 one-hundred dollar bills hidden under his mattress. Printed currency held outside commercial banks is, of course, part of high-powered money, entering equation (2-3) as "C." If the individual decides to deposit the $2,000 in his checking account, then the printed money is taken out of circulation and it enters the vault of the bank as reserves. Thus, the variable "C" in equation (2-3) falls by $2,000, while the bank reserves "R" go up by a like amount, leaving total high-powered money "H" unchanged. Also, as long as banks stay fully-loaned, the value of (D/R) does not change as individuals choose to hold more-or-less printed currency; if the reserve requirement is 10 percent, the value of (D/R) stays fixed as 10.

So, how does a switch in individual preference toward fewer demand deposits relative to printed currency affect the total money supply? That is, a decline in the ratio of demand deposits to currency? The quick answer is that a collective preference by individuals to withdraw their money from bank accounts and hold it as currency will cause the money supply in a fractional-reserve banking system to disastrously collapse as it did during the Great Depression. To more formally answer this question we go through a minor math excursion that can easily be avoided by the "mathophobic" reader who can skip the following paragraph and proceed on to the next.

Define the ratio of demand deposits to printed currency to be $x = (D/C)$. Then, equation (2-4) is re-written as follows:

(2-5)
$$M = \frac{H(D/R)(1+x)}{(D/R+x)}$$

Now, it is a simple matter to determine how the money supply responds to changes in (D/C) by differentiating M with respect to x while holding high-powered money H and the ratio (D/R) constant. Taking the derivative, one obtains:

(2-6)
$$\frac{dM}{dx} = \frac{H(D/R)[(D/R)-1)]}{(D/R+x)^2} > 0$$

The derivative shown in equation (2-6) is positive as a consequence of fractional reserve banking; that is, $(D/R) > 1$, which means the numerator in equation (2-6) is positive in sign. Thus, an increase in the public's desire to hold checking account balances rather than printed currency, which is an increase in $x = (D/C)$, causes the money supply to expand, whereas a preference to switch back to printed currency (which amounts to a decrease in x) will decrease the money supply.

Let's examine each of these values and ratios that define the stock of money, equation (2-4), during the deepening part of the Great Depression, the period 1929-33. The ratio (D/C) fell precipitously as individuals tried en masse to get their money out of banks. The result was that the numerator of (2-4) fell by much more than the denominator. In fact, if (D/R) is approximately 10, then the "money-multiplier" catastrophically operates in reverse when individuals scramble to convert their bank accounts to cash.

The 1907 theory leading to the creation of the Fed was that the Fed could counteract a falling value of (D/C) with an offsetting increase in H, with the result that, system-wide, the total money stock, M, would be stabilized. In theory, since H appears only in the numerator of equation (2-4), it could be readily increased by the Fed in whatever magnitude was required to prevent a fall in M. However, as Friedman and Schwartz famously note in their book, the Fed did not do this—at least not during 1929-33. The result was a historically huge decline in the total U.S. transactions money

48

stock. Fluctuations in (D/C), driven by rational individuals correctly suspicious of what a fractional-reserve banking system might have done with their deposits, has been a historic and continuous source of volatility in the U.S. banking system. Ironically, fluctuations in (D/C) and the resulting economic volatility could be structurally removed by making illegal the fractional-reserve practice of the banking system, at least so far as checking accounts are concerned—that is, by placing the Fed in the front seat of our car on ice rather than the back seat. Not only would the removal of the banks' fraudulent practice of transferring property rights of depositors without compensating or informing them be the right thing to do, it would also help to stabilize the monetary system and thereby the economy in the process. A 100 percent reserve requirement for banks would also greatly simplify the conduct of Federal Reserve monetary policy.

As Friedman and Schwartz subsequently discuss in their book, large open market purchases and the robustness of a free market economy adjusting to extremely large institutional shocks eventually led to a recovery from the Great Depression. One could say much the same concerning the current period (2008-2012) with the caveat and grudging nod to the Bernanke Fed that it, at least, never did allow a 50 percent contraction in the money stock. That is, the U.S. economy is apparently finally modestly recovering despite the shocks of successive ineffective or inept monetary and fiscal policies. The biggest issue currently for the Fed is that practically all of the increase in H over recent years has languished in banks as an increase in "excess reserves" rather than generating lending activity. That is why the recovery response to a historically expansionary Federal Reserve monetary policy has been so weak.

Interestingly, in the Great Depression as well as the more recent economic downturn, the level of nominal interest rates could not be used as an indicator of the ease of monetary policy. Following both the Great Depression and the current credit market collapse nominal short-term government interest rates were then and are now close to zero. Instead, the actual sustained growth rate of the broad money supply (M2) is a more reliable measure of the ease or tightness of monetary policy. Since, in a fractional-reserve banking system, actual money and credit expansion relies on the lending activity of banks unleashing the effect of the money multiplier (D/R), even strenuous expansionary open-market purchases by the Federal Reserve can be initially disappointing in their expansionary impact upon the economy. The reason ironically is that the very same banks and lending agents that helped to spawn the credit expansion and collapse in the first place through their "irrationally exuberant" loan underwriting, will typically become nervous and excessively conservative in stimulating money and credit expansion that is desperately needed during the recovery. Sadly, this effect has been worsened by the badly-timed passage of additional and more stringent government regulation and oversight upon banking and credit activity.

You will by now have inferred that we are critical of a monetary system that finds its basis on a fiat money that has been over-extended through the dubious lending mechanism of a fractional-reserve banking system. In particular, we believe that the pyramid of poorly underwritten, weak, and over-speculative loans that occur when a fractional-reserve banking system is responsible for the allocation of society's scarce savings has led to an inefficient allocation of savings and repetitive systemic instability. The Great Depression period and the more recent credit market implosion are but two examples of this system-wide inherent instability. Further, support for this system, whether it is in the form of the Federal Deposit Insurance Corporation, the Federal Reserve System itself, or government bailouts in which the government makes itself (and thereby the public at large) the final guarantor of excessive, bad loans is simply window-dressing—putting the best front on a fatally flawed system. These solutions respond to the symptoms of an endemically unstable money, credit, and banking system, but do not address the root causes of the economic instability.

Let us step back for a moment and consider the division between consumption and saving at the individual as well as the aggregate level. In the simplest context, the motive for saving is very clear.

Individuals face the problem of maximizing their welfare through consumption over time. When an individual is very old, he is probably not going to be as productive as he was previously, and thus his consumption will depend on his previous saving behavior. Therefore, an individual or a household saves in order to smooth or maximize consumption over time. There is some real expected additional return which at the margin is sufficient to entice each of us to defer present period consumption in return for a higher level of consumption in a future period. The higher the expected return to postponed consumption is, the more likely it is that a given individual will defer more consumption today for greater consumption later. For an aggregate economy, the total of saving is the sum of that proportion of production or income that is not consumed. If it is not consumed then it is invested in the tools, factories or education that allows individuals to produce more efficiently in future periods. Thus, we view aggregate saving as equal to aggregate investment and we could and will use these aggregate terms interchangeably.

This is where the aggregate and the individual concept of saving can and do differ. An individual might direct saved income to a savings account, an investment in a CD, a loan to Uncle Bert for a snowmobile, or they could channel savings to a business that uses it to increase its stock of tools and equipment. Only if the funds flow into a capital good (tools, equipment, education, etc.) that actually enhances future production is the individual's saving viewed as part of the economy's aggregate saving. Otherwise one individual's saving simply flows back into another individual's consumption—through an opaque loanable funds market—and adds nothing to the economy's stock of productive capital.

Our contention, explored in greater detail later in this book, is that the aggressive, poorly underwritten, and over-expanded lending market encouraged by our fractional-reserve banking system does an inefficient and wasteful job of allocating our economy's scarce and valuable savings. The inefficiency occurs in part because bankers, brokers, and other intermediaries in the credit market are typically not compensated on the basis of directing the available saving of individuals to the best and highest use. The recent excessive and aggressive lending in the U.S. residential housing market is simply one of the latest illustrations of this. A fractional-reserve system encourages a multiple expansion of leverage which may not be justified by the actual available production of the economy, at a given point in time, to consume and invest. It can create the dangerous illusion that more is available than has actually been produced; or, put another way, it encourages the illusion that claims on property or output exceed what actually exists. When this happens it is the definition of a "bubble" that sooner or later is unsupportable and must burst. At the worst, this illusion risks implosion of the credit market at any time (as we have recently experienced and as the country previously experienced during the Great Depression). At the best, it generates a historically observed bias toward inflation as the fiat money supplier (the Federal Reserve) is forced to choose between validating weak lending decisions by printing more money or risking a severe recession.

So how do severe economic downturns, such as the one we are currently living through, happen and persist? We are vulnerable to recessions, in part, because any trade or exchange doesn't just take place at a point in space, it also takes place at a point in time. Arranging an exchange often requires the specification of contracts, which look forward over time, between buyers and sellers. Whether we are talking about restaurant menus, prices listed in a catalog, interest rates on loans, or labor contracts, we have no choice but to try to estimate future economic conditions. For example, determining the interest rate that will be charged on a loan requires a forecast of the inflation rate over the loan's life. If inflation turns out to be surprisingly high, then the interest rate being paid by a borrower will not keep up with rising prices; the lender can end up earning a negative real rate of return. On the other hand, surprise deflation during a loan's life would mean the borrower is paying a cripplingly high real interest rate. Turning to labor agreements, when negotiating a long-term labor contract, the parties need to determine whether the wage paid will go up each year during the life of the contract, and if so how much based upon inflation, increasing productivity and so on. So, economic forecasting is a necessary part of contracting trades over the future. The absence of such contracts is inconceivable—all production would be tied up in continuous negotiation and argument.

Once such a contract is in place, the economic forecast that formed the basis of the agreement will typically turn out to be wrong. Contracts in efficient markets may be rational in the sense that they are not systematically wrong, but they will still be wrong in an uncertain world in which not all shocks are systematic or predictable. Mortgage re-financings, unemployment, and labor strikes are evidence of this. So, if contracts are typically wrong, why are they not quickly revised? One obvious reason agreements are not constantly revised is that the time and resource costs of day-to-day rewriting of every contract would be enormous and unthinkable. There is another reason. Whenever an economic forecast is off, there will be winners and losers; the winners are understandably going to have little interest in revising the contract's terms.

Consider a labor contract that has a built-in schedule for an annual rate of increase in wages of 4 percent each year. The increase in wages might reflect the expectation of an equivalent rate of increase in the economy's Consumer Price Index. If inflation ends up being only 1 percent, then workers delight as the value of their real compensation is increasing. "Finally," they may say, "our true worth is becoming recognized." From another perspective, as a result of the forecasting error, labor is becoming more expensive to employers who are surprised by the low inflation rate. If workers wages are rising at 4 percent, but the price of the company's output is only growing at the overall inflation rate of 1 percent, then labor's "real wage" is growing at 3 percent. Should the real wage become large enough, employers will either be more reluctant to hire new workers or they may go a step further and lay workers off. Naturally there will be resistance on labor's part to revise the contract because those workers who remain employed are doing very well; they have received a windfall they did not expect in terms of inflation-adjusted compensation.

As another example, suppose general inflation is higher than had been expected when contracts were negotiated. That is, suppose wages are scheduled to go up by 4 percent, but inflation comes in at 7 percent. Then the employer reaps a windfall because the compensation to labor is rising more slowly than prices. The company profits since the price of its output is growing at a faster rate than is its labor expense. Although labor will wish to re-open the wage contract to negotiation, the employer will be in no hurry to do so because the firm is harvesting unexpected profits.

In an efficient and rational marketplace, contracts will not waste easily obtainable information that can be used to forecast future economic conditions. That is, the economic forecasts reflected in contracts will be as correct as they reasonably can be based upon the set of information available when the contracts are negotiated. The systematic or predictable portion of the information is available in the past series of the variable we are trying to predict (see, for example, "Rational Expectations and the Theory of Price Movements" by John Muth). Information considered in contracts would include systematic components of inflation and consistently applied Federal Reserve monetary policy rules. Those things that can be predicted will be included in efficient and well-written contracts either as expectations or contingencies.

Since contracts will reflect predictable information, the sad conclusion is that the Federal Reserve can only exert real effects from its monetary policy if it makes its policy rule secret and unsystematic—thereby surprising the participants in the private economy and upsetting their contracts. For instance, maybe the Fed prints money much more quickly than expected and thereby creates some surprise inflation. The shot of inflation causes the real wage to fall, making profits jump, and enticing companies to hire more people. We should emphasize that the inflation will only result in a lower real wage if it exceeds the forecasted rate built into labor agreements; it will only have an impact if it is a bolt from the blue. "How can such surprises really be good?" you may well ask. As was discussed above, any unexpected shock to the economy will result in winners and losers. In the case of surprise inflation, companies see profits increase but workers suffer a decrease in their real wage. Rather than making a value judgment as to whether company profits are more important than workers' real wages, what should be stressed is this: The only way monetary policy can have an impact on the real economy is when it is unpredictable and adds volatility to markets and to economic growth. Unfortunately, the history of Fed policy during its first hundred years has shown that it has not lost the ability to surprise and shock us—and, therefore, make its monetary policy rule, if it has one, indiscernible.

As we saw in the 2008 credit market collapse, one of the most important, forward-looking contracts in our economy is the contract involved in a loan or a mortgage. And, of course, banks are the most important players in the mortgage market. In a fractional- reserve banking system there is an uncompensated transfer of property rights occurring when most of a demand depositor's funds are loaned out without her awareness or compensation. However, this is not the only uncompensated transfer that occurs. When a bank makes weak loan underwriting decisions in lending these "excess reserves" in an attempt to make a profit, then the bank has transferred risk to all its depositors and in the age of taxpayer-financed bail-outs—to society at large. The coupling of a frenzy of fractional-reserve lending with a profusion of default risk, because too many loans are being made to individuals who are unlikely to be able to repay them, can lay the groundwork, as we have witnessed, for a huge catastrophe.

How does this actually work in the case of an individual loan? Consider a story that closely parallels many "real-world" examples from the period of the housing boom and subsequent collapse. Visualize two married school teachers living in a prosperous community who decide in the midst of the 2005 housing boom to take a shot at buying a $600,000 home. The teachers' joint income is in the range of $70,000 and they have little accumulated savings. However, they are pleasantly surprised when a mortgage broker is, with some effort, able to place them into a "teaser" rate adjustable mortgage that is large enough to mitigate the need for a significant down payment. Alas, stories similar to this were commonplace during the 2001-2005 "crazy" years in real estate.

For many loans made during the period, the initial or "teaser" rate of interest was set below the going market rate for a few years in order to allow new borrowers time to increase their household earnings before the loan payments got high. The end result of very low payments early in a loan is called "negative amortization." That is, the excess interest owed which is not paid during the early part of a loan is simply added to the unpaid principal balance of the loan. Thus, added to all the unhealthy aspects of this underwriting process is the fact that the principal balance of an already top-heavy loan will actually increase during the loan's early years.

The loan made to the school teachers was then packaged with other similar mortgages and securitized, stamped with approval by a bond-rating agency for a fee, and then, as a AAA-rated security sold to an unwitting investor—say a small community retirement fund in Norway (another real-world example).

What unfolded is drearily familiar to many of us. The Federal Reserve held the price of credit artificially low from 2001 to 2003 (with a target Federal Funds rate of 1 percent), and thereby provided a green light for such an expansion in the lending market that a $600,000 adjustable rate home loan could be made to two school teachers with a straight face on the part of the lending intermediary. Later, the Fed suddenly reversed course and decided to apply the monetary brakes to the credit market frenzy, as it believed the low price of credit had unacceptably raised the risk of future inflation. So the Bernanke Fed started ratcheting-up the target Federal Funds rate from 1 percent to 5.25 percent. The cumulative effect of these incremental rate policies was to raise short-term interest rates and slow monetary growth. The impact of this action was felt when the interest adjustment period was reached on our schoolteachers' loan as well as on a myriad of other similar adjustable loans. They, like many other irresponsibly lent-to borrowers, simply did not have the income available to meet the increase in monthly loan payments as their "teaser-rate" period ended. Of course, an adjustable rate mortgage adjusts up when rates rise, and monthly loan payments increase. Borrowers who were stretched to the limit to finance their loan in the first place had no choice but to default on a mortgage that arguably never should have been made. Multiply the school teacher example by thousands of other such loans and it is clear that the Fed wittingly or unwittingly ignited a powder keg again during the first decade of the 2000's just as they did in 1929.

So who are the culprits in this sad story? There are many accomplices, and the structure of the banking and lending system is partly to blame. The fractional-reserve lending system encourages and allows questionable loans to be made without providing transparency to or obtaining agreement from the original source of funds (the depositors). The intermediaries in the loan approval or underwriting process, who are likely compensated based upon the volume of loans originated rather than the quality of those loans, also are key enablers of questionable lending. The bond-rating agencies deserve a special share of the blame. Rating agencies are supposedly performing the function of providing protection to the investing public rather than simply rubber-stamping approval on anything that is thrown to them (for a fee). The lesson here for an investor seeking transparency is clear: Beware of any due diligence provided by a government agency or any third party—the best and ultimately only reliable due-diligence is accomplished by open-eyed investors themselves. A regulatory watchdog market could work, but only if the approving institution is fully aware that its compensation comes from the buyers and not sellers of securities. Of course, blame is also attached to many borrowers who either provided fraudulent information or willingly entered into loans that, under even the likely circumstance of modestly rising interest rates, they would be unable to repay. Finally, a large share of the blame attaches to the Federal Reserve and its conduct of monetary policy. The manipulation of the price of credit and artificial pricing in such a key market, as that for saving and lending, is fraught with peril. It is not clear why the Fed, with the mandate for providing a fiat currency as a medium of exchange and value, and with the objective of stabilizing inflation or the value of that currency, should persist in manipulating what should be determined in a free market—the price of credit.

Starting from the credit market collapse, and noting the rigidity of contracts, the rest of the story of the recent economic contraction is easy to set forth. Initially the Fed followed a policy of artificially holding the price of credit at an absurdly low level. This caused an expansion of credit and allowed the stock of loans to go through a period of frenzied growth, eventually filling every nook and cranny in the aggregate credit market with good loans or bad. Then the Fed inevitably took away the "punch bowl." In the fall of 2008, mortgage defaults started to spike to historically unprecedented levels. The epic level of loan defaults and write-downs brought the collapse of banks and brokerage institutions (Lehman, AIG, etc.) to the forefront in a way that was eerily reminiscent of the credit collapse during the Great Depression.

As a result of these shocks, combined with an expectation of declining earnings, the stock market experienced an eventual decline in value of over 50 percent. As asset values fell and leverage pinched the typical consumer, aggregate consumption and investment spending began their inevitable decline. To a typical business, it appeared that sales and revenues were on a downward trend, but expenses were not falling because of labor and other forward-looking contracts that were in place. Therefore, the average business had no choice but to reduce output and lay-off workers, creating a rise in unemployment. In the aggregate this was all a recipe for the strong recession we are still experiencing. Rarely do we observe a collapse of 30 percent in average housing values. Such a dramatic decline in the main store of aggregate wealth has historically corresponded to unusually severe economic contractions—again, for example, the Great Depression. Not surprisingly, while consumers will readily increase their personal expenditures based upon the rising value of their homes, they will also reduce their personal expenditures when the value of their homes decreases. The collapse was and continues to be deep and long—extended by inept and wasteful debt-financed government policy responses and reluctance in many markets to immediately write-down assets to their true market values. The cost of delaying the re-valuations, bankruptcies, business failures and write-downs is a delayed and disappointingly slow economic recovery.

The government and the Federal Reserve responded to the credit and housing market collapse by once again reversing direction on a dime. Together, the U.S. government and the Federal Reserve effectively bought billions of dollars of toxic debt through Treasury debt swaps and Fed open-market purchases. The skeptical amongst us observed that they had forgotten one important thing: Transferring default risk from the specific banks and security issuers—while it may be helpful to them—does not eliminate the risk. It simply passes the problem, which was theirs, on to the government—that is to say on to all of us as taxpayers— and makes it ours.

Reacting to the most recent economic collapse, the Fed responded by increasing the monetary base by over $1.5 trillion dollars from September 2008 through December 2011. And it lowered the target Federal Funds rate to the absurd level of 0.13 percent (approximately zero). This Federal Reserve policy appears to reflect an unstated understanding that the best way out of a debt crisis is to inflate it away. By creating a flood of new money, those pesky debt obligations that are stated in dollars can be reduced to the extent that the real value of them, relative to the rest of the economy, simply doesn't matter.

These wild policy swings to "stabilize" an economy experiencing successive volatile shocks are reminiscent of the famous 19th century story of a tour boat upon the Hudson River. Seeing an interesting sight (perhaps a whale), all the passengers scurry to the port rail. As a result, the ship begins to roll dangerously in that direction. In a panic, the passengers all scurry to the starboard rail with the result that the ship rolls even more violently in that direction—both because of the imbalance and the fact that it is already starting to roll back in that direction anyway. After several panicked rushes, the un-dampened oscillations of the ship rolling actually resulted in its capsizing. To make matters even worse, suppose that in addition to the panic of the passengers, the Captain (the Federal Reserve in our case) is actually shouting through a bullhorn, encouraging them to rush even more strenuously from rail to rail. During the past decade, the Fed has taken us on a round-trip from a target Federal Funds rate of 1 percent, to a high point of 6.5 percent, and then back to almost zero. The skeptics amongst us can be forgiven for wondering whether we might have been better off during this period, and the economy and financial markets more stable, if the Fed had simply held the target Federal Funds rate at, say, 3 percent during the entire period. Ask yourself, did this Fed "round-trip" policy stabilize the economy or destabilize it?

At the time of this writing, the U.S. economy has been struggling through a deep recession/depression since the onset of the credit and financial market collapse of the fall of 2008. It has been 50 years since the Nobel prize-winning economist Milton Friedman first articulated his sharp criticism of tax and debt-financed fiscal policy. During the period 2008 through 2012 we have seen countless attempts at "stimulative" fiscal policy on the part of two presidential administrations. The result has been a ballooning stock of U.S. Treasury debt as well as burgeoning federal deficits. Sadly, there has been little discernible positive effect of all of these policies upon the U.S. economy. Unemployment remains stubbornly high and economic growth remains disappointingly low. Banks and the lending market still appear to be in a hobbled state of disrepair. The heart of Friedman's criticism—when a government makes a new expenditure it extracts from the private economy an equal and off-setting private expenditure that would have otherwise occurred—appears as true today as it was when he first stated it fifty years ago. The actual result of government expenditure is worse than a zero-sum game. It is a negative sum game because the government's expenditure is less likely to stimulate growth of the economy than the private expenditure it displaced. That displaced private expenditure would have tended to flow to more productive uses and higher returning investments. Particularly inefficient are the bailouts and gifts that reward the weakest and least deserving entities—thus reversing the economic benefits of free market competition. The fact that any growth at all is occurring is testimony to the robustness and natural ability of even a partial market economy to recover from almost any shock.

At present (2012), we observe the machinations of the European Union with great interest. Credit problems and irrational government policies know no national boundaries. A single central bank (the European Central Bank), with a single currency (the Euro), operating over many different governments—each with independent expenditure, taxation, and debt-financing policies—is sooner or later a recipe for disaster. Those who run prodigious government deficits (Greece, Italy, Spain, etc.) must be ultimately bailed out or subsidized by the taxpayers of the more prudent (e.g., Germany) if the Union is to survive. The alternatives are stark. Dissolution of the European Union appears politically unacceptable. Allowing the weaker members' government debt to go into default implies a crisis in the foreign exchange value of the Euro. It could also make all Euro-denominated debt toxic in the international bond market, making this alternative politically unpalatable as well. Therefore, what the more solvent members of the European Union are left with is either buying up and assuming the toxic debt of their less responsible brethren, which results in a future tax burden being transferred to their citizens, or inflating the supply of Euros to pay the debt service of their spendthrift partners—resulting in higher future inflation and Euro depreciation. Either case represents a transfer of wealth from the prudent to the imprudent—from the ants to the grasshoppers. Doubtless, after all the accords, meetings, beseechments, and understandings of Euro-zone officials, a form of one of these last two alternatives is likely to be what actually happens. Of course, appropriate window-dressing and promises and/or stern admonitions and finger-wagging from all on future expenditure restraint and austerity will be generously provided. Much back-patting and congratulations on the diligent efforts of all in curing the "euro-crisis" will doubtless occur. What will be lost is recognition of the irony that all this effort went to repair what was a fundamentally flawed and perhaps indefensible institution in the first place.

We believe that a rational market economy has incredible self-stabilizing characteristics. But the disastrous combination of a flawed banking and lending structure coupled with destabilizing central bank policies is a bit much for any economy to endure. There has to be a better way to manage and maintain a rational money supply and to provide a more transparent loan market. Describing a better way is the purpose of the remainder of this book. To see how it could work, let's return to the island.

CHAPTER 3

THE DINNER

Years have passed since we last looked in on the island economy. A group of islands have joined together into a larger nation and trading area called the "Island Confederation." Bob Jr., now chairman of the Central Bank of the Island Confederation, is nervously awaiting his daughter, Roberta. Under Bob Jr.'s direction, the Confederation Central Bank has become responsible for controlling the supply of fiat currency for the islands and for regulating the banking industry. His earlier dream of managing a pure fiat money supply, at this point independent of any silver or commodity backing, has become reality. However, his life is still filled with confusion and complexity. Currently, Bob Jr. is somewhat baffled and overwhelmed by the apparently necessary expanding role of the Confederation Central Bank in trying to respond to a Confederation credit crisis, equity market meltdown and a deep, severe, and lingering recession.

On the home front, Bob Jr. is having dinner tonight with his daughter, Roberta. The front door opens and Roberta energetically enters the room. She gives Bob Jr. a warm hug and then sits down at the dining table. They are eating alone as Helen, his wife and Roberta's mother is off on an expedition to photograph and paint birds with the island bird-watching society. Jessup, an aging retainer, brings out a tureen of green turtle soup (a local delicacy) and begins to serve them.

"Well Dad," his daughter begins, "I have just come from a meeting at the Economics Club and you can bet there was a lot of discussion about the current situation in the Island Confederation. Many are of the opinion that we have brought this crisis on ourselves through a combination of misguided policy and structural flaws. However, most members think that you are just reacting the way you have to react at this point. They are disappointed that you don't come around much these days and have not responded to their invitations to speak. Your old friend and mentor Jim always comes to the meetings and is a frequent participant. He always asks about you. Gramps also comes to most our meetings. For a fisherman, he knows a lot about 'common sense' economics. Sometimes his comments create quite a stir."

Bob Jr. looked at his daughter and sighed inwardly. Why did she always have to be such a rebel and a critic, such a thorn in his side? It had been that way since she was very young. They had always argued good-naturedly and sometimes, truth be told, not so good-naturedly about almost everything. Nevertheless, he was very proud of her sharp intelligence and great beauty. She had matured into a confident woman and a gifted economist.

He responded, "Please give them my apologies at the club, but I am somewhat distracted presently with all the public responsibilities of managing a rescue of the Confederation economy and the banking and credit sectors. I have always felt the Central Bank plays the major role in protecting the economy from the threats of unemployment, slow economic growth, and inflation. But, I give you my congratulations; my spies tell me that you have recently become the president of the club. Imagine this of a club that used to be restricted to only male members in my day."

"Ah yes," his daughter replied to his comments on economic policy. "The government's charge to the Central Bank still clings to the old fallacy of multiple targets, unemployment, economic growth and inflation, with only one instrument—monetary policy. It doesn't require a great intellect to realize that one policy tool is only compatible with one target—don't say you don't realize that Dad because I've often heard you lament on it before. The goal you are politically charged with is logically unattainable before you even begin. Dad, you need to simplify your life at the Central Bank and confine yourself and the Board of Governors to following a monetary policy that is simple, transparent, and predictable.

"Many at the Economics Club believe that the Central Bank's attempts at 'stabilization' aren't helping. Instead, they think what the bank is doing is actually the main source of volatility and instability in our economy. The bank's active monetary policy is sending mixed signals and is interfering in the efficient allocation of resources to Confederation markets. You are artificially setting the price of savings, which is the interest rate, in a way that distorts the natural allocation of output between current consumption and investment, or, if you will, between current consumption and future consumption."

"Roberta, you sound like you've been talking far too much to Jim, again. He never understood the need for a fractional-reserve banking system—thought it was some kind of 'fraud,' much less the need for a Confederation Central Bank to control monetary policy in an increasingly large and complex economy," Bob Jr. replied. "For God's sake, I had enough trouble trying to get him to understand the concept of money backed by a silver stock that had fallen to the bottom of the lagoon."

Bob Jr.'s mind involuntarily wandered back many years to the images of being with Jim and crossing the lagoon with the original bank's silver reserves on the large log raft. He recalled the beautiful sunny morning with the glaring bright sunspots reflecting off the choppy water; his daydreaming inattentiveness being abruptly snapped by his shocked awareness of a large, fast-moving swell suddenly appearing on the horizon. He remembered the sinking horror of realizing there was absolutely no way to maneuver the raft to avoid it. He precisely recalled the sudden rush of water raising and then flipping the raft over, tossing them both into the water, the taste of salt-water in his mouth and throat, and the vast hoard of silver coins sparkling and fluttering in the water as they lazily disappeared toward the bottom of the Great Lagoon. The image was surrealistically beautiful—like a flock of iridescent birds heading home over a sea-blue meadow. He remembered Jim's almost comically distraught pale face as he came sputtering and coughing back to the surface with the several coins he had managed to catch—his eyes as big as saucers. It was tough on the poor guy, he had actually been asleep before being tossed into the lagoon. He could still hear Jim's retching, sobbing and wailing on the beach as if his world had ended. He, himself, had remained stoic with the growing firm realization that exactly where the silver was, and ultimately whether it existed or not, really didn't matter. He knew that after their extended argument on the beach, even after all these years, Jim had never really accepted the idea of a fiat money. He had bowed reluctantly to it at the time because he simply had no other choice.

Roberta interrupted her dad's internal reverie. "Well, since you mention Jim, he is doing well. He has gained a new lease on life at the club. His ideas have stimulated a lot of discussion and many of the members agree with his thinking. His views on the superiority of commodity money, the fallacy and danger of a fractional-reserve banking system leading to excessive lending, and what he calls the paradox of what 'is,' have become quite popular with many of the current members."

"And popular with you, too, I suppose? Since you were little you've always enjoyed being a contrarian to my points of view," her father snorted. He contemplated how it had complicated his life that the Economics Club had become sufficiently 'modern' to begin admitting female members, which resulted in Roberta's joining and ultimately shaped much of her thinking on matters of economics. Maybe Jim did have a point when he had observed years ago that the island economy would be better served if the young drones who were Club members would find useful employment rather than idly hatching utopian schemes. But he had been one of them then. Of course, he could not admit any of these internal thoughts and doubts to his daughter.

Roberta replied, "Well, I don't agree with everything Jim says. But, I think that the paradox of what 'is' is just simple economic logic. We cannot magically make more output by simply shifting the claims on existing output around, or making more of them, stacked on top of one another. Even worse, we cannot create more output by creating excessive layers of borrowing fueled by a fractional-reserve banking system. Jim is right in saying that an unnaturally low price of credit, natural human greed, a fractional-reserve banking system, and poor quality of loan underwriting have combined to lead to the current implosion of the Confederation credit market. In turn, the credit market collapse has created a slump in output and employment because forward-looking trading contracts could not and did not anticipate it. I do agree with Jim's point of view that banks should play no role in expanding the money supply. Nor should they be the agents controlling the allocation of savings and credit. However, I firmly disagree with Jim that commodity money, specifically a return to silver, is the best solution."

"I think you are very naïve," Bob Jr. retorted, in spite of himself growing irritated. "If you actually spent some time with me down at the Central Bank, instead of coming up with cockamamie theories at the club, you would be amazed at the level of sophistication and detail of our discussions. While you and the other Club members are pontificating, someone has to consider the actual situation at every single individual bank—and in what precise way we should intervene or regulate. Someone has to consider the conditions in every market in the economy and what they collectively imply for the optimal role of monetary and interest rate policy. Someone has to come up with real answers to hard questions and policy responses to ruthless reality. Tireless, unappreciated public servants have to turn over and scrutinize every leaf in a staggeringly complex Island Confederation economy in order to determine the specific optimal policy or regulatory response in each case. Speaking for myself, the task is so daunting that I hardly get any sleep any more—I take it home with me every night. You should 'job-shadow' me for just one day and observe the staggering array of questions, decisions and crises that I must respond to on a daily basis."

His daughter's eyes had softened with sympathy as she listened to him. Whether she saw him as mistaken or not, he was her dad. She thought he was misguided, but she knew him well enough to know that his heart was in the right place. "Dad, you just don't get it, do you? Nothing can manage the outcomes and markets of a complex economy better than the operation of free markets in that economy. Any attempt to supplant or replace the function of a free market by a single controlling committee, central bank board of governors, or government, even with the best of public-spirited intentions, is doomed to failure. That is the well-known fallacy of top-down central planning or socialism.

"Attempts to intervene and manage, in detail, the outcomes in an economy as complicated as that of a single island, much less the entire Island Confederation, lead to increasingly complex layers of questions and further actions required. It is the profound genius of a market economy that the expertise about markets, production, investment and pricing is at the bottom of the pyramid, not at the top.

"You know Dad, in the 1700s Adam Smith observed that the economy's engine is the simple optimizing behavior of individual participants leading in the aggregate to a social optimum—the power of the 'invisible hand.' It is pointless and hopeless to try to manage or anticipate that hand. The Central Bank would do better to adhere to a predictable and transparent monetary policy— expand the supply of fiat money at the same rate as the average rate of real growth of the Confederation economy. This, of course, is much more easily done with a 100 percent bank reserve requirement. In this way, the Central Bank really would be part of the solution to economic growth and stability rather than a big part of the problem. If you followed that prescription, you could simplify your life, get out of the way of an efficient market economy, and you would get to sleep at night. You need to see that every intervention in private markets inevitably spawns the need for ten more, as does every rule or regulation. The problem of our economy is we currently labor under a flawed, bureaucratic institutional money, banking and credit structure—one that has evolved institutionally and by the accident of bureaucratic design. Its later development has not been determined by the market. It sorely needs to be revised or, more bluntly, largely demolished. You should simplify your life."

Ah, the arrogance and naïveté of youth, Bob Jr. thought. He remembered that as a young man he had had a good measure of it himself, until the complexity, necessity, and 'busy-ness' of the real world had hammered it out of him. The young always had such a simple and clear solution for everything until the need to respond to actual problems and crises caused them to cast aside their utopian visions. To be truthful, his mind had wandered and he had ceased paying attention to his daughter's diatribe about halfway through as he returned to his own immediate concerns at the Central Bank.

Roberta looked at him again with real concern. "Sorry about climbing on the soapbox Dad. I didn't mean to get so long-winded, but with the current state of the Confederation's economy, needless to say, I think a lot about such things. I suspect most of us islanders do. I really do believe that Gramps has a point in longing for the days of the old island economy when we all worried about our own business and not about everyone else's. I really do believe that the expertise lies at the bottom of the pyramid with the individual producers and their trading—not with bankers, managers, and politicians."

"Well we certainly disagree on that point," Bob Jr. quickly replied. "I believe that the free market economy is a beautiful but fragile flower—one that must be cared for and guarded from the shocks and storms of the real world as well as from the irrational behavior of its own participants. Nurturing and protecting the free market economy takes the patient intervention and regulation of experts, the government and the Central Bank. The 'free market' you and your grandpa so much admire is healthy only with careful and diligent attention. It is a delicate mechanism that thrives only because it is tended and protected analogous to a plant in a green house. Now Roberta don't you patronize me. I knew about and studied free markets and knew how important it was to protect them, sometimes from themselves, when you were in diapers."

His daughter nearly exploded with a derisive snort. "I'm not patronizing, I'm disagreeing. You should say that the free market somehow survives in spite of all this careful and diligent intervention, this tinkering. Free markets are the natural trading arrangements between humans. They are like weeds—robust, strong and hard to kill, not fragile. They continue to spring up and thrive despite the repeated tinkering, intervention and regulation of so-called experts. They thrive despite the fact that 40 percent of the product of the free markets of the Confederation economy is now siphoned off by government taxation and expenditure. Think of the prosperity that would result if the amount expropriated was reduced to 20 percent or even 10 percent."

"Yes," bellowed her father, "and think of the disaster spawned by speculative bubbles and excesses that would lay waste to the entire economy without our intelligent control and intervention in the marketplace. We have seen stock market pricing bubbles, housing bubbles, and credit bubbles—fueled by over-zealous speculators— that have burst and would have brought our entire economy down to a smoldering ruin. It is the job of the Central Bank, *my* job, to intervene to restore sanity and reasonable prosperity. What thanks do I get? Apparently not even my own daughter can appreciate what I have done."

This was dangerous ground, so Roberta diplomatically softened the decibel level. "Dad, of course I thank you for your selfless efforts, and I know you well enough to realize that you always operate with the best of intentions. Further, I know that, with things and institutions as they regrettably are, your efforts and the efforts of the Central Bank are probably necessary to reduce human misery and to return the economy to stability. But don't you ever wonder to what extent the Central Bank, the regulators and interveners, and the institutions they have designed, might be responsible for creating the very problems they must respond to? For example, don't you ever wonder to what extent the target interest rate manipulations of the Central Bank lead to the excessive speculation and bubbles to which it must later react? Don't you wonder how strong and self-stabilizing a market economy might be, if it was not subject to and shackled by such a set of institutions, regulations and interventions as we now have—if it were left to its own devices?"

"I don't have the luxury of time for such idle wonderings," Bob Jr. retorted. "Some of us have to work to assure the future and survival for all of us instead of hanging out at the Economics Club discussing alternative utopias.

"But, I must admit you sound much like me at your age—although, of course, I then held very different ideas. I still hope you will, with enough education, experience, and serious-mindedness, ultimately choose to follow my career of public service at the Central Bank. It is a thankless task but critically important—as you will eventually come to realize. You are a very capable young woman and you could choose a worse career.

"Again Roberta, I just wish you could observe the sophistication and detail that goes into our discussion of rational inflation-targeting of current monetary policy. You would be surprised at hearing some of your very same arguments and points being hotly debated in the private meetings of the Board of Governors. The economy is so large and so complex, and has so many hard and serious questions for even the most able and educated of us to manage. It requires almost superhuman and increasing efforts by the intelligentsia for the unknowing benefit of the little people in little markets.

"The current crisis is a perfect example. Roberta, what do we do with all the bad loans and toxic debt produced in all the individual markets by individual decision-making—simply let it fail? This would surely bring down the whole economy, a human catastrophe from which we might never recover, left to the market's own workings. The result would surely be a far more severe collapse than what we are currently enduring. Avoiding that dire outcome is the enlightened benefit of strong and intelligent policy intervention."

"My point precisely Dad," Roberta responded. "This debt would not be there in the first place had the Central Bank not artificially manipulated the price of credit, the target interest rate, to such a low level. The bank caused a feeding frenzy by a crowd of moronic lending market intermediaries, or bankers if you prefer, who make their fees off of loaning the hard-earned savings of producers and savers. These bankers responded to low lending rates with a great deal more enthusiasm than intelligence. Their actions, coupled with a fractional-reserve banking system created a predictable unstable pyramid of excessive leverage—in many cases, layers of loans to individuals with neither the ability nor the intention to repay them.

"When the Central Bank created an artificially low cost of borrowing, it created the ideal conditions for an expansion of a bubble of 'toxic' debt. The result is that the Central Bank and the Island Confederation Treasury is now busy buying up that predictable profusion of debt and sadly making it an obligation for our society at large, for future generations. Of course Dad, you know the stock of bad debt will not simply vanish; it will mutate from an individual obligation to a Confederation obligation. This outcome provides exactly the wrong lesson to markets. The borrowers and lenders of bad loans have been absolved from the responsibility for making them; they have been insulated from the cost and consequences of their own bad decisions. It is natural and healthy for participants in free markets to be punished for poor judgment and to learn from it. In free markets, every company and every individual must enjoy the sacred right to fail as the result of their own bad or irresponsible decisions. Ultimately, when the public sector assumes our weak debt, the way to make the enlarged stock of government debt inconsequential will be for the Central Bank to inflate it away by new money creation, effectively imposing an inflation tax upon all of us. I would never want to be responsible for that.

"And, by the way Dad, I don't see much of a future for myself in banking. With the exception of you and Jim, there is something about hanging out with bankers that seems to dull my intellect and depress my outlook."

Bob Jr. was becoming increasingly frustrated with this conversation. "So what would you have us do at this point? Simply let lenders and businesses fail and default, resulting in general economic collapse? Or should we try to respond with enlightened policy to minimize the shock to the economy? I have my own view of the paradox of what 'is.' In the real world, we do not have the luxury of what should be, we have to come up with solutions and policy responses to address what 'is.' Surely, the Confederation Central Bank held interest rates at historically low rates. But the low interest rates were caused by an unprecedented set of events, starting with a massive surprise terrorist attack upon us by the head-hunters. It is our amazingly bad luck that such barbarians actually still share the world with us in the present day. What a horribly dreadful mixture! It would be comical if it wasn't so tragic. They are technologically advanced enough to bomb us and destroy our valuable infrastructure while at the same time backward enough to boil us in pots. Many of us were killed, and some were actually eaten.

"The results would have been far worse had we not intervened with heroic expansionary monetary policy and very low interest rate targets in order to revive a devastated economy and a general collapse of public confidence. This is a perfect illustration of the real world need for optimal macroeconomic policy and the need for active intervention—not for benign neglect. Whatever you may think of it, the banking and monetary system, be assured, is exceedingly complex and requires constant attention and fine tuning in order to optimally serve our economy. This is the real story of what 'is.' Not Jim's threadbare old paradox."

"I couldn't disagree more," Roberta replied. "I believe the economy is far more robust in adapting to and recovering from shocks than you think. If markets had been left to naturally respond, we probably would not have created the next 'crisis'—the overhang of an unnatural expansion of the credit market, and a bubble that was bound to burst. In my opinion, the cure is all about risk, return, and transparency. Each of us should be responsible for their personal actions."

"And should we have allowed the fish-net and canoe industry to collapse, as it would have done without rescue?" Bob Jr. angrily retorted. "This is one of the Confederation's largest industries and largest employers. It is simply too important to fail. It was a correct and well-reasoned response by the government to provide a debt-financed bailout to such a critical industry—such a mainstay of Confederation employment."

Roberta started to reply and then bit her lip. She had started to say "With all due respect" when she realized that this was one of those peculiar, oxymoronic statements people use when they want to signify that the measure of "respect due" is, in fact, quite small. Instead she said, "Yes, in a market economy all industries or individual businesses should have the right to fail through competitive pressure. Other islands have long shown that they can produce fish nets more cheaply and efficiently than the Confederation can. It benefits us and them if we buy their nets instead of producing our own. By supporting an inefficient, uncompetitive industry, we are violating the basic benefit and rule of a market economy: Productive inputs and investment always will and should be allowed to move toward their best and most profitable uses. Instead, the heavy hand of government bond and tax-financed intervention is moving scarce, precious savings and investment to one of its least productive uses—in order to save jobs and votes in a non-competitive sector. A sector that is ultimately doomed to disappear in any case. This is 'life-support' and is precisely the wrong sort of intervention by government. It impairs economic efficiency rather than promoting it and it lays the groundwork for further 'necessary' interventions and, ultimately, failure."

Roberta looked at Bob Jr. for a moment before continuing in a quieter tone. "As I said before, the economy has grown too large and complex to manage or to understand from the top down. Why don't all you big people—you managers extraordinaire—at least consider the obvious solution in money and banking? Give up, get out of the way, and try letting a large complex economy accomplish what, to you, is an apparently impossible task. That is to manage itself through efficient, transparent markets working their magic from the bottom up."

Bob Jr. retorted, "And I say again that the money and credit market is too important to every individual's welfare to be left to chance! President Abomo agrees—he believes in the social goal of every Confederation citizen pursuing his or her own dream of credit-financed home ownership. It is a tough but noble goal. Moreover, it is one that will not, cannot happen without astute management."

"And one to be financed by an inflation tax imposed on all of us," snorted his daughter. "Politicians, like Abomo, cling to power and wealth by expropriating wealth from those who vote against them and transferring it to those who vote for them—essentially legalized stealing. If it is, indeed, a noble goal for each to own their own home, then let them pursue it and obtain it, themselves, through their own efforts and their own earnings. Don't guarantee it as a gift or obligation from the rest of us—delivered to win votes. This is the sad anti-market tragedy of representative democracy left uncontrolled."

Her dad reddened and vehemently objected. "As you well know, I did not vote for him and I was appointed to my position by his predecessor. You may also know that I disagree with some of his policies. However, as Central Bank Chairman, I have worked with him and come to know him. You are unjust in painting him as just another self-dealing politician. As a result of personal contact, I have grown to respect and like him. President Abomo is, in fact, a noble person and a man of good intentions and high integrity. Many in both parties, who put public interest before self-interest, support his attempts to re-float the Confederation economy and credit market. I think it is grossly unfair of you to attack and besmirch him when you do not personally know him. It might come as a surprise to you, but there actually are politicians who care about the public. I know him now and I believe that he works just as hard and spends as many sleepless nights as I do worrying about the welfare of the general public."

"Perhaps I over-spoke that time Dad, and for that, I apologize. I suspect that many misguided politicians are good people at heart. But don't you see that, even with the best intentions on the part of managers and politicians, the result is always the same. In their view, the responsibility for failure does not lie upon those individuals who have made bad decisions, rather it lies upon markets that are under-controlled and need more rules and regulations. As the old saying goes, the road to hell is paved with good intentions. At the individual level, I'm sure that politicians are not necessarily bad people, they just almost always produce bad policy. It is the problem of even well-intentioned politicians and bureaucrats that they are trying to manipulate and control an economy too complex to understand and to manage. Of course, they must be honorable enough to execute the policies that they stood on to get elected. Policies which can't help but result in a transfer of real wealth from those who voted against them to those that voted for them. The failure is not with the elected politicians, who are only human, but with the institutions that continue to enable them to operate such a 'spoils' system. What we are missing in the constitution of our Confederation is the critical clause that would simply restrict or limit the abilities of elected politicians to tax and spend—to deliver bread and circuses to their supporters at the expense of their foes."

"Well Roberta, I shudder to think where our economy would be right now without the direct stimulus the Abomo government created by stepping in and providing 'cash for canoes' and the first-time hut purchasers' housing credit, to name two specific examples. And, yes, I know that I have not always been a strong supporter of such fiscal policies in the past, but I am also enough of a realist to understand that extraordinary times call for extraordinary policies and interventions. Imagine where we would be without emergency loans to many of our largest banks. You would say they should have the right to fail. I would respond that if they had failed, we all would have gone down with them. These programs have helped keep two of the largest sectors of the Confederation economy afloat. Without them, we would be stuck in a slump or, worse, an implosion of aggregate economic demand and expenditure. What you 'free-market' types cannot seem to understand is that sometimes in a market economy, when individuals and businesses have become too fearful to spend, it is necessary for a courageous government to step up and confidently spend and, by doing so, to save our economy, our society."

"That doesn't sound at all like you, Dad. You were always the one who expressed doubts about fiscal policy, the one who spoke of monetary policy as the 'big gun'."

"I know, Roberta, but I as I said, the magnitude of this economic crisis has really made me doubt my previous position. Frankly, the current situation may call for every hand on the oar, monetary and fiscal. I'm honest enough to admit I don't understand how our economy collapsed so hard and so fast. Are you?"

"What you central bankers and government interventionists can't understand is that it is usually you who have created the very economic volatility and crashes in the first place to which it appears that you must respond," Roberta replied hotly despite herself. "The private market, left to its own devices is not inefficient or unstable. Rather it is the peculiar and awkward set of money, banking, and credit institutions that the government and the banking sector have fashioned, validated, and protected that causes volatility and inefficiency in these markets. It is time to move back to rationality, simplicity and transparency in the money, banking, and credit markets. Then you will see how efficient the private market can be. A good sign is that with all the post-crash bankers and lending intermediaries frozen in fearful inaction—a private, direct lending market is finally beginning to evolve. As the need arises, a beautiful new market mechanism is starting to arise. With our current technology to aid the direct lending market, the old indirect lending market and conventional

77

banks hopefully will become an anachronism—an inefficient relic of the past.

"Moreover Dad, in patting itself on the back for providing spending stimulus, the government forgets one crucial point: The 'cash for canoes', bailout of the banks, and tax credits for first-time hut purchasers must come from somewhere. As you well know, every dollar of government expenditure, stimulus or otherwise, must be dipped out of the bucket of funds that would otherwise be available for consumption or investment expenditure within the private sector. There is no other way to do it. Stimulus spending is like a man trying to lift himself by his own bootstraps. I think it more likely that stimulus spending is justification for the feeble-minded in exercising political power and influence. As an aggregate economic stimulus, taxing or borrowing from ourselves in order to pass on transfer payments to a weaker alternative is less than a zero sum game—once the inefficiency of government bureaucracy and administration is factored in. I fail to see how using taxes assessed on the private sector to buy and destroy old canoes which are property of the private sector creates wealth or adds to welfare in any way."

"It creates jobs in a stagnant and underemployed economy, in an economy that lacks the confidence needed to generate its own recovery," Bob Jr. retorted. "That's just the kind of jump start we needed to return us to growth and prosperity!"

"Excuse me Dad," said Roberta. "I am confused. I thought the logical goal of a market economy was to produce maximum wealth and prosperity, while minimizing the need for back-breaking labor or jobs. To me, destroying part of our property or wealth just to keep us busy seems a foolish and duplicitous goal."

Her dad interrupts to signal Jessup, to refresh the caviar and wine. "I think you have a sad and cynical view of public service and politics, if you think that selfless public servants, such as President Abomo and I are simply feathering our own nests at public expense—living off the fat of the land, so to speak.

"You have spent a great deal of time criticizing our money, banking, and credit system," he continued. "I happen to think that its management is a complex and necessary activity, required for our aggregate economic welfare. I know you don't. On this point, we appear to have reached an impasse. So, besides the unfettered operation of the free market, how do you propose we achieve your vague goals of 'simplicity and transparency'?"

"Dad, just as the day of commodity money passed, so now has the system of intelligently or unintelligently managed fiat money. It's sad, but predictable, that we have a bunch of bright people working increasingly hard on a pointless and impossible task. They are using their short-sighted ingenuity to maintain fiat money and its associated obsolescent institutions on life support—when a better and more transparent solution for managing our monetary transactions, savings, lending, and investment lies right in front of us.

"The quest to hang on to the old system grows out of an old familiar story that spawns and expands bureaucracies not only in money and banking, but also in many other areas as well. Humans desire freedom. However, with freedom comes a frightening exposure to and responsibility for the full consequences of our individual decisions. In a free society, we bear the full risk for our actions and are unable to pass part or all of that risk to someone else. As a result of our fear, we engage in another typically human behavior: We make rules. At first the rules seem reasonable as a necessary step to civilize markets and provide desirable protections to private property. Soon we put in place more advanced rules to protect those of us who may be more vulnerable or less astute. The problem with this well-meaning behavior is that most rules are pregnant and yield multiple offspring. Even worse, as complexity grows we find that not all rule creators have good intentions. Many simply are seeking to create profitable, protected niches for themselves. Eventually the bureaucracy becomes so big and the rules so complex that we all become rule breakers. The bureaucrats complain of impossibly mounting burdens of enforcement work;

the system becomes unworkable and its drag on productivity intolerable. I think we are close to that scenario now within our current money, banking, and lending bureaucracy."

"I suppose that you are including me amongst these bright but misled bureaucrats?" Bob Jr. interjected ironically. "I'll admit to you that we created our fractional-reserve banking system and a fiat money partly by fortuitous accident when Jim and I lost the silver at the bottom of the Great Lagoon. But, I think you're living in a dream world if you think any other market monetary system could possibly work better. Our current system supports a massive volume of transactions as well as a modern and efficient credit market. An ironic measure of our system's efficiency—arising from the real-world hard work and thankless dedication of people like me—is that young people like you are afforded the wealth and free time to make such windy, philosophical, criticisms of the system."

Roberta smiled and continued, "The Island Confederation economy may have benefited from the money and banking system that evolved in the past, but now the volatility and employment cost of its mismanagement is simply too great. Our technological capability for free market trading and exchange has advanced to the point where fiat money and fractional-reserve banking are simply no longer necessary. You mention the gigantic volume of trade as if that explains the requirement for an equally large volume of fiat money and bank deposits in order to accommodate it. I believe your argument is based upon an obsolescent view of the velocity of money. With current technology allowing instantaneous record-keeping and transfer of funds, the velocity of money can become whatever it needs to be, a notional variable. We no longer need a 'bricks-and-mortar' banking system with armies of back-office functionaries making tedious entries in accounting ledgers. In fact, continuing to chain ourselves to such a crippled, limiting money and banking system only creates a drag upon our economic potential. It is possible to consider a large number of alternative monetary goods that could accommodate all the exchanges required—and the size or supply of any of them no longer is a valid objection."

Her dad thought he knew where this utopian discussion was headed and he gently mocked her. "If we abolished money and banking as we know it, then what would happen to our old banker friends, Smitty, Jerry, and even your Uncle Paul?"

"Exactly," said Roberta. "They might have to increase the gross domestic product of the Confederation by actually going out and producing some real income, instead of abusing everyone else's property rights by loaning out depositors' funds for a profit—what Jim always, correctly, called a fraudulent transfer of property rights. But, Dad, even you must admit that the fractional-reserve banking system constitutes a 'ponzi' scheme and that it makes you uneasy. A sound banking and lending system must rest upon something fundamentally stronger and more transparent than this."

"By the way Roberta, when are the members of the Economics Club going to go out and increase the gross domestic product of the Confederation? I agree only with your last statement. The need for a sound foundation is precisely why we manage and regulate money creation and lending now. As you surely know, under current regulations banks must hold a minimum amount of reserve cash in their vaults. In addition, we have required that the funds of every depositor be insured."

Bob Jr. was interrupted by his daughter. "Insured by whom? The society self insures depositors funds, which means we are, all of us, on the hook for validating and supporting illicit lending behavior and bad underwriting of loans by banks for profit. What a masterstroke! Banks get to rob their depositors through an uncompensated, unapproved transfer of their property and they get all of society to be unwitting accomplices in robbery. On your first point, you might be surprised at how many of our club members have vigorous careers and businesses."

"I see the twinkle in your eye, Roberta, and I know that you have always engaged in hyperbole in order to get my goat, but please remember, you are impugning my industry, and a noble profession. And, of course, you are forgetting that the banking and lending industry doesn't exist by accident, it exists by necessity. You have overlooked the basic fact that the fractional-reserve system is necessary to multiply lending because the vast majority of consumers in our society, in any society, often buy things that are too expensive for them to purchase out of their present income or wealth. The best example of such a purchase for most is a house. If we eradicated the banking and lending market, with power multiplied by a fractional-reserve system, what would happen to the housing and mortgage market—would they disappear?"

His daughter sighed, "You've never really grasped Jim's concept of 'what is' have you? An economy, an aggregate society of trading individuals, has in it, at any point in time, a specific amount of real output and real wealth that is actually available. Multiplying the number of loans between individuals or between banks and weak borrowers doesn't somehow magically increase this—there is no black box. An extensive quantity and variety of real materials and labor hours are necessary to build a house. If the grand sum of these inputs exceeds the ability of a typical house purchaser to pay for them at once, then a loan, or mortgage, is required for the transaction to take place. However, it requires some other person, a saver or investor, to defer present consumption in return for providing that loan. The borrower gets the house and agrees to pay off the lender over time at a mutually agreed upon interest rate plus return of principal. The lender accepts this deferred consumption and risk of loan default only because her future consumption or wealth can be higher as a result. There is no mystery here—both the buyer and the lender have entered into a transparent mutually agreed upon transaction with their eyes open.

"There is nothing wrong with the lending process I just described, it is time-honored and admirable and necessary to the efficient functioning of an economy. What I do object to is that currently this process is brokered by an intermediary, a banking system, which removes the transparency. This banking system thrives on an uncompensated and uninformed transfer of property rights to depositor's funds. I object to a profit structure that provides an incentive to banks to make excessive and poorly-underwritten loans while transferring the risk of failure of those loans to either uninformed depositors or to the society at large through either a central bank printing a fiat currency, borrower bailouts, or a national government providing guarantees to depositors. I object to the fact that most of the profit for those loans goes to the agents who set them up while most of the risk is transferred to the unwitting depositors or to society at large. I'm impugning the structure of the industry, not the honorable motives and beliefs of individual bankers. It is the structure of money, banking and credit that is flawed and obsolete—and that we must change. Most of the Economic Club members currently hold this view, as I do."

"You have still avoided my question with your long-winded answer," Bob Jr. replied. "How can we meet President Abomo's goal of a house for every family without a large and aggressive fractional-reserve banking system? If only 'sound' loans are made, the lending result may be grossly inadequate to meet this noble goal. Left to its own devices a private credit market will probably not be able to provide enough funds."

"That is exactly the problem," answered Roberta. "The blunt, logical truth is that however hard the banking system may try, it cannot create a larger real share of Confederation production to be available for lending than actually exists. The limiting factor is aggregate private savings—not what bankers or politicians think should be lent. Sadly, what the central bank and government policy can do is produce an artificially low price for credit through low target interest rates. These low target interest rates will result in over-eager, greedy lending intermediaries attempting but failing to lend more savings than are actually available. This, of course, they cannot accomplish. However, what they *do* accomplish is to steer too much of our scarce and precious saving into consumption loans and away from its best and highest use as productive investment. When that happens, we all bear the cost in terms of lower future prosperity. As I stated before, these loans are often directed to inefficient uses and to borrowers who lack the ability or intention to repay them. That is what has created the mountain of toxic debt and defaults under which the economy currently labors.

"The straight answer, but one unpalatable to those who believe they have the natural right to broker the wealth of all individuals, is probably that President Abomo's attractive goal is ill-considered and unobtainable. There are already too many houses, and trying to obtain even more houses comes at a severe and hidden social opportunity cost. Pursuing more houses may be steering some or much of our economy's scarce savings and scarce inputs away from their best and most productive uses. Some houses should not be built and some mortgages should not be carried by their borrowers—especially by those debtors who are unlikely to be able to make the future payments required to service their loans. Again, bankers—whose eagerness is not necessarily matched by their astuteness—loaning the savings of others to individuals unlikely to be able or willing to repay is precisely the problem that has led to our current credit market collapse."

"Whoa," objected Bob Jr. "I've caught you at last in a false statement. Let's be more precise and careful in our use of terminology. In your emotional attack upon our 'archaic' banking system you have shown a lack of understanding of how lending actually works. Let's go back to basics, my dear daughter. Perhaps you can learn something from your old banking dad after all.

"You are critical of fiat money as well as the system of fractional-reserve banking. But, they are two different things, and your arguments get muddled when you are indicting them both simultaneously. So, let's just focus on one issue at a time, shall we? Suppose that our money was backed entirely by silver coins. In that case, I fail to understand how you can argue that fractional-reserve banking is a problem."

Bob Jr. continued, "Consider the following Economics 101 thought experiment. Suppose our economy's stock of real wealth consists of four silver coins, a hut, and a canoe. The initial owner of the four silver coins deposits them in his checking account, and receives in return a document saying he owns four silver coins that are available upon demand. To further simplify things, let's assume there is a 50 percent reserve requirement. With a 50 percent reserve requirement the bank loans out two silver coins to a borrower, call him Fred, who uses them to purchase a hut. Note, that the bank now has first lien and title on the collateral of this loan—the hut! The builder, who sold the hut to Fred, places the two silver coins in his checking account. Again, with a 50 percent reserve requirement, the builder's bank loans out a single silver coin to another borrower, George, so he can purchase the canoe. Note again that with customary and prudent bank lending practices, that bank also has first lien and title on the collateral against which its loan to George is made—the canoe. No matter how many times this process is repeated, the total stock of lending is backed by a stock of collateral of total value that exceeds it. If this process has been followed then there is no inherent instability in the banking and credit system, there is no inevitable implosion of credit that is likely to result, and there is no 'mountain' of excessive or toxic debt. In your enthusiasm you have carelessly overstated your argument and your indictment of the fractional-reserve banking system. If the lending has been done correctly and carefully, then there is always sufficient collateral to back every single loan made within the system. If there is a problem then it lies in the degree of regulatory oversight that should have been applied to keep the lending market prudent, rigid in its underwriting rules, and secure."

"Good job Dad! Thank you for so aptly illustrating my argument," Roberta smugly replied. "Your textbook explanation of the lending multiplier precisely illustrates exactly what is rotten at the base of our current banking and lending system. In your example—which is really better than any I might have made up myself—the economy has real wealth consisting of four silver coins, one hut, and one canoe. But look what has happened as a result of fractional-reserve banking: The illusion has been created that there is greater wealth than actually exists. As Jim might say, we're violating the rule of what 'is'! Your story began with an initial deposit of four silver coins into a checking account. The depositor has every reason to believe that the four coins are available on demand—he perceives his wealth as consisting of four silver coins. The builder, who sold the hut to Fred, gets two silver coins, which he placed in his demand deposit account. So he rightly thinks he is the proud owner of two silver coins. Finally, the seller of the canoe ends up with the last silver coin, which he owns. So, the illusion has now been created that the economy's real wealth consists of seven silver coins, along with the hut and the canoe! But more silver has not magically materialized out of thin air. What 'is' is four silver coins.

"Further Dad, despite your contention that all the loans are collateralized, I still stand by my indictment of fractional-reserve banking in each and every respect. It is not just the illusion of greater wealth that is the problem; it is also the loan quality and the incentives
that caused all the loans to be created in the first place. When the Central Bank holds the price of borrowing at an artificially low level, then there is an excessive demand for credit and loans. When these loans are made by intermediaries or bank lending officers, because they receive fees for the quantity of loans they make with other people's funds, the predictable result will be a mountain of probable-default debt. The problem is the quality of the collateral and therefore the low probability of the repayment of the loans.

"The difference between you and I is that I see the structure and misplaced incentives of the current fiat-money, fractional-reserve banking and credit system as a key culprit in generating a pyramid of excessive and unstable credit. Worse, when the pyramid starts to collapse, as you well know, the market value of *all* the loans comprising it will decline precipitously as does the market value of all the collateral that backs them. This results in a market panic and an implosive collapse of the credit market, such as we have just witnessed. The incentives and structure of the current lending market is wittingly or unwittingly designed to make us all feel as if we are sitting on a powder keg. It's no accident that when bankers stand to make record profits on loaning depositors' funds because their interest costs are excessively low, they will engage in 125 percent loans to value of collateral, and I mean shaky collateral, and there cannot be enough regulation or regulators to stop them."

"Bad or irresponsible lending practices will occur under any money and banking system," replied Bob Jr., sagely. "Such lending practices are the reason the Central Bank will always need to be vigilant in providing appropriate oversight and regulation of the banking system."

Roberta's eyes glowed at him briefly with the affection and frustration of an offspring who is loving, yet also aware of its intellectual superiority. "Let us return to the crux of the problem that creates the *mountain* of toxic debt to which I referred—the fractional- reserve banking system. Please follow me closely in my argument, which you believe I have overstated.

"When an individual depositor makes a deposit of funds into a bank, they do so under the belief that those funds are not necessarily offered up by bankers to the loan market for a profit—but rather are available, in full, for their consumption at any time they choose. This contract is the one that bankers provide to short-term depositors. The depositors do not particularly care that, if bankers operate under a 10 percent reserve requirement, then 90 percent of the funds that they deposited may be loaned out in a short or long-term obligation. It is precisely this legalized ponzi scheme and the resulting over-expansion of leverage pursued by bankers seeking profit that produces the aggregate over-expansion of total debt and the intrinsic instability of our credit and banking system. If and when those depositors seek to consume a portion of their deposits in the aggregate economy, there will not and cannot be sufficient funds or bank reserves to meet the potential sum of their claims. It is this characteristic that creates the potential of implosion in our banking system at any time. It is this overextension that makes us all uncomfortable with the fraudulent heart of our money and banking system. Dad, it is this overextension that is the real reason we must have a central bank and a flexible emergency supply of fiat currency.

"As you well know, meeting the potential claims of depositors can and sometimes does require that the fraudulent, uncompensated transfer of depositors' property rights be validated by a large injection of newly printed fiat money from the central bank—to prevent a credit market collapse. The printing of new money results in inflation and the devaluation of the purchasing power of the currency. In other words, the theft of the depositors' property by bankers is validated by reducing the value of the currency in which depositors are repaid, essentially by an inflation tax on all of us. Greedy lending and weak loan underwriting is only made possible by a cheapening of the quality of the assets in which depositors were simply intending to store short-term value. Although they may not realize it, they were thwarted in safely storing the value of their money; first by the lending of their deposits and then by the cheapening of the currency or property they stored."

"Whoa, again!" Bob Jr. interrupted. "You impugn our current banking system, but what is so superior about your alternative—a private, direct lending market, if I understand you right—that would be responsible for allocating consumers' excess savings to borrowers? Such a system would be exactly analogous to the current banking system. There would be a lending multiplier that would be very large or even infinite, because there would be no brake of a minimum reserve requirement. You cannot tell me that there is a unique aggregate volume of loans that would occur in a private, unregulated direct lending system. You cannot guarantee that there would necessarily be fewer loans or better loans in an unregulated, private direct loan market than there would be under our wise oversight. Individual lenders could and would make mistakes making loan contracts, pricing their loans, and evaluating the quality of collateral or borrowers' guarantees behind the contracts. It would be chaos! What makes you think that they could do a better job making loans than does the system of regulated banking and lending professionals? Finally, I object to your continued use of the word 'ponzi' scheme to lend an illicit air to the honorable and traditional necessary activity of saving, banking and lending."

"Faith in the average efficiency and rationality of a transparent free market driven by the aggregation of individual decisions optimizing their self-interest is what makes me trust a direct private loan market," calmly countered Roberta. "Again, you need to follow me closely, Dad. There is no paradox. The aggregate sum of all the lending that will occur between those intending to save and those intending to borrow in an economy that consists of two, a hundred, or a million individuals is exactly the split between savings and consumption that is intended. This will be true, whatever the exact market-determined volume and pricing of loans is that gets us to that end point. You are absolutely right in observing that a free market is no guarantee that all loans entered into will be good, well underwritten, or correctly priced. Loan defaults will occur, and, of course, people can and will make foolish decisions under any lending system, even the lending that would occur in a transparent, free market. Free exchange does not guarantee that credulous or naïve individuals will not be vulnerable to being talked into bad deals. Again, one virtue of free market trade is that it provides a harsh, but valuable, education to fools."

Roberta continued, "In rare cases, even the aggregate market may generate a speculative boom in the volume and pricing of a particular type of loan or asset class, but the speculative boom will tend to be self correcting in a non-illusionary marketplace that always converges to rationality and efficiency over time. Also the pain of 'excessive speculation,' if it happens, will come to rest as it should on exactly those who participated in it. Such a lending market will be naturally self correcting and will not be aided by or require policy intervention. Its outcomes will certainly not be clouded by government or central bank policy that tends to validate the irrationality of a fraction of its constituents by transferring the cost of their speculation to the economy at large. Such interventions unfairly and arbitrarily reward the foolish at the expense of the wise and thus teach exactly the wrong lesson.

"History has repeatedly shown that individual-maximizing behavior trumps a regulated and opaque market with perverse incentives every time. 'Transparency' simply means that when a managed structure has grown too complex to understand, it should be rejected and replaced with easily understandable individual-optimizing trading behavior. Lazy individuals may want 'experts' to be responsible for the allocation of their savings to the lending and investment market, but they shirk this responsibility at their peril. Some of them might make mistakes in loaning out their precious savings, but, again, a free market never guarantees that some people will not make stupid or unfortunate decisions. The truth is that no one can guarantee that in a free, direct lending market that all loans will be of high quality, correctly priced and made to strong, honest borrowers. However, in the aggregate such a system will certainly be more efficient than the current money, banking, and lending system. It appears to have been created mainly to serve greedy bankers and shabby loan underwriting, reward fraudulent borrowers, exploit naïve depositors, and artificially price scarce credit at too low a level.

"The inevitable conclusion of our current system is the bias toward an inflation tax imposed upon all of us by too rapidly expanding the stock of fiat money—rewarding the wrong motives. The school of hard knocks is a good school as we see in other, unregulated markets. Some poor fishermen fail to make money, as you surely know, but the aggregate fish market is nonetheless a model of efficiency and productivity. The lending market is no different than any other market—the expertise is again likely at the bottom of the pyramid and not at the top. In my opinion most of our problems in credit volatility have come from making it a 'top-down' rather than a 'bottom-up' market. The good news is that now we have both the incentive and the technology to offer a better free-market solution than the current system.

"Finally, Dad, I insist that 'ponzi' scheme or the fraudulent transfer of property rights is exactly the right way to describe a fractional-reserve banking system. The correctness of the term is apparent in the discomfort it creates. Any banker instinctively knows that at any instant his bank could face a total demand for withdrawals that exceeds the available cash on hand—that is, he knows that his bank's cumulative lending activities constitutes a scheme that could collapse. Isn't that the fundamental characteristic of a 'ponzi' scheme? A scheme supported only by faith, illusion, and hope. Truthfully, all bankers must have occasional nightmares about runs on their banks. When we validate or institutionalize such a process by back-stopping it with a fiat-money printing central bank and regulation, all we have done is made a precarious, dangerously speculative and inefficient system blessed and permanent."

"You always were a very glib child as well as a great debater and tonight you appear to have danced your way all around the ring," Bob Jr. wearily replied. "I never did fare very well in conversational chess matches with you and I take a perverse pride in that, as a parent. But I probably would have saved myself and others a lot of trouble in simply drowning you as a child." At this Roberta and her dad both smiled. "Alas, I didn't. So, I ask again, let's get down to brass tacks, what is your grand solution? I throw myself upon the mercy of the Economics Club, knowing full well that the opinions that you attribute to that group are in fact most likely the product of your own mind."

"As I said before, Dad, a sound money, banking, and lending system is quite simply about risk, return, and transparency. Look at it from the perspective of a typical individual who has accumulated income, wealth or money that exceeds his immediate consumption needs. Each of us is sometimes a saver simply because of the nature of consumption over time. The only question is how long we choose to save or to defer the consumption of our accumulated wealth. Banks arose simply because individuals believed, perhaps mistakenly, that banks could store their silvers for future consumption more safely and conveniently in vaults than the non-bank public could by storing them under their mattresses. Thus, the depositors thought they were increasing convenience and reducing risk.

"An obvious alternative to storing their silver in banks was loaning out their excess silvers to others who might then use them for consumption or investment as a loan to be repaid after a fixed period of time. Of course, the rate of return would be commensurate with the length of time the funds were borrowed and the speculative risk associated with the use of the loan and the borrower—with the well-understood result that risk and required return to the lender should be positively related. Ideally, such contracts would be legally stringent and binding and entered into voluntarily and with full understanding of terms by both lender and borrower. That is the essence of a fair and stable credit market and the essence of what I mean by transparency.

"When the beautiful, simple financial agreement is corrupted by layers of fee-driven intermediaries, or when the process and its terms is not well-understood or agreed to by the depositors or borrowers, then we have a potentially unstable credit market. This is what I mean by a lack of transparency. Put simply, when the distribution of risk is either not well understood in the lending market or it is transferred to other individuals than those who profit from making the loans or using the funds, then the credit market, financial system and the economy is almost certainly headed for catastrophe.   First, let's get rid of the fraudulent transfer of property rights that began with you and Jim getting dumped in the lagoon, when the silver sank to the bottom. Let's go back to a 100 percent reserve requirement for banks, immediately. Let's get back to a straightforward lending system in which the individuals who are making loans with their own wealth are fully aware that they are making them—and making them voluntarily for an agreed upon rate of return."

"I certainly agree that a 100 percent reserve requirement would destroy the money, credit and banking system as we currently know it," Bob Jr. interjected wryly.

"Perhaps not a bad thing," Roberta smoothly responded.

Ignoring his daughter's sarcasm, Bob Jr. continued. "But short of that recommendation, which I consider short-sighted, utopian and unpractical, I think your description of the complexity of the lending system and the distribution of risk has elements of correctness that call for a pragmatic, appropriate solution—namely a powerful central bank with the capability of oversight, strong regulation, and corrective action. Government is the appropriate vehicle to protect lenders and borrowers against unforeseen risks. I see the same problems you do, I just have a different, a more pragmatic, answer."

Roberta bristled. "Dad, I can't believe you just said that. Don't you realize that government is a fiction, an illusion? When 'Government' takes on a responsibility, simply translated, it always means that all of us collectively, in the aggregate, have shouldered it. You don't remove risk or bad debts by making the government the final guarantor. You simply imbed the flawed lending decisions more deeply in the collective economy. Worse, you provide a strong and continuing incentive for future bad lending decisions to be made by validating them. Such a system is headed for certain failure because it violates the basic principal of sound lending. It rewards those who make or receive excessively speculative loans and punishes those—the rest of us—who had no part in the making of them. It's much better to place the responsibility for sound lending upon those who individually benefit from making or receiving the loans. That is the fundamental risk, return and transparency that I have been speaking of tonight."

"What you have failed to understand, Roberta, is that the design of a fractional-reserve banking system arose of necessity and genius—my 'genius' if I may modestly say so. Without a fractional banking system, how do we get enough money, enough of our trading good, to actually accommodate all the trades made on a daily basis and required in our Confederation economy? Your argument about technology fails to convince me. Velocity is not just limited by technological capacity for recording transactions, it is limited by human behavior and intentions. Without the size of the money stock being magnified through a fractional-reserve banking system, I still believe the velocity of money is simply inadequate to allow a small stock of commodity money to accomplish the volume of trading required by a healthy economy. I, and no doubt others, will be reluctant to try some half-baked, grand experiment of yours and the Economics Club's design in which the entire economy is the guinea pig. We could try out a new monetary exchange system and fail. Mandating every half-baked utopian idea for a new money and credit system is a sure recipe for disaster."

"That's your fundamental problem, Dad. You continue to believe that the only thing that could be proposed is a new monetary 'system' to be imposed or mandated, somehow to be managed and controlled from above by 'experts.' Mandates make me weary. Mandating a 'new monetary system' implies that it will be imposed from above on the poor market participants, below. It implies bureaucrats, regulations, and control. Mandates in a free market produce inertia, institutionalize errors, and stifle the genius of free market economies—natural evolution, adaptation to changing needs, and improvement. It is precisely the belief in a system that needs to be imposed, controlled and regulated that has led to the suboptimal money, banking and credit system that we now suffer under. I—we —would propose no such authoritarian solution. What we propose instead is a market evolution toward a new money and lending solution, rather than a mandated program. No step that doesn't work would be irreversible and every best outcome is not known in advance. Let voluntary experiments occur, let a thousand flowers bloom, and let the best competitive solution win by public choice not by mandate.

"I believe velocity is a canard in today's economy. I state again that, with our current technology of electronic record-keeping of trades and exchanges in asset ownership, velocity can approach the speed of light, if necessary. The velocity of money is currently only limited by, as it should be, human behavior, desires and trading frequency—not anything else. Technologically, a very small volume of money can accommodate all the trades required within a very large economy. If, for behavioral reasons people trade faster or slower, then so be it. That does not change the fact that modern technological constraints are non-traffic sensitive. Today's technology can accommodate any volume of trades generated in a given period of time. A minimum required size of the stock of money is, yet, another example of the archaic, pen-and-ledger thinking endemic to bankers. Once a logical monetary good is found, velocity in its exchange can and will be just whatever it needs to be. Exchanges of ownership of the monetary good made electronically and instantly, coupled with portable, electronic communication devices can allow trades to proceed at the speed of human thought—at the speed of human desires. If you disagree, let the market provide the test."

"Well, no one's going to argue with the speed of your thought, although we might doubt its direction. I'm still waiting on the edge of my seat," scoffed Bob Jr. "The difference between you, the idealist, and me, the pragmatist, is that you seem to always see the 'free market' as some kind of magical plant that thrives best on its own with no control or intervention. This is just the simple idealism of youth which my younger self was also guilty of. I, being older and wiser, again realize that all plants must be nurtured and pruned to realize their optimal outcomes. I believe that the 'market' is really just children at play, desperately in need of direction, rules and oversight. So, again, what is this mysterious trading good proposed by the Economics Club—returning to silver, the original commodity money of our island economy, I suppose? Oh, that's right. You did say you disagreed with Jim on that point earlier."

Roberta stared at him for a moment. "Dad, if you have really irretrievably lost the imaginative idealism of youth, then that is so sad. I, for one, refuse to believe it. I believe that you are just so swamped with working to save an unsalvageable system that your vision and imagination have been squashed. They are still in there somewhere waiting to emerge.

"However, responding to your question, we are no admirers of the natural price fluctuations of any single commodity. And we know that volatility in prices and output growth can be caused by unexpected fluctuations in the value of any single commodity money. Our current preference has narrowed to a trading asset of recognized and stable value that will tend to grow at the same rate as the growth of the economy itself. We believe that such a good is the most natural and optimal unit of valuation and exchange possible. Of course, the ultimate monetary good we are speaking of is nothing less than the freely traded shares of the ownership of the means of production of our Island Confederation itself. That is, not the shares of single companies but, rather, the shares of a broad index of capital or equity ownership."

Her father squirmed and literally almost fell out of his chair. "I can't believe you're saying this. You would recommend a monetary good, a store of value and exchange, which is the very mother of all market volatility—equity shares? You're inviting the devil to dinner. The equity market is the poster child of instability, volatility and excessive speculation! Much of our Central Bank policy intervention has been an effort to stabilize it. I must say I am disappointed! After your big build up, I expected a much more grandiose and complex effort at monetary, banking and lending reform from the vaunted Economics Club. I expected a revolutionary proposal from you. This seems ridiculous and outright dangerous!"

Roberta listened unflappably and then responded. "No, it is not dangerous. We agree that the stocks of individual businesses are speculative and volatile. However, we believe that the *real* value of the economy's means of production is, in fact, quite stable. The value of the aggregate capital market only appears to be volatile because it is viewed through the volatile lens of fiat money and a wildly unstable banking and lending system. Put simply, the stock market's monetary valuation is unstable, depending upon the rate of inflation and interest rates among other things, but the real value of ownership of the economy's means of production is not. Moreover, a stable credit and money market based on the value of real assets could well lead to much less volatility and much more stability everywhere in the economy—including expectations of the growth of future earnings to shares of broad ownership of the companies that constitute the economy. It is revolutionary— though it is also an elegantly appealing, market-based vision.

"I must confess when tradable capital market index shares first appeared, others saw a beautiful and simple tool for diversifying capital investment in retirement accounts. I saw, instead, a broad-based asset that, when coupled with electronic exchange and accounting, could lead to a perfect way of keeping score in a market economy. I saw an ideal and logical unit for valuation and exchange. Finally, I saw a money that really made sense. It is an adaptation and innovation of the market toward greater simplicity and transparency in exchange that our current technology of custody and trading has now made available and practical to us. What the economy needs now is for the traditional banking, lending, and money-controlling institutions to just kindly get out of the way."

"Now wait a minute, Roberta, I cannot fathom that you seriously believe that most individuals would be comfortable holding their money balances in the form of equity market shares, no matter how broadly defined. Just think for a moment of trading a unit of our current money, with which everyone is familiar, for a share of some stock index with all its well-known volatility of returns and value. I have this absurd of vision of people running around trying to buy pizzas with flapping paper stock certificates. It's crazy! The public will not accept this. Next, I suppose, you will be trying to convince me that the average rate of return to a broad stock index should be viewed as the risk-free rate of return?"

"I doubt that there will be flapping paper stock certificates. I, personally, visualize something more along the lines of individuals using plastic cards that electronically trade the agreed upon quantity of index shares from the account of the buyer to the account of the seller. As to your point about how they would rather hold their hard-earned wealth, turn it around the other way, Dad. Why should rational people feel more comfortable holding their wealth in the form of meaningless pieces of currency, whose value is stable only insofar as a central bank can be trusted with its printing presses and the banking system is not too aggressive with loaning out deposits? Talk about fluctuation in value—nothing beats the sorry historic record of fiat money and fractional-reserve banking. And, worse, the trend direction of the value of fiat money is always down. Attaching any value to a fiat money is blind faith and trust on the part of the public, and a faith and trust that, sad to say, has always been betrayed. The real rate of return to holding a fiat currency is simply the negative of the rate of inflation— historically an almost assured negative rate of return to currency holders. Given the choice, wouldn't you rather hold your wealth in the form of a productive asset, whose sustained rate of return over time is positive? Moreover, doesn't it make sense that the risk-free opportunity cost or return to saving over time should be the benchmark of the broad, sustained real rate of return that can be expected from holding productive capital? Isn't it strange that we are viewing things so backwards that we think the risk-free rate of return should be some central bank-managed, inflation-adjusted rate of return to a short-term government bond—with all the risks to real value that entails?"

"I suppose you would have no role at all for a central bank under this utopian system," Bob Jr. responded. "Who would be responsible for controlling outbreaks of price volatility, interest volatility or inflation under your proposed system?"

"I can't believe you just said that Dad," Roberta quickly responded. "It shows how hard it is for you to even briefly shed the mantle of a central banker. You still don't get it, do you? You of all people should realize that, by definition, inflation can only be a problem when our medium of exchange is a fiat currency whose supply is regularly abused by the government or authority controlling the printing presses. Inflation is simply the mirror image of the devaluation of a fiat currency when the supply of it is growing faster than the economy in which it is used as 'money.' In a system of fractional-reserve banking, the situation is even worse because we have allowed a banking sector to pursue additional fraudulent profit by loaning out most of the funds placed in its care by depositors. This creates a further motive for expansion of the fiat money supply that lies outside the direct control of the central bank. It is scarcely surprising that with such a system of fiat money and fractional bank reserves that the primary monetary problem becomes 'managing' inflation.

"For you, as Chairman of the Confederation Central Bank to moan about controlling inflation is just simply incredible. It is analogous to a fire chief wringing his hands about the difficulty of putting out fires that only the fire department can start. Don't you see that, with a unit of trade and valuation that has a real and stable value in itself, inflation is an illogical concept? Inflation can't happen when prices are measured in terms of units of capital—in terms of real things. I repeat, sustained general price inflation is only possible when prices are measured in units of fiat currency."

"It seems to me you're repeating a lot of things tonight," said Bob Jr. "Well it's all very 'airy fairy.' Just the kind of thing we might expect from the Economics Club. I'll play along with you momentarily, just for laughs. If all the 'market stability' you anticipate comes to pass the world could get very boring. What happens then to the time-honored tradition of investors taking on additional risk for additional return, I suppose that would disappear too?"

"Alas, no," replied Roberta. "Unfortunately, the real world will always have plenty of uncertainty, plenty of risk to the future and the abrupt intrusion of unknowable events. As a result of unforeseeable future shocks, there will always be plenty of price volatility in the shares of individual companies. And, when used to purchase consumption goods there will likely be some baseline volatility in the purchasing power of an index share as well. There is no escaping that fact. There will always be storms, wars, diseases, earthquakes, fraudulent schemes, dishonest individuals and, of course, sneaker waves. I might be wrong, but I doubt that you and Jim were bored when the sneaker wave doused you and dumped all the silver reserves to the bottom of the Great Lagoon. All we are saying is that the unavoidable natural risk of an uncertain world is enough. To it we do not need to add additional unnecessary layers of risk and uncertainty through ill-designed or archaic institutions and bad policy rules."

"So if we used this new vehicle of exchange," Bob Jr. mused, slightly intrigued despite himself, "the banking structure and system would be violently changed, perhaps disappear altogether. Again, seriously, what *would* happen to Smitty, Jerry, and Uncle Paul?"

Roberta answered, "At rock bottom, bankers and banks only serve two needs: Banks provide a safe and temporary storage of the transactions good, which is money, for the depositors, until it is used by them for either consumption or investment. Moreover, bankers have operated as so-called 'experts' in the loanable funds market—acting as intermediaries. I am suspicious of the need for this second function because I am generally suspicious of those who get between the 'wallpaper and the wall'. However, if individuals continue to desire it, banks, could still act as intermediaries in the loan market as long as there exists disclosure and full awareness of what they are doing and what fee they will receive for it—that, again, is what I mean by transparency. I think the second function would probably be better served by a direct loan market, but that is just my opinion. As a free market economist, I can have no objection to 'experts' receiving fees for services rendered, so long as the services and the fees are well understood and agreed to by both sides."

Roberta continued, "And yes, the banking system will be fundamentally changed by a dynamic free market, and the challenge of a robust direct, transparent lending market—whose volume of lending is unrelated to the creation of the stock of money. The banking system may not vanish, but it will likely evolve to an electronic custody system—tracking the ownership and exchange of monetary assets in trading—rather than one based upon brick and mortar buildings, desks and vaults. The need for and convenience of this custody, trading, and recording function can be fulfilled for a competitive fee. As regard to the need for lending 'experts' acting as intermediaries, again, I have no objection to it, if a market generates such a demand. However, it is my view electronic technology and information flow makes the demand for and the hold of such 'experts' on the marketplace precarious and, likely, temporary.

"Ironically, the current archaic and suboptimal banking, credit and monetary system is held in place only by tradition, regulation and the inertia of a controlling central bank and fiat money. I believe that the Confederation economy is technologically and ideologically ready for the evolution to a direct loan market, the abolishment of the fractional-reserve banking system, and a monetary good based upon real value instead of a fiat currency. Our economy is ready for it. We just need to free ourselves from the existing, mandated structure. This simplification and this return to the credit market being free-market rather than institutionally determined will result in the price of lending, the interest rate, finally being market-determined, not bureaucrat-determined."

"What about safety and what the public will accept? Do you think that many individuals will be comfortable with their stated wealth floating around in cyberspace where it is subject to mistakes or hackers?"

"That is an interesting observation on your part and one with some validity," Roberta responded. "There is danger of thievery and distortion everywhere and this danger should never be discounted and can never be totally eliminated. However, as long as we cannot carry around all the assets we may own, in part or in entirety, in our pockets, shares of factories, for example, why are paper records showing our ownership necessarily more secure than electronic ones? A paper document or a paper asset can be altered,

101

stolen from a mailbox, lost, or destroyed as easily as an electronic one, and in many cases more easily. Alternatively, electronic records can be recorded in multiple locations and made subject to multiple safeguards. While less familiar to many individuals, it is not clear that electronic transfer and record-keeping is innately less secure than one based upon paper records. In fact, careful consideration of the problem leads to the opposite conclusion: that electronic record-keeping and exchange can be made much more redundant and secure."

"So I have finally caught you in a position of hypocrisy and contradiction," Bob Jr. smugly observed. "I knew that, given enough rope, you would eventually go too far! You're like the rest of the young utopian reformers and activists. How do you reconcile mandating such a radical change to the money, banking and credit market while at the same time imposing yet another institutional structure upon your much admired and precious 'free' market?"

"Once again Dad, we propose *mandating* nothing!" Roberta retorted hotly. "This happens to be the most logical and natural exchange good we could think of in a marketplace that is currently bogged down with creaky, cumbersome, illogical institutions and incomprehensible regulation. Capital is a beautiful, natural money because intrinsic to every trade would be a visible reminder of the real opportunity cost between consumption or saving and investment, between current consumption and future consumption. We are simply suggesting this to the economy as an alternative to the current flawed money and banking system. It is not for us to dictate how a rational free market in credit, money and banking could and will evolve. A market economy that moves to some other solid basis for its monetary good and gets rid of the fractional banking system would still be far superior to what we have. Even a fiat money printing central bank, without the ponzi-scheme of a fractional-reserve banking system would represent an improvement to our present system."

"Since you have such an abhorrence for 'bad loans,' I suppose that you probably also agree with Jim that abolishing the debtor's prisons was a bad idea?" Bob Jr. snidely interrupted.

"Well actually his thinking has some logical merit. If one individual steals property from another individual at a given point in time, the individual stolen from has had his consumption possibilities impaired. Few object when the thief is placed in prison for that crime. When an individual defaults on a loan obligation, they are stealing the lender's property or future consumption just as surely—therefore there is a symmetrical logic to debtor's prison, or at least in insisting that the debt be eventually paid off in full. However, what made most of us, including me, abhor debtor's prison was the fact that lending and borrowing over time is an uncertain activity, even with the best of intentions. It involves risk of unforeseen or unfortunate future events, death or illness, for example, which can render it impossible for the borrower to pay off their debt.

"Actually, I believe a return to debtor's prison is not required, transparency and free will exercised in loan contracts between borrower and lender is sufficient. It is better to let lenders and borrowers knowingly share the risk of loss and default in their mutual agreements, than to mandate a visit to prison for any loan default. Such contracts can place some non-performance risk on the lender as long as the terms of default and the risk adjustment to interest are set subject to voluntary agreement between borrower and lender. Even a stupid loan contract, willingly entered into, is really none of society's business. 'Drunk Uncle' loans entered into by word of mouth agreement, with no interest required, no penalty provisions, and an almost certain default, while foolish should not be illegal. However, when loans are made by a third party without the consent of or compensation to the actual lender or when there have been fraudulent presentations by the borrower concerning ability to repay, then someone should go to debtor's prison—in some cases it should be the banker or intermediary who engineered and derived fee benefit from making a particularly weak or egregious loan with someone else's funds. When the government or central bank forgives bad debt to 'save' the credit market they implicitly steal from and impose the loss on all of us. In that broader perspective perhaps they could be candidates for debtor's prison."

"You're revisiting old ground for us," wearily objected Bob Jr. "We will not agree on the assertion that it was unnecessary to save the economy and we certainly will not agree on the implicit assertion in your argument that, as head of the Central Bank, I should go to debtor's prison. You still haven't answered my question. What are the nuts and bolts? How will you begin to implement your utopian dream?"

"Once, the fractional-reserve banking system is eliminated, simply by example," said Roberta. "Perhaps the members of the Economics Club will begin with exchange and trade amongst themselves being accomplished by trading broad index shares of the public capital market. As it works in demonstrating practical exchange and a stable store of value, it will spread like wildfire to the rest of a free market economy starved for monetary transparency, freedom from the insidious tax of inflation, and credit-market sanity. What turns and developments the free market may take in generating a high-tech solution to the problem of evolving an efficient new monetary good is impossible to predict. We will watch them with interest and we will be as surprised by some of the innovations as you."

"Not as surprised as me, because I know your scheme could never happen," Bob Jr. interjected acidly. "Playing along again, what of the possibility of getting back to precisely where we are now? In fact, didn't the workings of your much-vaunted free market result in the evolution of the very money, banking, and credit system we currently have—including the Central Bank?"

"Anything's a possibility, but staying with or returning to the present system is probably a slim one. The institutions that you and Jim created might have seemed necessary at the time, and perhaps even seemed to work for a period. However, technology and the complexity of the economy have moved beyond the point where our conventional fractional-reserve banking system is an appropriate solution—it now is just a sad archaic anachronism awaiting replacement and held in place only by institutional inertia and mandate. There is no good justification for making bad loans with someone else's property. That is the fundamental, fatal flaw of our current—that is, *your* current—banking system. Moreover, the technological capability that we now enjoy allows us to meet the need for a stable store of value and unit of exchange in a far more efficient way than fiat money and the obsolete traditional banking system. In fact, it is likely that not just the velocity of money but also its supply will ultimately be market-determined."

"I fear your dependence upon and love affair with technology," interjected Bob Jr. "Surely a monetary system must be more stable and permanent than something that is dependent upon what is in vogue at the moment. You speak of the technological wonder of electronic funds transfer and the creation of capital index funds as if they were some wonderful 'deus ex machina.' I can't see it. Personally, I would hate to have the fate of our economy rest upon such a slender reed."

"Nonsense, Dad! The evolution of human trading economies has always been due to the convergence of technological capability, applied human knowledge, and market need. That used to be as true of the old banking and monetary system as it will now be with the new one. The base of human economic activity is trade— whether it occurs at a given point in time or over time. Anything that makes trade easier to accomplish, simpler and more transparent to participants provides enormous productive benefits to the economy. When it helps us accomplish this, technology is a wonderful tool. The key lies in allowing natural efficient evolution of the marketplace to occur, rather than blocking it with the imposition and inertia of bureaucracies, rules, and interventions."

"Youth wants change, while experience values stability, predictability and permanence. Even if the current system isn't perfect, it's still a very good system—a proven system. And fractional-reserve banking adds to the efficiency of the economy by allowing banks to put otherwise idle wealth or idle balances of depositors to work—by loaning them to those who would use them immediately for consumption and productive investment. How does your proposed stock index monetary good replace that?"

A frustrated Roberta thought for a moment, trying to phrase her response in the best way for her dad to finally "get it." "The problem in a nutshell, Dad, is basically Zeke. I know what I think of Zeke, but what do you think of him?"

After a long debate with Roberta, her dad appreciated and enthusiastically jumped at this diversion. "I try not to think of him! He's the worst neighbor I've ever had—with all his junk, wild dogs and even improperly controlled sewage regularly leaking across my property boundaries. Last week I'm sure his pit bulls ate your mother's cat. We found its tail, but, of course, Zeke wouldn't admit it. He's a pathological slug who admits or accepts responsibility for nothing! His cultural shallowness and sleazy lifestyle is deplorable."

"Exactly!" exclaimed Roberta. "At the individual level, Zeke characterizes much that is wrong with our money, banking, and credit system. However, let's try not to behave like snobby elitists Dad. We should be careful not to condemn his consumption choices and lifestyle and feel superior just because they are not the ones that we would make."

"I can," grumped Bob Jr., "especially when his lifestyle imposes severe negative externalities upon me or my property."

Roberta continued, "However, we can and should criticize his lack of responsibility in repaying debts he has incurred with the aid of lending agents. Whenever Zeke comes up with some half-baked scheme, such as the pit-bull training center you just complained of, he is always able to find some banker stupid enough or greedy enough to loan him somebody else's wealth in order to accomplish it. In the aggregate, such loans are a horrible outcome for the

Confederation economy because they represent an inefficient allocation of the economy's scarce wealth and savings to a use unlikely to be best or highest. Even worse, when he predictably defaults on his loan, as the 'Zekes' almost always seem to do, your President and Congress and forgives his behavior by swapping Confederation debt for his debt—thereby making it the obligation of all of us. When this behavior is repeated by armies of 'Zekes', just imagine the inefficiency of such a system in steering scarce saving and investment away from their most efficient use. Because of misplaced incentives to lending agents and a system that produces an excess of leverage at artificial returns, the loans to individuals such as Zeke are likely not disciplined by an efficient lending and investment market as they otherwise would and should be. Over time, such a system and such a policy costs the entire economy a staggering sum in lost output, prosperity and growth— and it fails to allow the marketplace to punish all the 'Zekes' and those who lend to them for bad financial decisions."

"Well," Bob Jr. replied, "it's hard for me to argue with you in the case of Zeke. He's been a thorn in my side for years, but what about the other part of my argument. How does the monetary system you propose replace the essential banking function of putting idle wealth to productive work in funding trades and investment?"

"Think about it carefully, Dad. Have patience, I'm going to repeat my earlier argument. Remember the days of hand-written double-entry banking ledgers and the snail-like delay between the accomplishment of a trade and the actual recording of the change of ownership of funds. Back then anything that could speed up the process appeared to make the banking system more efficient. One unfortunate attempt to speed things up and magnify the available stock of money was to allow bankers to loan out depositors' reserves that they thought were likely to be idle—excess reserves. Since this was a fraudulent transfer of property rights—there is no other way to paint it—it was fraught with risk and it caused many sleepless nights for bankers. Now listen closely, Dad—and don't keep moving your mouth in preparation to interrupt. The advance of electronic technology has vastly sped up the process of recording trades and the ownership of monetary goods to accomplish them. In fact, it is only a slight exaggeration to say that the transfer of funds in response to a trade can now take place at the speed of light. Thus, the bogus augmentation of the supply of money through a fractional-reserve banking multiplier is clearly unnecessary to the efficiency of the exchange economy. I personally suspect that the practice of lending out 'idle' reserves always had more to do with subsidizing bankers' greed as intermediaries in the lending market than with achieving optimal efficiency of a money-based trading system."

"So what happens with your unconstrained, unmonitored electronic monetary exchange system? Does human trading accelerate to the speed of light and the economy then either explodes or flies off the rails?"

Roberta coolly responded, "No, not at all. The natural speed of exchange, consumption and investment in an economy is and should be driven by the speed of natural human intentions, behavior and desires. It is not, and should not, be constrained by the physical limitations or flaws of the monetary exchange and recording system. An optimal monetary system should be easy to understand, painless to use with no inflation tax or delays, unnecessary to manage, and should not impair people by limiting their future prosperity or destroying their wealth. Clearly Dad, we have reached a point in our economic evolution where traditional banking needs to either evolve or disappear by free market pressure. We don't have the need for a bricks and mortar banking system anymore. All we need is a record of ownership of a monetary good that allows changes due to trades to be recorded accurately and instantly. We need a lending market that allows those producing more than they wish to consume to lend or invest the excess at a competitive market-determined price. And the lending should be directed by expected return and risk incentive to the most efficient and productive borrowers or users. Moreover, the moral hazard of that agreement should then stop there—to rest, as it should, only on those individuals who entered knowingly into a mutually agreed upon loan or investment.

"I take it as a very encouraging sign that, since the recent collapse of the Confederation's credit market and banking system, to which you and President Abomo have been so energetically responding, the electronic direct lending market displays unprecedented growth. It seems already to be transforming the lending market away from the traditional intermediaries of the banking system. This, in my opinion is a natural and desirable evolution."

"Ah Roberta, it all sounds very utopian. What if we bankers use our political pull and make the use of any alternative type of money illegal? That would certainly halt your experiment in its tracks. I'm not so sure that if we unleashed the lawyers on it right now, we wouldn't find that what you propose is already illegal."

"Of course, you could do that. If you unleash lawyers on anything, they can find it to be 'illegal.' But don't you see that this kind of regulation—using law to replace market forces—is exactly how we got into our current mess? Institutionalizing idiocy and imposing further bureaucracy and regulation is not the way to achieve economic efficiency. I would rather start removing the rules and regulations and start trusting, once again, market efficiency driven—as always—by optimizing individuals. Let's stop making bad rules that don't work and then responding to their failure by layering on yet more bad rules and interventions that don't work."

"So you are an anarchist too? Do you actually believe in any rules for the economy?"

"Certainly," Roberta replied. This was a return to familiar ground in their ongoing debates. "Law and the legal system should protect the right of individuals to free trade. There should be no coercion and no fraud, and certainly not institutionalized fraud. Again, speaking of fraud, we should have one law that clearly makes it illegal to transfer property rights without the knowledge, consent, or compensation of the individuals from whom they are being transferred. And, of course, on the other side of the coin, good law should make it illegal to purposefully transfer risk to individuals without their knowledge or compensation. In our Confederation, the best and most commonplace example of violating this law is the fractional-reserve banking system, although it is clearly not limited to just the banking system. Any loan that has involved a fraudulent presentation of collateral or ability to repay, or any loan that has placed a claim upon another's assets without their knowledge or consent, is also an example."

"But, again Roberta, tell me how would we stabilize the economy if the banking structure and Central Bank disappeared—with all its capabilities for stabilizing the Confederation economy from shocks? When you realize that we lose our most important tool, monetary policy, for economic stabilization, what is so optimal about your proposed money anyway?"

"You mean how would you destabilize it?" Roberta mocked. "The health of our economy is too important and valuable to be managed top-down. The market for savings, borrowing and investment is too critical to our future growth and prosperity to be anything but market-determined. The function of money is too important to be managed by anyone—no matter how benevolent their intentions. Economies, markets and technology can evolve, but political and bureaucratic institutions typically don't—at least not in the direction of greater economic freedom and prosperity. That is why government bureaucracies impose increasing costs upon an economy that has moved far beyond needing them—the Island Confederation Post Office is a good illustrative example. It is time for the ponderous, archaic money and banking structure to be moved out of the way.

"What is optimal about our proposal for capital as money can be summarized in three simple attributes. Again, I am repeating my arguments to list them. First, money based upon broad shares of capital ownership is easily recognizable, has intrinsic real value, and literally eliminates aggregate inflation. Second, if capital is money, the opportunity cost of saving or lending versus consumption is made crystal clear in every trade. Thirdly, the price of credit, which is the interest rate, and the money supply, are naturally market-determined, without the artificial intervention of a central bank and the instability of a fractional-reserve banking system."

"Roberta, I know it is getting late and you are just giving me the same answers over and over again apparently restating them as articles of faith. Needless to say, I am not convinced by them. You certainly seem to love the natural, unconstrained evolution of the free market, but you fail to realize the basic fallacy of your argument. The marketplace and the rules and structures we place upon it are not some natural jungle plant, but, rather, are the deliberate creations of human thought and behavior. Like a plant, it is a work in progress that requires control, pruning and intelligent redirection when it goes astray. The 'free market' is an artificial, hypothetical concept. We built it and we can certainly change or supervise it. Even, heaven forbid, *your* proposed system would require supervision and control if it was to have any chance of being successful."

"You are absolutely right, Dad, the free market can change! The free market is a great human concept and it can operate with a minimum of rules and intervention. When manuals are required to conduct our economic affairs that, after all, reduce to voluntary trading between individuals for mutual gain, we can be sure we have gone off the rails. The key word is 'free.' When there is not enough freedom in the operation of the free market, it will have lost its capability to evolve through human ingenuity into a form that better serves our needs. This is no better illustrated than in the cumbersome cul-de-sac we have created in money, banking and lending. Let's get back to the bigger and simpler view of what we are always trying to accomplish as individuals maximizing our own welfare—production, investment and trading. Let's never lose sight that the purpose of money is simply to facilitate exchange, storage of wealth, and investment more simply, efficiently and transparently. Put very simply, money is just a convenience that allows individuals to accomplish trades more efficiently and more easily. That's all, whether the trades facilitate consumption at a given point in time or whether they allow consumption to be deferred to the future for an appropriate, market rate of return. Once again, the pace and ease of this trading should be driven by human utility and intentions—not slowed, constrained or thwarted by mechanical flaws or complexities of an imposed, cumbersome money and banking system. Moreover, the traditional 'banking system,' the very word 'banking' sounds like a drag, is ripe to be competitively replaced by a more efficient, natural monetary system. A chance is all we're asking for."

"Extinction in your view, I suppose, extends to the Confederation Central Bank itself?"

"Well, you said it, Dad. The need for a fiat currency and the regulation of a central bank is simply testimony to the fact that the monetary system we have in place is fatally flawed and operates on the basis of misplaced incentives. A direct lending system and a monetary unit based on real value, no fractional-reserve mirage, would be far more efficient and clear, and the supervision of a central bank would become unnecessary. The benefits of direct lending of savings would be profound."

Bob Jr. objected, "You keep talking of the superiority of 'direct lending.' What theoretical reason is its superiority based upon? Bank lending officers are experts at underwriting and lending. Most other individuals are not. Why should bankers not accomplish the most efficient allocation of society's 'scarce savings?' If the bankers who do their lending most efficiently get the greatest rewards, then tell me why that market is not efficient? Once again humor me, why does it not work?"

"You've provided the argument to me yourself many times," Roberta smugly replied, "and I listened. You remember your tirade about the business of stockbrokers when your equity portfolio, which you put in the trust of one, earned lamentably low returns? The problem, I remember you saying at the time, was not the efficiency of the market for stockbrokers, but, rather, the misplacement of incentives for their performance. The equity market is designed so that stockbrokers are compensated based upon the number of transactions that they make with their client investors' funds rather than upon the investment performance of those funds. Other things equal, brokers, of course, would prefer higher rather than lower investment performance for their clients, but their first allegiance is toward maximizing the number of transactions and, therefore, their fee income. The argument is exactly analogous to the case of bank loan officers. Most, if not all of them, are rewarded based upon the volume of loans they originate and the fees and interest they thereby harvest for the bank. Of course, they do not desire the loans to fail, but they are compensated only secondarily on the quality of loan underwriting. This misplacement of incentives is why their recent lending activity led to a crisis and collapse of the Confederation lending market.

"Think about it, Dad. You've answered your own question. What I just said constitutes, of course, the very essence of your argument as to why the bank-driven lending market fails as a free market. Why you believe, at your core, that banks and the credit market must be managed and regulated. Why your life, as a central banker, is therefore so complex. You complain about my views on economics, Dad. But you must remember, you planted most of the seeds for them yourself when I was younger."

"Alas, what a monster I created! Are you telling me that bankers and lending officers cannot discriminate appropriately and rationally between short-term and long-term profit maximization— when their long-term profit maximization should naturally tend to lending market efficiency?" Bob Jr. dryly interjected.

"Come on Dad," snorted Roberta derisively. "You work with these people. Better yet, you, yourself, perceive and argue for the need to regulate these people. By your perceived need to regulate them, you've again already answered your own question! You know that if you started talking about short-run versus long-run profit maximization to the typical bank loan officer, they would glance at you dully and then return to slurping their soup and the business they understand best—getting the loans, or depositors' 'excess reserves' out of the window as fast as possible and into the hands of the 'Zekes' of the world. The worst of this is that, in the aggregate, the 'Zekes' wish to borrow only to fund their short-run consumption because they are too lazy or unproductive to obtain sustenance through their own efforts.

"The cost of this behavior is a crime. You remember my old friend Ted. He has an interesting argument on how the cumulative efficiency cost might actually be measured. He is going to present it soon at the Economics Club.

Bob Jr. interjected, "How is Ted? I haven't seen him since his internship at the bank. Like you, another bright but misled youth. I remember him as a precocious child around our house always into everything, but I liked him. Give him my best."

"Give him your best in person. You should come to his presentation. His view is that inefficient allocation of savings results in an economy that tends toward over-consumption and underinvestment—thereby forfeiting future growth and prosperity. Contrast this to an economy with direct lending and shares of the capital stock being the monetary good. First, the incentives will not be misplaced in the lending market. Those with excess savings will only be interested in offering them to borrowers and investors, deferring consumption to the future, for the highest possible future risk-adjusted rate of return. The benefit of deferred consumption will be clearly evident to all because it is embedded in the monetary unit itself. By deferring consumption you automatically earn the real rate of return to capital. There is nothing idle about capital money balances."

Roberta continued with her explanation of the benefits of using capital as money. "Likewise, when capital is money, the opportunity cost of borrowing to finance current consumption is at least the real rate of return to capital—more if default risk is considered. That is a formidable hurdle rate which, sorry Zeke, will tend to steer precious loanable funds away from idle consumers. Moreover, every time a unit of the new money—a share of capital—is offered in exchange for current consumption by its owner, the opportunity cost of that current consumption will be starkly evident. The aggregate result of this will likely be a steering of more current production toward efficient capital investment and future production in the Confederation economy— with an exemplary outcome for our future prosperity and economic growth."

Bob Jr. sighed, "Oh the idealism of youth! I guess I just have enough real-world bumps and bruises to not quite accept that everything could be so rational and optimal. Your view, Roberta, is just a few tweaks, stand back, and everything will come up roses. I honestly wish it was so simple. I think it is part of our human condition to irrationally speculate, chase rainbows and generate investment bubbles based on wishful thinking. I am so convinced of the replication of that sad behavior that I think it will continue in any world you and the Economics Club can dream up. Moving to your vision of capital-based money will not change that."

"You may be right Dad. As I said before, I certainly don't claim that a monetary exchange system based on the value of capital will cure all ills or protect all markets and individuals from misperceptions, irrational speculation or scams. All I am saying is that a simpler, more transparent, more intuitive money and lending system can't hurt economic efficiency and will probably increase it. If people are sometimes irrational and chase speculative booms, why confound the problem with a complex and irrational money and credit system that encourages and bankrolls their worst motives?"

"Let's get back from a utopian future to the present problems in front of us—the ones that confront me as a central banker," objected Bob Jr. "You are eloquent about the problems and paradoxes of the present banking system and you are contemptuous of the central banking and political decision to bail it out, but isn't it an obvious recognition that, at the present time, the private banks have simply grown too large to fail? Like it or not, they must be bailed out by the government, the Central Bank, and, ultimately Confederation taxpayers for one very pragmatic reason—the survival of our Confederation economy."

Roberta stared thoughtfully at him before answering. "In an ironic way, Dad, I suppose in a market economy when an industry or an institution becomes 'too large to fail,' it is a way of saying that, in fact, it *must* fail. Not that we must force it to fail, or nationalize it. Regulatory control, protection, or nationalization, as we have seen in the past, simply doesn't work. All it does is preserve and make permanent a monopoly or an industry that would otherwise be on its way to extinction or, at least, evolving to a more efficient competitive substitute. Wouldn't it better serve the interests of the economy if the outdated institution was simply allowed to wither and atrophy away and be replaced by a more efficient, economically democratic, competitive mechanism? How many times must we repeat this sorry, but predictable story? We are caught in an endless cycle of booms and busts engendered by our fiat-money-augmented, fractional-reserve banking system. A cycle of excessive and weakly motivated lending, asset price bubbles, market collapse and recession, and then 'enlightened' costly intervention. How long before we finally admit that our money, credit and banking system is fatally flawed? That we need an alternative?"

"But, again," Bob Jr. retorted, "if a better market solution exists, why can we not evolve toward it without your design, intervention, and direction?"

"That's a good question, Dad," Roberta replied. "Honestly it is one that has given us a good amount of debate at the Economics Club—especially amongst the free market types. I, myself, believe that even market economies, such as the Confederation, can get into a habit or regime that has its own inertia once in place. The money and banking system that has evolved is a good example. It may require a nudge, encouragement, and a road-map, for the

116

economy to move to a more efficient way of managing its trades and lending. Put another way, the idea we are now offering as a substitute for our money and banking system may be a good illustration of exactly how a market economy *does* evolve to solve its problems and needs. That is, even in a very efficient and rational economy the idea for an improvement had to occur somewhere, or to someone, first.

"Of course, our idea for capital as money may be imperfect itself, or likely only partially developed, and the final solution that emerges to replace fiat currency may be something that we can't foresee. We can never let pride of authorship cause us to oppose a market evolution that is brilliant but quite different from what we initially proposed. What I do know is that we should encourage a needed evolution of the Confederation economy to a better valuation, exchange, and lending system. But the worse problem is that, once institutionalized and regulated, such 'natural monopolies' as our current money and banking system are very hard to remove. We are not really starting from a free market position in advocating a fundamental change in our monetary system."

Bob Jr. replied, "Probably it's because our dinner has gone on to the wee hours of the morning, but I must admit, I am intrigued despite myself. However, being a pragmatist, what is step one in getting your proposed monetary system in place?"

"I suppose step one is what we have done tonight, but on a bigger scale," Roberta answered. "First, lay out the template and proposal we have suggested and the reasons for it in a public arena—for all to consider and debate. Secondly, encourage and allow, in the early stages, a voluntary dual valuation system in which fiat money and our capital-based monetary unit are both used as units of pricing and exchange. Then, we must allow market evolution toward the preferred monetary exchange system to occur unimpeded. In fact, we must aid and support it in its early stages—if there is enthusiasm for its adoption. Traditional banking interests will, of course, oppose a transition because it threatens

117

their long-term survival, but that is nothing new in a competitive, evolving market economy. Alas, those threatened will seek to protect themselves—by political, non-market means if they can. Finally, I believe, our capital-based unit of trading and wealth, coupled with a direct lending market, will win the day and lead our economy to a more logical monetary exchange system. One in which individuals no longer suffer an inflation tax imposed upon them, or the fraudulent transfer of their property rights and wealth."

Not responding, her dad motioned Jessup to refill Roberta's wine glass. Jessup rolled his eyes at the ceiling and pointedly yawned as he did so. He had been around the family long enough that he could get away with such behavior. It was, after all, very late.

"Gee Dad, the dismal condition of our economy has certainly not adversely impacted your wine cellar—this dessert wine is just the right sweetness. Excellent! Speaking of the Confederation economy, by the way, doesn't it seem like it is taking a distressingly long time for any kind of recovery to appear? Shouldn't your monetary policy and President Abomo's budget-busting massive economic stimulus policies have begun to work by now—if they ever will? It seems like many years since the economy felt good."

"Don't think I can't detect your less than subtle jibes, Roberta, as you well know there has been an austerity program applied to my own travel and entertainment in solidarity with the rest of our suffering population. One of our cooks, Sheila, we sadly had to let go. Jamie had to fix this excellent dinner, we just enjoyed, all by herself—alas there is belt-tightening everywhere. No one is immune.

"Speaking to your question on monetary policy, we have followed two directions. First and foremost, we have put stringent oversight regulations in place over the banking and lending system to avoid the unfortunate excesses and poor lending practices that led to the credit market collapse. It has been a detailed and exhaustive

118

process. But at last, I am confident that what happened before cannot happen again. Secondly, as you are no doubt aware, we are kick-starting the economy by expanding the money supply very aggressively. So aggressively I must admit it scares even me a bit. Given a little time, I am confident that this will reinvigorate the Confederation economy as much as it is in the power of monetary policy to do that. Now we just need to get overly cautious consumers and investors to start spending again. The fact that they won't, even with interest rates close to zero, has us, at the Central Bank, pulling out our hair. Many say that monetary policy is at the end of its rope. They're calling it a 'liquidity trap.'"

"Dad, who are you kidding? You just contradicted yourself in your last statement. First, you constrain the banking system with the handcuffs of excessive regulation, and then you flood the system with freshly printed fiat currency. The poor unimaginative, terrified bankers! Does it really surprise you after all the collapses, defaults, public whippings and new stringent regulations that they are now afraid to lend their excess reserves—your freshly printed currency—to anyone? Look what has happened to excess bank reserves, reserves above and beyond those required to meet minimum fractional-reserve requirements to back depositor's accounts. They have sky-rocketed! Your fresh fiat currency is not finding its way into the hands of private consumers and investors—it is just sitting idly in bank vaults—jealously hoarded by panicked 'deer-in-the-headlights' bankers."

Bob Jr. rolled his eyes. "It sounds like you are talking about the old textbook bromide of 'helicopter money,' printed and dropped on the population at large to stimulate their spending."

"Why not? I am not a fan of fiat currency, as you well know, but if you really want to stimulate private spending directly, I can think of no more effective way to accomplish it—admittedly with a price tag of inflation lurking just around the corner. The mistake is relying on a chastened banking system to make the first step—that is the real liquidity trap, if there is one. As to your other recent policy that you haven't mentioned, tell me it isn't true!"

119

Bob Jr. looked puzzled. "Tell you what isn't true?"

"I understand that you are now, of all things, actually paying interest to banks on the excess reserves they hold. What could be a more bone-headed policy than that? First, you bemoan the fact that monetary policy is not stimulating private expenditure and then you actually are rewarding banks for holding excess reserves that they do not lend out. How do you justify this? It seems to fly in the face of what you are actually trying to accomplish. In any case, if you must pay interest on bank reserves, why not pay it to the actual owners of them?"

Bob Jr. blinked uncomprehendingly. "Excuse me?"

"Pay the interest to the long-suffering depositors, who get ripped-off in a fractional-reserve banking system every time their deposits are lent out by banks without their knowledge, approval or compensation. If interest should be paid to anyone, it should be to them—not to the banks. Paid to the banks, it just provides a further incentive for them not to lend excess reserves which, if I read you right, is the opposite of what you want them to do."

Again, her dad replied with weariness. "It might surprise you Roberta to know that I made very nearly the same argument you just voiced before the Board of Governors last month. As much as you may think so, I do not run the Confederation Central Bank as some kind of misguided benevolent dictator. But the Board disagreed with me and voted against me. They felt that because banks were pressured by our stringent regulations, and since the interest available on the inter-bank market for loanable reserves was effectively zero, that it was only fair that banks should receive some relief and reward for their prudence. Thus, they should be paid interest on reserves held in excess of what is required."

Roberta flared. "And you still wonder why, with increased scrutiny and policies such as this, they are not lending? You ask me to explain why I think our money, banking and credit system is incurably flawed, illogically designed, and an institutional nightmare ready to be scrapped. I rest my case. The tragedy is that if it were not institutionally mandated and controlled, I believe that a rational private free market would have evolved past it long ago. It is folly to attempt to cure this system with additional layers of regulations, what-ifs, and bandages."

"Let's not stir that pot again. I have heard far too much of your diatribe against our money and banking system tonight. It is often the fate of children to rebel against the ideas and institutions of their parents and then, as they age, to adopt them. It would be the height of ironic justice if you were to one day end up as the Chairman of the Confederation Central Bank."

"Never!" Roberta hotly replied. "Actually though, if it ever *did* happen, it might be an excellent opportunity for me to actually disband it. But I fear the institution and the Board of Governors is such an octopus, it might actually consume anyone."

"Returning to the basic problem, Dad, the transmission mechanism of monetary policy has failed. Going through banks, the linkage between the currency the Central Bank prints and actual spending by the non-bank public is broken. The Island Confederation Central Bank monetary policy you describe is analogous to firemen pulling up in front of a burning house and tying a knot in the front of their hose before they strenuously start trying to pump water through it. Money has not ceased to stimulate spending. Money must be allowed to flow. Never fear, people will certainly spend and invest your freshly-printed currency if ever gets into their hot little hands. If they are too cautious at first, simply give them some more and I guarantee sooner or later they *will* start spending—but it must go directly to them. In our present system, you are right to be scared. The potential inflationary overhang is tremendous. Once the pendulum starts swinging the other way and greed and our fractional-reserve banking system works its multiple expansion of deposits and our money supply—watch out!"

"Roberta, you keep harping on the uncontrolled expansion of our money supply resulting from our fractional-reserve banking system. In fact, right now, as you probably know, the situation is exactly the opposite. Even with the legal minimum reserve requirement for banks set at 10 percent, we cannot induce your so-called 'greedy' banks to loan their excess reserves. As a result, it may surprise you that right now, as we speak, the money base or stock of high-powered money is actually larger than total transaction quantity of the non-bank public's total money supply— currency held by the non-bank public plus their checking account balances. The bank money multiplier has ceased to exist. I confess, I never thought of that as even a remote possibility. If we at the Central Bank had not been resolutely expanding the supply of base money, the money supply would have catastrophically collapsed along with our economy! Fearful bankers have stopped lending and have simply absorbed absolutely all of our epic monetary expansion as excess reserves. We pumped up the money supply so that the total money stock was stabilized despite their sorry lack of cooperation. What do you and your wise friends at the Economics Club say to that!"

(The reader should note that a similar state actually prevails in the U.S. economy at the time of this writing, Spring 2012. That is, the monetary base exceeds currency held by the public plus checking accounts, which is the money supply as defined by M1. In terms of the money equation, (2-4), the fraction D/R is less than 1.)

Roberta stared at him with widening eyes. "Oh, Dad, don't you see? You are inadvertently making my strongest argument for me. When will you realize that the furious swings, chaos, and inherent instability of our monetary system, which requires such extreme interventions and currency swings by the Central Bank, is proof that it is the monetary system itself is the problem? Right now the banks are so regulated, so scrutinized, and so scared as a result of the credit market collapse, that, as you just stated, bank reserves actually exceed their demand deposits. At this point in our money and credit crisis, your minimum legal reserve requirement of 10 percent is clearly irrelevant. It is a meaningless behavioral constraint. I ask you again, what are you going to do after your historic booming of the supply of the fiat money base, when the hunkered-down banks reverse their timidity and start 'swash-buckling' and lending 'excess' reserves again with a vengeance? You know they will! Roaring inflation will return then. Again, you are right to be scared. You really are smoking in the powder room!"

Bob Jr. looked smug and waggled his wine glass suggestively at Jessup for a refill. "Why then, of course, you at the Economics Club and the rest of our economy can thank your lucky stars that they have such a vigilant and strong central bank on call. We're aware of the obvious inflation risk and ready to step in and shrink the money base as needed to stabilize the total transactions money supply and to avoid inflation. That's exactly our job and fortunately we are there, alert and ready. While the rest of the economy sleeps, our work goes unappreciated, but it is critical and never done. 'Heroic' is perhaps not too strong a word to describe it."

"Dad heroic or not it's a job you wouldn't and shouldn't have to do if we had a simpler, more rational monetary system. Can't you see the futility of the Central Bank worrying about and trying to stabilize the money supply, given the volatility of the notional ratios that determine our transactions money supply? There are way too many moving parts between the Central Bank, the money supply and the ultimate impact of monetary policy—the ratio of deposits to bank reserves, the ratio of deposits to currency held outside banks, the velocity of money, etc.? Your job is complex and futile simply because you are saddled with a money and banking system that is complex and futile."

"Well, while you idle young pups at the Economics Club have the luxury of discussing your utopian schemes and making such statements, it's a job that in the real-world economy must be done and, thanks to us rolling up our sleeves, it is being done."

"What a great system, Dad," replied Roberta sarcastically. "As you describe it yourself, you have to pump in reserves like mad when things collapse because the banks stop lending when lending is most needed. But they lend like drunken sailors in the exuberant times when more lending is definitely not needed—regardless of how you set the minimum legal reserve requirement. All the bankers ask of you is to shut up and leave them alone so they can pursue their unjustified profits when times are good, but to bail them out without question during the bad times when excessive weak lending causes economic collapse. Don't you realize that you, that the Confederation Central Bank, is being gamed?"

Bob Jr. smiled tolerantly at his daughter. "You always did have a unique and blunt way of putting things Roberta."

"Wow, Dad! I just had the most incredible thought! Inadvertently, you and the Central Bank have just performed that critical test to show that the practice of fractional-reserve banking is not actually necessary to the operation of our monetary system! Recent Central Bank policy has clearly shown that a movement to a new system of value and exchange, such as our capital as money system, is not only possible, it is very achievable."

"What do you mean?"

"I mean that the Central Bank has just demonstrated that it can maintain and stabilize the total money supply even when private banks fail in the aggregate, as they have, to loan out any excess reserves. At the very least wouldn't it make your job, the Central Bank's job, so much simpler, in trying to control the total money supply, to just issue fiat money and not have a fractional reserve banking system at all—to simply set the legal minimum reserve requirement to 100 percent, as it effectively now is anyway? You bet it would!"

Bob Jr. stared thoughtfully at her and was quiet for some time before beginning, "In all our debate and discussion tonight Roberta, I must grudgingly admit that what you just said might just

124

be the most intelligent and valuable observation you have yet made. I never looked at it that way, perhaps because as you say I am too busy trying to make the system work to step aside a moment and observe it, but now I'm going to have to think pretty hard about that. Your 'capital-as-money' ideas still sound pretty kooky to me, but this last observation of yours is thought-provoking. It, alone, may be worth this dinner. As you say, recent history proves that we at the Central Bank are fully capable of providing whatever money stock is necessary even without the fractional-reserve attribute. Moving to a 100 percent reserve requirement is an appealing idea and no doubt it would vastly simplify my life as a Central Banker and allow us to really hit our monetary targets. For once, the implementation of our monetary policy could be simple and accurate. Of course, there is still the question of lending, but banks could be restricted to lending only from the balances of their depositors savings accounts, as distinguished from checking accounts. Food for thought, I must admit."

Roberta's eyes glowed slightly. She disagreed with her dad on many issues and would probably continue to do so, but she deeply appreciated this evidence of his intellectual honesty. It was a good time to say nothing else.

Bob Jr. mused on quietly for a while. "Finally a central bank able to firmly direct and precisely control monetary policy—it's quite a vision. And, at least after the crisis, the government will reduce its emergency spending and the growth rate of government debt can start to diminish as well. That will take another external pressure off of us."

"Oh please, Dad, I know that you know better than that! I've heard it from you. Nothing is as permanent as a temporary, emergency level of spending. It always has and always will create new bureaucratic structures and new populations of nervous dependents. Once the precedent is set, any temporary, emergency expenditure becomes absolutely essential, only reasonable, and permanent. The administrators and recipients will squeal like scalded pigs at any attempt to reverse and reduce it."

"Actually, Roberta, I kind of agree with you on that—I have to since much of what you just said has in the past been words out of my own mouth. Families are the same way. On any scale, human behavior is predictable. Countless households have got into debt difficulties because it seems easier for them to face that than to face the dissension and push-back that occurs when they try to rein in family expenditure once it has been increased. At least it is a fiscal problem of the government and not another direct monetary issue for the Central Bank—we have enough on our plate."

"Denial on your part again, Dad, and I suspect you well know it. In fact, I have heard you lecture on this very point before. Emergency government expenditure, made permanent by political design or expediency results in growing deficits and a ballooning stock of government debt. That coupled with the political unpopularity of tax increases, inevitably results in pressure upon the Central Bank for inflationary financing. Implication: get the fiat money printing presses fired up. Irresponsible fiscal policy eventually will come to your monetary door and you well know it."

"Yeah, you're right again Roberta. Thanks for mercilessly destroying my brief illusions sought in aid of my digestion tonight. That is why, I suppose, not just me, but central bankers everywhere have always gone down the hopeless path when they testify before their governments. Universally, we beat the drum for prudence, fiscal austerity, and tax increases. You can imagine how well that plays with almost everyone but it is a required script for us. To politicians and their constituents it's a dismal message guaranteed to ensure the continued broad unpopularity of central bankers. Still, during this epic downturn, I must admit that I still believe that expansionary fiscal policies had to be tried along with everything else. They just might work. The risk of economic collapse is simply too great not to try all the tools at our disposal. When the economy is imploding and people aren't spending, inflation seems a rather remote fear."

"Roberta, you and I largely believe in the benefit of free markets. Now stop smirking. It's true. Our difference is while you firmly believe markets are always self-correcting, I am not so sure. Where we really part ways is that I believe that the economy cannot function without a healthy banking system strongly controlled and regulated by a well-run central bank. The work of the money, banking, and credit sector, in my opinion, is the exception because it is too critical to the health of the entire economy to be left solely to the transitory winds of a free market."

"You couldn't be more wrong than on that last point Dad. There is nothing partial about a commitment to the concept of economic freedom and free markets. They are either free or they are not. Accepting the concept that free markets cannot work in one sector of the economy is the 'foot in the door.' It eventually expands and leads to the destruction and constraint to free markets, which is simply free voluntary transactions between individuals, throughout the economy. Surrender of free markets *anywhere* is eventually a surrender of free markets *everywhere*. And make no mistake about it. Free markets are inextricably individual freedom. Surrender free markets and you surrender freedom, period."

It was getting very late. Bob Jr. stared at his daughter across the table. This was the longest talk with her he could remember. She must have had a lot to get off her chest. She returned his stare with a level, self-assured, yet slightly amused, stare of her own. Her comfortable return stare signified an individual who was either extremely intellectually capable, and aware of it, or arrogantly ignorant and unaware of it. In his daughter's case, he knew it was definitely not the latter. She was a very formidable child. He had heard the concern expressed in the past that sometimes aggressive and capable parents can devour their young intellectually. He reflected, ironically, that the opposite could be the risk in the case of parents of very capable offspring.

"I love these discussions with you Dad, no matter how acrimonious they become because of two things," Roberta said interrupting his musing. "First, despite our different points of view on many issues, you are always intellectually honest and curious. Secondly, I honestly believe nothing is more important than the health of our economy."

With a slight smile, Bob Jr. said, "Since you were five, you've always been an egregious and tiresome child. You've obviously come well prepared to spring a quite a trap on your poor old dad. You've dumped quite a load on me tonight. Knowing you as well as I do, I shouldn't have been surprised."

"Well, in the end, almost all economics arguments finally come down to one thing," Roberta replied. "If we try to mandate, control, and manage any part of the economy, it eventually reduces to the solution of letting the smartest person amongst us determine what is optimal for all of us..."

"That would be you, I suppose," Bob Jr. couldn't resist interjecting with a twinkle in his eye.

"...or letting markets work," Roberta continued unflappably. "Since no one can be smart enough to dictate an optimal outcome, control is an impossible task, unfair to the individual given the responsibility to attempt it and unfair to the rest of us that comprise the economy. So the only solution is to let markets work."

"Well, let's finish on that point," Bob Jr. observed wearily. "Dinner with you is never dull. By the way, how are you getting home? It's getting really late. I guess I should take you."

"Oh, don't worry. Gramps was planning to pick me up anyway—speak of the devil, here he comes now!"

"What?" Bob Jr. sputtered, choking and coughing on the remainder of his wine he was trying to finish. In truth, relations between father and son had not always been a model of comfort and warmth.

"Hey!" Bob Sr., 'Big Tuna,' shouted in greeting as he bounded into the dining room followed by a flustered Jessup. He grabbed Roberta and gave her a big squeeze with his remaining arm. "How's my favorite granddaughter?"

Big Tuna was old, but still a large, impressive man as brown as a nut from sun and sea—still brimming with energy and enthusiasm. His loud clothes and casual manner made quite a contrast to his son.

Bob Jr. continued to sit and dourly observed the scene before him. He was still adjusting himself to the shock of his father barging in unexpectedly at this late hour. As a result, when he spoke, his tone was a little cold. "You should quit fishing yourself and leave it to others. It is a dangerous profession for a man of your age and I worry about you. You have plenty of money. That shark attack should have been a warning."

Big Tuna turned and beamed at his son. "Yeah that was quite the deal wasn't it? I was trying to boat one of the biggest blue fins I've ever seen and in the excitement slipped into a shark feeding frenzy. One of them got my arm clean off before I even knew what happened. Fortunately, Tony was there to haul me back in the boat. He was ready to gaff me if he had to. In retrospect it was sort of like dealing with a hungry pack of lawyers—or bankers."

"Losing an arm, going through rehab, and then continuing to fish with one hand, it sounds like a pretty tough last year to me. One you could have done without," Bob Jr. replied, blandly ignoring the jibe about bankers.

Big Tuna responded with a sympathetic smile, "All things considered, I think I had a better last year than you did. Things in the world of a central banker appear to be about as messed up as they possibly could be. That downgrade of government debt must have given you some real headaches."

129

"It was nonsense!" Bob Jr. retorted with more emotion than he intended. "There has never been a default on Confederation Bonds in our entire history. By definition in our economy, nothing is safer than the benchmark of our own Treasury debt. Therefore, downgrading it was an ignorant and irrelevant act. I'm going to have to take Nate to the woodshed over that one. Mark my words. Imagine him downgrading Confederation debt when he was criminally negligent in recognizing the weakness and warning signs in all the private debt and mortgages—unforgivable. In any case, suddenly defining what is the risk-free benchmark as having a degree of credit risk after all is clearly the height of idiocy."

"Oh, I don't know," Big Tuna responded. "I suppose Nate figured better late than never. You can define Confederation bonds as 'risk-free' if you wish, but I'm not so sure they are. At least Nate recognized that when your dog poops in the house, you can't get rid of it by just sweeping it under the couch—it's still there and it still stinks."

"Just precisely what are you trying to get at with that nonsensical analogy?" Bob Jr. bristled.

Roberta, who had been silently watching the interchange between the two men with growing amusement, interjected. "Oh come on Dad. Gramps is just crudely saying the same thing I said earlier this evening. If you have a pile of bad debt originated by fraudulent borrowers and incompetent bankers or intermediaries, having the government sector forgive it by bailing them out and absorbing it does not get rid of the problem. The debt is still there—but now it is public debt and has become the liability of all of us, not just those responsible for originating it. Given the size of the government bail out, we could argue it was Nate's duty not to lose track of it and, as a result, to downgrade Confederation Bonds."

"When you two get together, why do I always feel like my team's sole survivor in a tag-team wrestling match?" Bob Jr. wearily replied.

Big Tuna responded, "Oh we're gentle compared to what might happen to you and Abomo when the next election comes up. All kidding aside, there is real pain and discontent out there and, as the figureheads of one failed government policy after another, I'm afraid the voters will hold you two responsible. Nothing political is working and the recession has gone on way too long to the public's taste. In the old island days, you guys might not just get fired, you could literally end up as the main ingredient in a stewpot."

"Now I see why you are still just a simple fisherman," in spite of himself, a reddening Bob Jr. barked. "You have never understood even the simplest facts about me or my banking career. If you did, you would know that as chairman of the Confederation Central Bank I am not elected. I am appointed with a seven year term—and the term does not fall on election years. I work with President Abomo, as I would work with any president, but I am not part of his political team or a member of his party. In fact, you might recall that I was appointed by a President of the opposing party. Great effort has been made to protect the independence of the Central Bank—so that it may only serve the greater good and not the whims of a particular politician in power. You may make snide remarks about me if you wish, but I will not accept your attacks on the honorable institution of our Confederation Central Bank."

Big Tuna sat silently for a moment and then smiled warmly at his son. "Sorry Bobby, I really didn't mean to get your goat. It seems like this always happens when we talk. Surely you can forgive me for not immediately realizing that the Central Bank was such a pure, non-political institution. After all, seeing you hobnob all the time with President Abomo, testifying every month as chief bureaucrat of the Central Bank in front of the congress and reassuring them that you are adhering to their demands and legislation, and all your rubber chicken speeches in front of bankers' organizations, hopefully you can understand and forgive a simple fisherman's confusion."

131

Bob Jr., who had not missed the sarcasm implicit in his father's words, did not reply, but simply scowled.

"Bobby even you have to admit you've ended up in a strange job—trying to decide how fast to print up the little worthless pieces of paper you call 'money.' That is essentially trying to decide how fast to swipe real wealth from the rest of us by inflating the currency."

Bob Jr. addressed his father, "Again it shows how little you really know Dad. I take the responsibility of fiat money expansion very seriously for the greater good of our economy and the elimination of sustained inflation. I always have. That is why I've been labeled an 'inflation hawk' by my critics who think my policy positions are not sufficiently expansionary. The fact is, as I was telling Roberta, we've been printing money at a pretty high rate for the last few years with unfortunately very little effect on the rate of inflation or on renewed economic growth. The old relationships between money and growth that we thought we knew well have apparently broken down."

Roberta had meant to stay out of this corrosive interchange between her dad and her grandfather. But as usual, the unstable, weird chemistry between the three of them seemed to spawn increasingly competitive and irascible exchanges. It had been that way as long as she could remember. It never ended well. An observing psychologist might smile and shake his head in weary familiarity. Roberta knew all this but now she couldn't help herself and hotly interjected. "As I said before, you know the answer to your own question, Dad. You have been printing money with most of it showing up as ballooning bank reserves across the system. You have the private banks so cowed and hobbled with tight, new lending regulations that their afraid to do anything or lend to anyone. Eventually, they will start lending again and the fractional-reserve banking system will increase the effective money supply beyond recognition. There will be hell to pay in inflation."

"And that's where you're dead wrong again in understanding our vigilance," Bob Jr. sternly replied. "The first objective of the Confederation Central Bank is always and everywhere to responsibly control the supply of money to target low inflation. The Board and I will never lose sight of that. If inflation starts to increase, be assured we will again step hard on the brakes of money growth."

"That's precisely what I've been arguing with you all night long!" Roberta replied with frustration. "When are you guys going to finally realize that your stop and go monetary policies are not the solution—but are in fact a major, if not the main cause of the current recession, the credit market meltdown, and the economic volatility our economy has had to suffer through during past decades?"

Big Tuna, who had been intently listening to this father-daughter interchange, interjected, "I'm not saying that you and your board don't believe you're doing the right thing for us and our economy, Bobby. I just think that eventually the temptation of inflating away the real value of the huge stock of government debt by inflating the currency will prove too much for any politician to resist. I'm not saying that it won't work in the short run either. I know the current public perception of Abomo, the government, and the Central Bank is that nothing has been achieved during almost his whole first term. Employment and output growth remain shitty. However, politically it's always better late than never. If your monetary policy starts to take hold before the election and the economy starts to improve, public perceptions, as always, can be counted on to be fickle and short. You guys might still pull off getting re-elected!"

Why me? Bob Jr. thought as he cringed at his dad's last statement. "You still don't get it, do you Dad? You might recall I just described in detail to you how and why the Central Bank and I are independent of politics. I hate to say it Dad, but I guess it's true that old age doesn't come alone."

"Whatever. Anyway," Big Tuna continued, "the truth is I really did worry about you, Bobby. I remembered what a hash you could make of things, even with the best of intentions, when you were a teenager and in college and it appeared to me that maybe you might be screwing the pooch again."

Bob Jr.'s mouth started to open in shock and outrage.

Roberta, quickly seizing her grandfather's hand, tactfully interjected. "Gramps we've got to get going. I have an early day tomorrow. Good night, Dad. Thanks for a great evening and a great dinner. Love you."

Bob Jr.'s eyes warmed as he regarded his daughter. "Good night, Roberta."

CHAPTER 4

EDWARD'S VISION—MOVEMENT TO A CAPITAL-BASED MONEY

Not long after Roberta's lengthy dinner conversation with her father, a meeting of the Economics Club is about to commence. Roberta is standing at the podium next to a nervously smiling, diffident young man. She is the president of the Club, after recently trouncing another club member named John Tompkins in the Club's annual election. Under her leadership the organization has thrived and become the premier source of free market analysis and criticism of the Confederation economy and its institutions.

Roberta taps on the podium, ignores the amused sounds of the membership, and begins speaking. "Quiet please. Tonight we are continuing our series of presentations on issues facing our monetary system. The Economics Club has had a long-running discussion of the inefficiency and intrinsic fraud of our fractional-reserve banking system backed by a fiat currency. This evening Edward will present what I think you will find is an interesting and compelling argument. Now be quiet and stop smirking and listen courteously to what he has to say. I realize that most of us know him as "Ted" but on this occasion we're standing on a little more formality so I'm introducing him as Edward. His premise is that the inefficiency of our institutionally imposed banking system results in a very high opportunity cost for our economy—that is the inefficient use of our scarce savings and the resulting underinvestment in capital. The result for our economy is a lower level of sustained consumption and quality of life than would be the case in a more transparent and direct system of saving, lending, and investing. He will propose a rather surprising and compelling alternative for a new unit of exchange and valuation—or money. You all know the rules of the game at our Club presentations. Please give him your full attention. May I remind you to save your comments and questions until after Edward's presentation."

Edward shuffles forward, glances nervously at the audience, and smiles shyly. He is wearing an ill-advised, screaming yellow bow tie. It is so large that, relative to his lean, gawky frame, it seems not a great stretch to imagine him flapping it and flying away. The garish tie is no surprise at all to the audience as Edward has a long-standing reputation as an island nerd, which he has done little to dispel. Someone calls out from the back of the crowd, "At least he dresses like an economist!"

Edward's nervousness and unease is due in part to his shyness and social vulnerability. But another portion is exacerbated by some recent unfortunate events relating to his relationship with Roberta.

Edward and Roberta had grown up together and were the best of friends from adolescence onward. The lithe, shapely Roberta with her long dark hair, emerald eyes, and perfect skin was clearly a stunner in the opinion of just about any male on the island. Moreover, her confidence and intellect were every bit as impressive as her appearance. The combination of brains and looks resulted in her being, without her conscious intent, a bit of a man-eater. Given Roberta's natural ease and appearance, she could not have been a stronger counterpoint to Edward. He had been an anxious, acne-challenged, introverted teenager with a horsey face. Through conscious and diligent effort, Edward was just beginning to overcome the self-consciousness and social ineptitude of his teenage years. As is sadly and tiresomely commonplace in human relationships, Edward's feelings for Roberta were not reciprocated in kind. Roberta deeply esteemed Edward as a colleague and friend, but she was not romantically attracted to him at all. Such was certainly not the case with Edward. He had mistakenly interpreted their long friendship as something much more and was hopelessly infatuated with her. Recently, in a weak moment, Roberta erroneously had seen little harm in finally acquiescing to a couple of dates with Edward to which she attached no special significance—thereby sending him precisely the wrong message.

136

This familiar and oft-played minor human tragedy would have been of no great significance and hardly worth mentioning, were it not for an unfortunate event that had occurred at an Economics Club meeting several months previously. Even in the most level-headed of individuals, infatuation has a tendency to destroy a sense of proportion, proper judgment, and appropriate inhibitions. Following this tradition of erroneous judgment in affairs of the heart, Edward, with what his most severe critics might have called his usual lack of social adeptness, had attempted to discreetly convey a written, intimate, and, indeed, an almost sickeningly sappy communication to Roberta. It is mystifying why he decided to commit such a witless endeavor to paper rather than using the currently available technology of electronic texting, but write it he did. Alas, instead of it being successfully delivered to its intended recipient, an event that would have been embarrassing enough, Edward's attempted communication instead followed an unintended trajectory.

As is the case in most sugary and witless missives of this type, Edward's note to Roberta was chock full of all sorts of dreadfully sticky endearments and indecipherable oddments such as "Kitty-pum" and "Snooter" and even worse, if such can be imagined. Clearly, the authors of such delicate and intimate terms would almost always prefer that they never see the public light of day. And, as is almost tiresomely predictable, they do—usually under the worst imaginable circumstances. In this instance, unnoticed by Edward, the note had fallen out of his front pocket during a particularly prodigious sneeze.

For Edward, dropping the note to the Club floor was a very unfortunate occurrence. While Edward's reason had momentarily departed in the temporary flush of infatuation, his sober judgment could almost certainly have been relied upon to return later. It is possible—perhaps even probable—that, with the return of balance and probity to Edward's mind, this disastrously lame note would have been carefully, rightfully, and mercifully destroyed rather than delivered. This, we shall never know. Instead, the note was picked up by the very club member that both Edward and Roberta would have least preferred—that is John Tompkins, also known by Club members as "the Tooth." To their very great discomfort, the Tooth saw fit to read the intercepted note aloud to the great interest, amusement, and glee of the rest of the Club membership, as if it was some sort of intriguing mystery—because, after all, Edward had at least had the good sense to not include any proper identifying names in the dreadful communication. However, although the note included no names, Edward had turned beet red during the enthusiastic public reading. Even the usually serene and imperturbable Roberta had become noticeably discomfited. Their response to the reading left little doubt as the note's authorship.

As a result of this recent debacle, it was now impossible for Roberta and Edward to appear in front of the Club at the same time without the accompaniment of widespread amused whispering and chuckling. Due to the difference in their personalities, Roberta seemed unbothered by this, but Edward still found it mortifying.

"Thanks, Roberta," Edward commences, doing his best to ignore the jibes and mirth from the audience. "I have titled my talk tonight 'Fractional Banking, The Agency Problem, and Underinvestment.' Most of my discussion comes from a rather mathematical paper I have recently written. I will give you a copy along with a transcript of my presentation at the end of our discussion. Tonight it is my purpose to discuss the intuition and common sense of my arguments without using math and graphs.

"It is usually useful to start off with a fresh examination of the simplest of concepts. Let's start with what we mean by savings and consumption and examine the motivations of individuals embarking in both behaviors. Suppose, for example, that Doug is a successful tuna fisherman with a boat and a net. As a result of his experience, Doug knows where to go and he catches a lot of tuna which he trades in the Confederation economy for the other goods that he wishes to consume. Doug trades tuna for units of the currency of our economy, which we still ironically call 'silvers' despite the fact that our money is now a central bank-issued fiat currency. Suppose that Doug is very successful as a tuna fisherman and after he has met all his immediate consumption needs, he still finds himself with income or a stock of silvers left over—a not uncommon situation among the more successful producers in our economy.

"The excess of current income relative to his current consumption allows Doug the luxury of saving his excess income—or, if you prefer to think of it this way, deferring or delaying part of his consumption to the future. Since the near-term future is uncertain and risky, and the long-run future is even more so, Doug will only postpone his consumption in return for some reasonable reward. We don't know the exact motivation for Doug's saving or deferred consumption. Perhaps he wishes to provide for the education of his children. Or, maybe he wants to work less and consume more at some point in the future. Whatever his reasons, most of us are taught to consider his behavior prudent or laudable and that we should emulate it if we can.

"Saving or deferred consumption can take many forms in our economy. For example, the amount Doug saved could be lent to someone else. There could be an implicit or explicit contract detailing the key elements of the loan, such as when the loan will be paid back, and specifying the exact reward to Doug for deferring his consumption. As an alternative, Doug could take his excess of current income over current consumption and invest it directly in his own fishing business—perhaps enlarging its productive capacity by buying another boat and hiring an employee so he catches more fish. This direct investment alternative is hugely important. After all, it is the savers in our economy who invest the excess of their production in their own or another's productive activity that allows for the steadily improving economic prosperity and growth of our overall Confederation economy. This is the productive genius of an optimizing market economy that uses human incentives and ingenuity to make our future, on average, more prosperous and more productive than our past.

"To make the outcome of his saving decision most optimal for him and for our society, Doug must spend some time and effort finding the best and highest available reward for his investment decision— a difficult challenge. Should he invest his savings in his own business? Or, should he consider the businesses of others that might produce an even greater positive return on investment? Should he invest his savings in a more speculative use that might offer a higher reward or in a less speculative one that offers a lower reward that has greater certainty? How should he diversify the use of his savings among different uses in order to reduce his overall risk of losing his future wealth and consumption? These are all questions we are familiar with as investors ourselves. Ultimately, because of the cost in time and investment expertise, will he conclude that he trusts an intermediary's or agent's investment acumen with his hard-earned savings more than he trusts his own judgment, as many of us do? In my opinion, the answer to this last question is far too often 'yes,' with the result that, in the aggregate, too much of our scarce savings and investment is channeled through the agents of banks and other intermediate institutions. The 'agency' problem is that these intermediaries will handle our scarce savings with their own varying motives and likely a considerably lower level of care for our welfare than we would. Using intermediaries can result in an expensive lesson.

"To a great extent, our savings are inefficiently employed when we use intermediaries to invest for us. The lending market is inefficient because it has been imposed upon us and regulated by the Central Bank and the government. It is my view that the institutionally-imposed fractional-reserve and fiat money-based banking system that we currently have results in a real opportunity cost upon our society in terms of foregone investment returns and future growth. Too often we are content to simply allow our savings to accumulate in a bank checking or savings account in return for the reward of a paltry level of interest or, at worst, no interest at all. Then, the bankers or lending intermediaries will aggressively make too many loans with these funds to too many borrowers who are not only unlikely to use them in the best and highest manner, but, in fact, may be unlikely to repay them at all. The faults inherent in our banking and lending system are readily apparent in the all too frequent credit crises, lending bubbles and collapses, and bank failures that litter our economic history. Since we are living in the aftermath of a credit collapse right now, I scarcely need to remind you of this.

"The worst and most ironic characteristic of our banking and credit system is its mandated inefficiency. Insult is added to injury. What would otherwise be our scarce savings and precious new investment in productive capital is further taxed away from us and allocated as bailouts to those who would otherwise fail. That is, we are called upon as a society to support precisely the weakest, least-deserving borrowers, institutions and lenders. Rewarding the worst, rather than the best, is contrary to the most basic premise of a competitive, free market economy. This practice is illogical and indefensible, but it is exactly what we do.

"So how we can change our current money and banking system to make Doug's saving and investment decision more clear and accountable to him? More importantly, how can the increased transparency and efficiency of a new monetary system result in more efficient investment at the aggregate as well as the individual level and a higher level of economic growth, consumption, and sustained prosperity for all of us?

"For Doug and for most of us the easiest and laziest thing to do is to allow the excess of our income over consumption to simply accumulate in a bank account. After all, we may well argue, we are busy with our own careers and are not professional investors. In behaving this way, we are putting off investment decisions we should eventually make ourselves, or at least monitor. Thus, by default we leave the allocation of society's scarce savings to the whims of bankers and other lending market intermediaries.

"Lending intermediaries—bankers—tend to direct scarce savings to the easiest, noisiest, and pushiest borrowers. In particular, they make loans to those who appear willing to pay the highest in loan fees and interest. Intermediaries are not loaning their own precious savings and do not exercise the sort of caution and judgment that occurs when an individual makes his own direct loan. Inefficient lending is, of course, heartily reinforced by the fractional- reserve banking system which allows banks to loan out almost all of the balances in our checking account deposits. Most islanders are probably not even aware that the basis of the banking business is the practice of lending almost all of their account deposits for a profit that goes largely to the bank—instead of to them. This practice is a transfer of the depositor's property to someone else who is unapproved by the depositor and for which he is typically not compensated. I say this practice is fraudulent. Why the system of fractional-reserve banking is not outlawed by the government as an illegal pyramid scheme is hard to understand. Not only does the government not prosecute bankers for this practice, but also the government actually validates and supports it. As a result of excessive lending the Central Bank and the government is effectively being 'gamed' along with the rest of us. Let me explain.

"The easiest loan for bankers to make with our surplus deposit balances is likely to be to someone I will call 'Uncle Bert.' All of us have an Uncle Bert. He is the black sheep in our family who consumes too much and produces too little. He is the one who borrows money to swill beer, join a bowling league, add on a room to his shack, or continue to subsidize a lifestyle of voluntary underemployment. He is the person who takes ten years to finish a bachelor's degree with a major in Sports Communication and accumulates enormous student loan debt. When too much of our economy's scarce intended savings is channeled to people like Uncle Bert, two bad things happen. First, too much of what should be seed capital investment for our economy is consumed by ne'er-do-wells instead of being invested in productive capital at its best and highest use. Second, Uncle Bert is precisely the individual who is least likely to intend to or be able to repay his loan obligations. Put simply, loans to borrowers like Uncle Bert are loan defaults waiting to happen.

"The inefficient allocation of our investment funds impairs the future growth rate of our economy and its future base of productive capital. This is bad business for our economy and bad for our future economic growth, production, prosperity and sustainable consumption. The inefficient allocation of our investment funds impairs the quality of life that would have been available to us had the best investment of our scarce savings been made. It is ironic that when our economy and its banking institutions make the macroeconomic error of allocating too much savings to consumption in the short run, it actually *lowers* the level of sustainable consumption available to all of us during the long run—a kind of restatement of the famous children's fable about the ants and the grasshopper. For this reason, I could just as well have titled this speech, 'The Tragedy of Underinvestment.'

"The second bad outcome associated with lending to Uncle Bert occurs when the inevitable loan default occurs. When lending intermediaries badly underwrite loans then loan defaults become epidemic. The credit market collapses, assets or collateral underlying loans plummet in value, the banking system fails, government feels politically compelled to intervene to absorb the bad debts at taxpayer expense, and our economy enters a severe recession, or worse.

"Who is to blame in this recurring mess? There is plenty of blame to spread around. First, we could blame weak borrowers—those who are more than willing to borrow funds that they are unlikely to be able to repay. They may even misrepresent themselves or their financial strength in order to obtain loans. We could also point a finger at individual loan officers at banks and other institutions. Even though Uncle Bert may argue that he is developing valuable human capital by earning his Sports Communication major, loan officers should know better. We could blame all of us who are lazy and who have effectively deferred the allocation of our scarce savings to inefficient or dubious uses by intermediaries, agents and bankers. Most importantly, we could blame the embedded, flawed design of our money, banking, and credit system itself for institutionally enabling the inefficiency and instability of our saving, lending, and investment process. Our system creates the illusion of more loanable funds than are really available through the fallacy of fractional-reserve banking. It offers misplaced incentives for the efficient allocation of excess reserves and savings by typically rewarding the volume rather than the quality of loans made. It places excessive layers of intermediaries or agents between the primary sources of savings and the ultimate disposition of them. For emphasis I restate, these intermediaries are people whose compensation is based upon the volume of loans they produce and who are not responsible for the quality and performance of their loans during the future. With such a convoluted system, do we have the right to expect anything other than inferior economic efficiency and incomprehensibility? Why does Uncle Bert always end up with your money? Why do the fruits of your labor get channeled as loans to long-term college students who spend ten to fifteen years drinking beer and climbing rock walls in the university's recreation center? It is because of the fundamental fallacy and unaccountability of agencies and intermediaries, whom you trust but shouldn't—to make loans with your savings. Nobody else will care for your money, wealth, and its disposition as much as you do.

"Further, we could fault our government, the Central Bank, and regulatory bureaucracies for enabling the current disastrous money, banking, and lending institutions to remain in place and for rescuing them at taxpayer expense when they produce predictable recurrent disastrous outcomes. The worst part of government institutional control of a fatally flawed system is the widespread belief that, when the credit and banking sector does implode, it is proof that yet more regulation and oversight is the answer. Those who agree with this point of view are seeing the trees instead of the forest. We rarely ask the threshold question of whether or not the system itself is the fundamental problem. The inevitable result of more and more regulatory bandages applied to a system that is fundamentally designed to fail is even more complexity and less transparency. The irony is that well-intended cures imposed by government of additional regulation and oversight of our credit market simply make the problem worse. These 'cures' embed more agents and intermediaries in the system, make our investment decisions less comprehensible, and actually worsen the problems they were intended to correct. A free market allows competitive evolution toward greater efficiency and clarity. However, this valuable function of a free, competitive marketplace is easily derailed by government oversight and control. Unfortunately, a regulated inefficient system can become a permanent fixture and an increasingly anachronistic burden upon our economy— tragically flawed and unable to evolve or to die.

"Let me emphasize this last point by focusing upon regulation for a second. In my view, regulation of a marketplace is one of the most obvious symptoms of a failed system. The need for regulation or oversight is an indictment of the design of the market or institutions themselves. The history of our money, banking, and credit system is a strong example. Bankers, agents, lending officers, and other intermediaries inject themselves into our transaction and savings decisions while decrying the government institutions, such as the Central Bank, that regulate them. Unspoken, of course, is the fact that bankers themselves originally lobbied for the creation of these institutions in the first place in order to validate their business, to protect their profits, and to limit competition. A banking system such as ours is inherently unstable and requires the regulation, oversight, and too often the actual bailout by a money-printing central bank. When the system crashes, or when its inherent contradictions become apparent, or when external competition threatens to bypass it and threatens its monopoly profits, the inevitable argument offered is that the cause is insufficient regulation. In the view of bankers and their regulators, and even well-meaning but misinformed individuals who are typically skeptical of free markets, more control is always needed. I believe this is how we can tell we are wandering down the road toward an economy crippled by institutionalized inefficiency and excessive regulation.

"But our problem with regulation is actually far more severe than the casual observer might think. The rules and regulations restricting our lending are unfortunately not just stupid but innocent. The instability of our credit market and the misallocation of savings within our economy have been exacerbated, because the government, or a bureaucratic agency acting on its behalf, decided for political or social reasons to mandate who banks or lenders *must* loan to. This mandate is enforced under the threat of litigation. Often the politically favored groups are the weakest borrowers amongst us, thereby flying in the face of sound economics and loan underwriting. Thus, sad but predictable political behavior dramatically increases the probability of loan defaults and failures and worsens the misallocation of our economy's scarce investment funds. The result is under-investment of our scarce savings into new productive capital goods.

"In fact, for the financial health of our economy, the opposite of more regulation is what we really need. Too frequently we fail to take the proliferation of regulation in markets as a reason to go back and press the 'clear' or 'restart' button. A return to simplicity and transparency in our monetary exchange, saving, and lending behavior is exactly what is required to solve our monetary system problem. Transparency requires a move away from a central bank-issued fiat currency for our money supply. It requires the ending of a fractional-reserve banking system in order to avoid providing false incentives for excessive or dubious short-term lending. It requires a new currency or money that not only has the usual attributes of a recognized medium of exchange, store of value, and unit of account, but some new ones as well, such as a solidly stable value. Better yet, a new money with an increasing value over time in terms of most traded goods. What is needed is a monetary good that always reminds those who are about to spend it of the true opportunity cost of current consumption relative to future consumption. This new monetary good should circulate successfully and accomplish all the required functions of money in exchange, valuation, and store of wealth without requiring the existence of a central bank or even the conventional banking system itself.

146

"Allow me to wax utopian for just a moment. Suppose that our new monetary good could be custodied and exchanged electronically—a capability that our current island technology allows. Further suppose that it actually embodies an intrinsic return to it that is close to the best and highest average return that can be obtained. Thus, those of us who are too busy to make our own optimizing investment decisions—most islanders, in fact— would be effectively realizing a good return by default, by simply accumulating or holding a greater stock of our wealth in terms of the new 'money.' What a beautiful vision this is. What if our new unit of exchange and valuation, our new money, was exactly the asset we would prefer to hold in any case in order to achieve the highest sustained risk-adjusted rate of return—that is shares of ownership in a broad index of our economy's productive capital?

"Let's back up for a moment. We all know the critical importance of a trading good that allows us to value all other goods and services and to easily accomplish exchange—that is, the critical importance of a monetary good. As an accident of history or perhaps an inevitable outcome, we have generated and institutionalized the monetary system we currently have. We use fiat money—pieces of paper backed supposedly by silver but, in fact, backed by nothing other than our trust in their imaginary value and our willingness to use them for transactions and hold them as a store of value between trades. Our money is a figment of our collective imagination, and it could fail at any time simply because we could wake up and choose not to believe in it—not to accept or value it anymore. Worse, the supply of this fantasy money is volatile because of the strange concept that we allow banks, acting together, to loan out much more of it than collectively exists in the original accounts or deposits—what we call the fractional-reserve banking system. This expansion of money banks may do to a greater or lesser extent, apparently as the mood strikes them, creating a money supply whose aggregate quantity is completely uncertain. As we have observed, this has allowed bankers the strange and exclusive legal license to steal from the rest of us and fraudulently transfer our property without our approval, compensation, or, in many cases, knowledge—a type

147

of activity that is generally frowned upon and excluded from all other types of legal exchange. In fact, regulators and overseers of our economy have generally disallowed such pyramid or ponzi-type schemes and imprisoned their instigators everywhere else they have occurred other than within the banking sector. But bankers are permitted to engage in fractional-reserve banking and are even smiled upon by our Confederation Central Bank.

"Given all this, should it be a surprise to us that we have recurring bouts of financial instability in our economy? The surprise is actually that such a monetary system works at all—it is almost beyond imagining. Moreover, as I have noted, it is tragic because of the destruction of wealth and recurring inefficiencies in production and employment that have occurred because of short-run financial volatility. Tonight, this familiar argument, valid as it is, supports, but is not my main point.

"This evening my focus is on the long-term consequences of our fiat money system. My primary contention is that our monetary structure is tragic over time because it inevitably blocks and impairs the efficient allocation of society's scarce savings to its best and most profitable use in future investment in our economy's productive capacity. The result is exactly as though the economy had chosen to save too little and had contributed too small a share of its current output toward investment and toward the production and growth of future output. We have an endemically inefficient structure that collectively encourages us, in the aggregate, to consume too much and to save and invest too little. It is inefficient because at this point in time it is not a market-driven and evolving system. Rather it is an antiquated, inefficient, bureaucratically imposed and maintained monopoly. It is embedded, regulated, institutionalized, and, therefore, unlikely to go away of its own volition or by competitive market forces. It is insidious because we do not see the long-run costs of our inefficient money and lending structure as clearly as we see the obvious short-run costs of economic volatility in the credit market, business cycle, and employment. We do not see or mourn the loss of prosperity and future growth that might have been. It is easy for us to criticize the individual farmer or fisherman who saves too little of his output to invest in expansion or support of next year's production. It is much more difficult for us to recognize the same problem within our aggregate society because of an inefficient lending market wasting our collective savings, but the argument is precisely the same.

"The solution, I believe, is to return to a more simple and obvious money that has a stable value as a real good. Imagine earning a real reward for holding money—the average rate of return to the ownership of capital—rather than incurring the opportunity cost of a typically declining value of a fiat currency caused by inflation. Money based upon a single commodity, such as the silver we once had, is better than a fiat money, but even the return to it over time is simply speculative. If we make the new money pieces of a broad measure of the capital stock, then the default or lazy decision of simply accumulating money balances would effectively place our savings in something close to its best and highest use anyway. A beautiful monetary solution emerges when our unit of exchange and valuation and the easiest way to hold wealth is also the asset that happens to generate the best and highest risk-adjusted average rate of return we could reasonably expect. Then, the opportunity cost of consumption is abundantly clear to all each time the purchase of a consumption good or service is contemplated.

"I can already hear the objections from bankers that the return to capital sets too high a benchmark. They will argue that our economy would be hurt because not enough loans will be made. Or, properly translated, not enough bank profits through loan fees and interest would be made. But I believe that, if the opportunity cost seems to be too high for most borrowers to meet, then that is precisely what we need and precisely the proposed system's advantage. The return to capital—factories, machines, and knowledge—is our society's true opportunity cost of current consumption versus future consumption. It is the fundamental truth that is hidden under the impenetrable veil of our current banking and lending system. Many, if not most, loans should not be made because they cannot meet this test and our economy would be better and more prosperous in the future for it. Of course, there would be no law against lending in a capital-as-money economy. The total volume of loans would be indeterminate and would depend on aggregate market lending behavior. Moreover, we would be foolish to promise that bad loans and loan defaults would disappear. We know they would not. There is no law against being stupid or making stupid decisions in disposing of one's assets. At the very least, however, we have the right to ask that such behavior not be encouraged and rescued by the embedded design of a flawed monetary system or by mandate.

"The long-run benefits of changing to a logical monetary good are staggering. The most desirable characteristics of a good economic solution to any problem is clarity and simplicity. An economy and economic institutions that are intuitively clear and readily understood by any sixth grader are always to be preferred. Using index units of capital as a trading good or a store of wealth passes this test. The numeraire or yardstick by which we measure the value of everything else becomes clear. The ownership of money becomes desirable not because of our trust in its imaginary value but because it yields a real and high average rate of return to its owner over time. We will save more because we will be reluctant to let go of a unit of productive capital every time we buy a pizza. Even a sixth grader, who would readily hand over fiat currency for a pizza, is going to think twice before he swaps his fishing pole for a slice. This behavior is a good thing and the way it should be because it reflects our instinctive understanding of the true opportunity cost of every current consumption decision we make.

"Let's contrast capital as money with fiat currency. Fiat paper is shoveled to the pizza maker as fast as we can do so because we are not sure of its value even in the near term. The only thing we know for sure is that its value is a mirage that typically rapidly diminishes over time as the central bank printing presses roll and as bankers loan out all available excess reserves. By way of contrast, frivolous consumption and frivolous loans will tend to diminish with capital as money. Bad decisions can and will still be made, but the opportunity cost of making them will be more clear to the individual saver and consumer—and the responsibility for the outcome of those bad decisions will and should rest with the consumer. Putting the responsibility on each individual trader is the most we can ask.

"We can also anticipate another classical banker's retort: 'There will not be enough of your capital money units to actually accomplish all the trades and exchanges that need to occur. That is why the genius of the fractional-reserve system arose in the first place!' This argument, at first glance, seems plausible. It may even have had merit in the old days of a double-hand-entry bank deposit and withdrawal system—a system that had long delays between actual trades and the recording of the monetary and checking account transactions that represented them. However, the argument that fractional-reserve banking is necessary is weak and growing weaker with our current technology that allows electronic, instantaneous transactions and the rapid recorded change in the ownership of funds required by those transactions. Since the limiting speed of monetary exchange is now the speed of light rather than the lamentable speed of bankers, the actual supply of the monetary good is interesting; but it is not a relevant constraint to the trading system. Current technology can make the old fractional-reserve banking shibboleths disappear.

"When the true opportunity cost of current consumption versus future consumption is clear, then the result will be that a higher level of aggregate saving and investment will occur in our economy. Along with your copy of tonight's talk, you will receive a paper presenting a simple model, whose original version was developed by Nobel prize- winning economist Robert Solow. The model and its various permutations are usually referred to as the 'neoclassical growth model.' It is a single-sector growth model with only two productive factors, capital and labor, and the basic assumptions of factor substitutability in production, declining marginal productivity of each factor when the other is held constant, constant returns to scale, and perfect certainty.

"The neoclassical growth model can be criticized, of course, for its rather heroic simplifying assumptions. Certainly, it is a model with a view of the forest rather than of individual trees. Despite its flaws, I believe that as a tool for understanding the broad picture of an aggregate economy this model is without equal. Many of its conclusions are robust and appear to explain our aggregate economic outcomes and situation well. I recommend you study this model. I will cover the neoclassical growth model, its assumptions, and its conclusions that are relevant to my arguments in much more detail when I continue this presentation tomorrow night. For our current purpose, however, it is sufficient to observe that with more efficient transmission of intended savings into investment capital, the tools available per worker would increase, and so would labor's productivity. The marginal product of capital, which is also the return to capital ownership, would move in the opposite direction, or decrease as the ratio of capital to labor is increased. That is, adding more tools per worker increases the productivity of workers but diminishes the marginal product of each additional tool.

"In our discussion, I am going to distinguish between growth in population and growth in what shall be called the 'effective' labor force. In our economy, over time the effective labor force grows for two reasons: first, the number of workers grows due to increases in population and second, the average worker's productivity increases as technology improves resulting in better tools and better knowledge. As you study the Solow model, the important fact to absorb is that the point of maximum sustainable individual consumption occurs when the growth rate of the effective labor force equals the marginal product of capital. This equality is the flag that signals attainment of what has been called the 'golden-rule' capital intensity. I have studied our island economy, and I believe that we have a level of cumulative capital investment that results in a capital intensity that is well below the golden-rule level that would maximize average sustainable consumption. I have reached this conclusion for the simple reason that our current average return to capital is significantly higher than the growth rate of our effective labor force—the growth rate of labor plus the growth rate of labor productivity.

"Simply speaking, our aggregate Confederation economy is strictly analogous to the farmer who is saving too little feed corn for next year's crop. For consuming too much in the short run he pays the long-term price of having lowered his sustainable level of consumption in the future. For this error in judgment, I blame the criminal complexity and self-serving inefficiency of our current money, banking, and lending system—and its regulators. I recommend a return to transparency and simplicity as well as a new monetary good, or numeraire, that is simply capital, itself.

"At the aggregate level the Solow model is a very simple—it doesn't even include a monetary good. What need would it have for money to facilitate exchange with the model's simplifying assumptions of perfect certainty and only one type of output? Attempts by economists to make the Solow model more realistic by introducing money seem contrived and pointless. In my paper, for added insight I take a look at some of these past attempts. Why not recognize that an appropriate valuation good, capital, is not only already in the model but, more importantly, in our hands? I recognize that a model, any model, is nothing but a simplifying abstraction. However, used wisely it can be a useful tool that points us in the direction of robust understanding.

"Please note that the solution I have proposed, units of capital ownership to be used as the yardstick for exchange and value, would alter our real economy in a way that makes the economy itself conform more closely to the intuitive insight of the simple neoclassical model. In a strange but ultimately appealing way, I propose that, rather than revising the assumptions of the model in order to make it conform more closely to our flawed reality, we change our economy and our money to conform more closely to the intuition and elegance of a powerful and intuitive model!

"In truth, there are many alternatives to our current money and banking system that would represent vast improvements to its

153

current dismal condition. A return to a type of commodity money instead of a fiat money would be one improvement, although not optimal because of all the demand and supply shocks that can strike any single commodity or good. Direct lending between individuals and minimizing the use of banking agents or intermediaries would be another huge improvement that would increase transparency in the credit market and stop making us bear collective responsibility for bad loans or bad decisions made by individuals. And finally, eliminating the fraudulent transfer of property rights by ending the ability of banks to loan out depositor's funds without their compensation or approval—the fractional-reserve banking system—is absolutely essential. Any or all of these changes would improve or eliminate the problem of misallocated savings and underinvestment. But, rather than returning to commodity money such as gold or silver, I would prefer to see us use capital as money. We now have the technology to do it. I believe that capital as money is not only practicable but is also the most logical, simplest, and most transparent good for exchange and valuation.

"I would now like to pause and invite your questions, comments and discussion."

No sooner than Edward utters these words, John Tompkins rockets out of his seat. It is fair to say that the orientation of the island Economics Club largely tilts toward those who believe in the virtues of freedom and free and efficient markets, but John Tompkins is the exception, the classic gadfly. In outlook he can be described as the nearest thing the club has to a Keynesian style economist, which partly accounts for Roberta winning the club presidency in a landslide over Tompkins. He believes wise intervention, planning and control are required in order to optimize the unfortunate outcomes and chaos of unfettered markets. He also believes market failure is commonplace, perhaps even universal. Most Club members think Tompkins believes so because his father's small, but prosperous fishing business had failed so abysmally and quickly when it had passed into his own hands. His formal name is John Tompkins II—oddly his name does not contain the more usual second generation "Jr." Possibly for this reason club members usually call him by his last name, which he finds acceptable. Less kindly, club members sometimes refer to him as "the Tooth," perhaps in reference to the unusual II he placed at the end of his name, which he does not.

"Ah, Tompkins," says Edward. "I was sure you would have remarks. I am surprised you were able to restrain yourself this long."

"It was difficult," retorts Tompkins. "I have never before heard such a concentrated and uninterrupted presentation of pure nonsense in a Club presentation, and I might add, in this Club I have heard a lot of nonsense. My questions and criticisms fall into three areas—perhaps the three main conclusions of your speech. First, what is wrong with the fractional banking system and loaning to your so-called 'Uncle Berts?' It appears to me that our economy can rise to fulfill the expectations of a far-seeing government and competent central bankers. Moreover, when it does so, that is a good thing. When we wisely expand leverage, loans, and liquidity, we really do achieve a higher rate of future economic growth than when we simply leave markets to their own crude devices. We enlist unemployed or underemployed resources and create a higher level of prosperity for all—more prosperity than unregulated private markets would have ever achieved on their own. Expanding the supply of money and loans to accommodate the 'Uncle Berts' is as good a way as any of stimulating an underperforming economy. Banks should do this and would be criminally negligent if they didn't. For this reason, today it is the lack of bank lending that I decry!"

Edward replies, "There are so many fallacies in your observation that I hardly know where to begin. First, as a true interventionist or planner, you have an unwarranted faith in experts imposing and operating from above. If there are unemployed individuals or resources—and we would be more prosperous and happier if they were employed—then wouldn't the private economy tend to exploit them as efficiently as possible for the profit of opportunistic entrepreneurs? Those who answer 'No!' to this question, as you do, put themselves into an untenable position as elitists or experts. You think you know better what is good for us than we do as individual and optimizing traders. That has been shown over and over again in our economic history to be a fallacious assumption. Wasted or unemployed resources imply entrepreneurial profit opportunities foregone. The argument ignores that unemployed workers always have the honorable option of working for themselves. It demeans them to assume they cannot work unless someone else, presumably higher up the food chain, deigns to employ them. Savings are a scarce and valuable resource to our economy that we are wasting through the implementation and maintenance of a horribly flawed set of institutions. Ironically, our flawed institutions are held in place permanently by law and regulation by the very experts, planners, government regulators, and, with apologies to Roberta, central bankers with which you are so infatuated. Without them and their stifling control, I believe market institutions would rapidly evolve and cure the idiocies, excesses, and inefficiencies of our money and banking system."

Tompkins smugly responds, "That's the problem with guys like you. You can't see the problems in the real world—even when they hit you on the head. You can't see—or you choose to ignore—the severe and sustained unemployment all over the Confederation and the long-persisting credit crisis. How do your efficient, profit-seeking entrepreneurs and free markets reconcile with that basic reality? I suppose you see no value or benefit from President Abomo's many wise stimulation packages and the expansionary Central Bank policies wisely executed by Roberta's dad. You probably believe that our large government budget deficits are egregiously wasteful and inefficient. I believe that they are the only reason our economy survived the last credit market collapse. Further, I believe that collapse could have been avoided with better, bolder, and more astute regulation of our banking and lending sector. In short, I believe that without the intervention, stimulus expenditure, and increased regulation, our Confederation economy would have collapsed totally while you people rambled on about private market efficiency. And, by the way, I'm tired of hearing over and over again of a pyramid of debt. Since, in the aggregate, loans within our banking system are from us back to us, if they are all good, solid, well-collateralized loans it really doesn't matter how many of them are made."

"Tompkins, I am amazed. You have unwittingly almost provided my response within your own observation. You correctly observe that the root cause of our current decline in output and employment is the credit crisis. How did we get a credit crisis? It was spawned by the very top-down-managed, central bank-imposed, fractional-reserve fiat money-supported banking system that I impugned throughout my presentation. If that doesn't make my point about the system's harms and inefficiency, then nothing will. And yes, Tompkins, I realize that if all the loans we make between ourselves in our banking system are perfectly underwritten and perfectly collateralized then, in theory, the volume of total loans in the pyramid of debt doesn't matter. But surely all of us realize that the bigger that pyramid of loans is, the higher the probability that some of them will fail—thereby generating a disastrous implosive death-spiral of loan defaults. This is because, as even you know, during the unraveling of a debt pyramid asset prices fall and the economy weakens, making even what used to be 'strong' loans weak and vulnerable to default. This is especially true when loans are aggressively expanded with demand deposit funds and when loan officers of banks are compensated based upon the volume of debt they originate rather than its quality. The risk of a debt default crisis becomes even worse when government lending regulations punish lending intermediaries for discriminating against weak borrowers. It is analogous to encouraging fools to light more matches in the presence of powder kegs. As I stated before, people have the right to make bad lending or borrowing decisions, but a free market at least should not endure an apparatus that promotes such behavior and then makes us all financially responsible for it.

Edward continues, "As to the sustained unemployment of people and resources, any market can and will be hit by shocks—including our overall Confederation economy. These shocks and their effects last for a finite time period because, in a world of uncertainty, we must plan for an unknown future by embodying our best guesses in contracts. For example, when future events make the expectations embedded in employment contracts incorrect, there will be winners and losers. As a result, the contracts will not be revised instantly and there will be an unavoidable, painful, but transitory period of adjustment. This period inevitably will be longer the more severe the unexpected shock or crisis is. It is also worsened and extended by successive rounds of shocks and inept or wealth-destroying government fiscal policy responses to those shocks. Unfortunately our economy has recently endured both a particularly sharp shock and an ill-considered government policy in response to it.

"You all remember hurricane Oscar five years ago. What peculiar bad luck that it should follow a circular path and hit our island full force four times in succession. What rational person among us ever would have imagined such a thing would happen? Yes, extraordinary natural shocks occur; and when they do they destroy wealth and create transitory recessions and unemployment until the marketplace adapts to them. Here at the Economics Club, all that most of us ask is that the government, the Central Bank, and an embedded, tragically flawed money, banking, and lending system shouldn't add to those shocks. We have enough natural shocks that hit our island, its economy, and our lives without adding man-made shocks of our own design or idiocy to pile on. As for President Abomo's 'wise' stimulus expenditures, I will ask only one question, one which we have batted around many times in our discussions at this club. Who pays for the stimulus and how can the expenditures exert a net stimulus upon our economy when the financing of them, by taxing or borrowing, inevitably reduces expenditure elsewhere by an equal and offsetting amount? Tompkins, I am saddened by this growing stream of record deficits that you admire so much. I know the enormous government spending has claimed a stream of private saving and investment that would otherwise have continued far into the future. The deficits represent a mortgage upon the future stream of prosperity that our economy could otherwise have enjoyed. Rather than helping our economy recover, I believe the 'stimulus' policies are the major reason that private markets are so restrained and pauperized and the main reason our recovery is so frustratingly slow. A market economy is resilient and can recover from many shocks—usually with a speed and vigor that surprises everyone. However, not this time around. It is hard to recover quickly from a shock and a policy response that claims such a large share of our precious savings and misallocates it for the foreseeable future."

"Well, I expected no less from you," says Tompkins wryly. "You have provided me the usual bromides and utopian free-market dialogue that I have come to expect at this club. We have gone around this particular bush many times. I recommend that you and the other members of this club who have their heads buried in the sand take a look at the outside world to see the persistent problems and suffering that call for optimal management and humane intervention. But now I believe it is you who have contradicted yourself, and that is my second point. You make a diatribe against central planning and what you refer to as 'management from above' while at the same time giving us the Solow neoclassical growth model, or some such nonsense, which you say should be imposed as the font of wisdom with its so-called golden rule consumption. You admit that the model is based upon heroic and unrealistic assumptions and yet you have the gall to ask us to make our economy more like the model! In my opinion, you are advocating top-down management in the extreme, although in your case I would certainly rush to agree that it is not by an expert. How do you reconcile this recommendation with your love of free, unregulated markets?"

Edward retorts, "Perhaps it is not surprising that you're trying to inflict quite a bite, Tooth. You seem to be attacking with even more than your usual animosity and vigor. I trust that the recent election results are not still a burr under your saddle." At this jab, the Economics Club erupts in hoots and chuckles. "I see I must patiently explain the intuition of the Solow model to you. And I respectfully suggest that those of us who are free market economists use models in a far different way than do those of you

159

who are instinctively interventionists and planners. Free marketers use models and paradigms for insight in explaining how markets work or should work in the absence of planning, control, or the sustained interference of bad or flawed institutions.

"For simplicity, think about a single farmer who grows a single output, corn. This farmer, call him Joe, eats some of it and saves some of it to plant for future production. His problem is how much to save given the size of his farm, his labor, and other constraints. Clearly, there will be some level of saving of corn, or investment, which will maximize his sustained level of future consumption; if he is a clever farmer, he will discover this optimal level. Joe does not need to be told that he is, as an individual, saving and investing in a way that if everybody, on average, emulates, we will arrive at the golden-rule consumption level of some model. He simply behaves the way he does in order to maximize his own welfare over time. For a free market economist, the Solow model is simply a useful tool for best understanding how he is behaving and why. It is not an attempt to mandate or control his behavior. When we aggregate farmer Joe with all his compatriots, farmers, businesses, and fishermen, for example, we derive the aggregate economy. All are attempting to maximize their welfare by choosing between current and future consumption. Assuming market efficiency in the allocation of savings, the result is strictly analogous to the golden rule prediction of the model. The assumptions of the Solow model are simple in order to keep the primary insight and intuition of the model crystal clear. The model and my discussion tonight are certainly not intended to provide some template or roadmap for control and intervention. I believe that if we remove the contrived and inefficient monetary monopoly of the Central Bank and the regulated banking and lending system, a capital-as-money economy can emerge as the natural and superior replacement for it by preference and adoption of the marketplace. It does not have to be mandated from above or legislated."

Tompkins snorts and sarcastically begins, "What foolishness. We don't have certainty. We don't have one farmer growing corn. We don't have only two factors of production; we have many. Facing the same constraints, different farmers would definitely not agree on the optimal amount to consume right now and the optimal amount to save for the future. Of what value is a model that makes such assumptions? Why should we use it as a guide? It is simply dangerous and naive to attempt to draw any insights from it. Why not build a model that is as complex as the world we live in so that we can really understand what we face? Locked in a fairy tale world as you are, Edward, you have not realized that to play with the big boys you need complex and realistic models."

In spite of himself, Edward's ire is aroused by the last few comments. "May I remind you, Tompkins, of the recent election? It was, if I recall, one of the 'big girls' who left you bleeding on the road. Heaven help you, if you were debating Roberta instead of me. You have only illustrated, Tompkins, that you do not understand the purpose and art of modeling. Complexity obscures rather than enhances correct understanding and intuition by using largely irrelevant variables. Insight and simple, robust understanding is the goal of a good economic model. Achieving this goal is best accomplished by abstracting away from what complicates but is of secondary importance in order to clearly and succinctly demonstrate key results, behaviors, and propositions. Once illustrated, the key assumptions, conclusions, and insights provided by a useful model should be plausible and appealing to our intuition—they should accord with our carefully considered commonsense.

"The Solow model is a superb example. Is it not reasonable to assume that the marginal product of labor rises when we provide more tools to a worker? Is it not reasonable to assume that the marginal product of a tool diminishes when we provide more of them to a single laborer? Is the result, at equilibrium in the model, that the growth rate of output equals the growth rate of the labor force plus the growth rate of labor productivity not appealing to our commonsense and intuition? Similarly, doesn't it appeal to our intuition that, in the long term, our individual consumption—our standard of living—can ultimately only grow at the rate of our sustained average gain in labor productivity? All these results

161

from the model, and more, accord with and reinforce what our thoughtful intuition already tells us makes sense. For this reason, when we have seen a good, simple economic model, we look at its results and conclusions and say, 'Of course!' and 'I could have thought of that myself.' That is the genius of a simple, powerful model as an explanatory tool. However, I must apologize to you, Tompkins. For those of you who are only happy when trying to understand the real world from within the cauldron of complexity that constitutes it, such moments of simple insight and discovery must occur only rarely, if at all."

"Just as I expected, Edward, your response is glib and sidesteps or ignores my main objections. I maintain my belief that we all try to control the economy and that so-called 'free marketers' amongst us simply have a different plan for control—one that would be disastrous if we adhered slavishly to it in the face of real world common sense. As a further example of your hypocrisy of being a planner without admitting it, let us consider your imposition of a preposterous monetary good, units of ownership of the broad capital stock, if I understand you correctly. What are they valued in terms of? Who controls their supply? Who are you to suggest that this form of monetary good be imposed upon the rest of us? Are we all going to be rushing around trying to buy haircuts with diverse capital certificates? I can only imagine how that would work! What an awful mess! I hope you are disingenuous when you state that you have no template or roadmap for control."

"Ah, Tooth, you are becoming too repetitive, strident, and combative. Again, as a free market economist, I do not mandate broad units of capital as a monetary good. I simply suggest it as a logical alternative with many desirable attributes—especially when compared with the fictitious value of fiat currency along with the arbitrary quantity of money created by a fractional-reserve banking system. The actual and precise form of the market monetary good that would evolve, if our economy were unconstrained with its current technology, would probably be more clever and more intuitive than anything I could imagine. I am suggesting a broad roadmap toward freedom and free markets. I am even suggesting

162

the consideration of a starting point, a route to consider, but I am not *mandating* it. All I ask of a new good for exchange and valuation is that it is simple and its value is transparent, real, and market determined. It must be free from as many of the negative or destabilizing attributes of our current money and banking system as possible. I am confident that an enlightened, unconstrained market can evolve to such a money. Tompkins, I know it is alien to your worldview; but the new money should only be valued by the market in terms of the things for which it is traded. Likewise, its supply should not be debated or managed but simply determined by the market. What we use as a trading good, a pricing good, and a store of value should be intuitive, transparent, and natural. Capital money is my best suggestion as to what could fill this role. I am not dodging your last question about the precise mechanisms that would allow broad capital shares to be traded successfully for all other goods and services—or perhaps I am. It is late and everyone here wants to go to bed. So remember that question, Tompkins, as I'm sure you will; we will return to it tomorrow.

"I believe that our trading technology has reached a speed and efficiency where any number of goods could become our monetary unit and have sufficient supply to accommodate the volume of our trade. Moreover, for those of you willing to come tomorrow night, I throw out a teaser. With the aid of the simple Solow growth model, I will explain why I believe that instantaneous trading and change of custody of asset ownership has made the velocity of money a market-determined notional variable. Unlike the old days, velocity of money is not subject to any physical limits. This lack of limits has profound implications as it relates to lack of effectiveness of central bank monetary policy. Tomorrow night I will explain why fiat money policy has become increasingly ineffective and neutral. As a corollary, I will also explain why the need for a central bank to attempt to optimally control the supply of money has become increasingly counterproductive and unnecessary."

Edward continues, "Folks, if you carry away nothing else from tonight's presentation, please leave with this fact. The two fundamental requirements for a capital-as-money economy have been met. First, the speed with which money can be exchanged for goods has been removed as a technological constraint. Electronic recording of transactions allows trade to occur at any speed we desire—up to the speed of light. Velocity of money is no longer a technological constraint but rather driven by the speed of our desires and intentions. Second, the broad market index shares of capital ownership allow an easily recognizable and easily divisible composite capital good to be used as a logical store of value and the medium of exchange. These two primary conditions remove all conceptual obstacles to using capital as money. If we get there, we will surely have a more robust, simpler, more clearly-valued monetary system than our current convoluted structure of a fractional-reserve banking system funded by a fiat-money-printing central bank."

"Aha," Tompkins gleefully responds. "I finally get it. Our island has always had an underbelly of crazies—tax avoiders and protestors who wish to disguise or hide their transactions and income from the government and individuals who trade within the underground barter economy. In doing so, these people break the law in trying to avoid paying their fair share of the legitimate collection of taxes and government expenditure for the overall public welfare. Tax avoidance—that is really what your proposed capital as money economy is all about. Right?"

"Sorry to prick your bubble, Tooth. But once again you could not be more wrong. There is no attempt to defraud or confuse the government in a capital-as-money economy. A more transparent and simpler monetary system makes life easier for tax collectors, as well. Since all transactions will be represented by a recorded electronic change in the custody and ownership of capital assets, the volume and quantity of exchange and income flows will be easier to monitor and record than ever before. When compared to the likelihood of unrecorded changes in ownership of paper

164

currency in a fiat-money economy, government tax collectors will be able to more easily track a capital-as-money economy.

"It is true, the Central Bank will be irrelevant and the tool of imposing a covert and, in my opinion, an illegitimate inflation tax upon the public will vanish with the disappearance of fiat money—again I will talk about this idea in more detail tomorrow night. However, the basic power of the government to tax and spend will not be diminished in any way by moving to capital as money. What is likely to happen is that any illusion on the part of citizens or voters as to the true opportunity cost of government taxation and expenditure will be removed. Further, the government may find that, in competing with capital as an asset, the hurdle rate or return required for individuals to voluntarily hold deficit-financing government bonds is likely to increase–which is a double-edged sword. A more transparent and simpler system of exchange and value will make the government's monitoring job simpler, but using capital as a trading good and store of value will also raise public awareness of the real opportunity cost of government taxation and expenditure. More transparency and less illusion in an economy is good for everyone."

Tompkins started to rise open mouthed and overflowing with further objections. But there was an irritable and loud grumble from the audience which had grown increasingly restless during the lengthy discussion. "Sit on it, Tooth!" someone shouted from the back.

Roberta rose and returned to the podium. "A battle between 'the Tooth' and 'the Tie'—we all knew it would eventually come down to this. I don't mean to be your fashion coordinator, but seriously Ted, you really need to lose that atrocious yellow bowtie.

"Well, Ted has given us a lot to digest. By the way, you will receive copies of his remarks along with, for those of you who are mathematically inclined, the formal Solow model illustration attached as an appendix. I also understand that tomorrow night Ted will run through his arguments in the context of the

165

neoclassical growth model as well as presenting an example of a neoclassical growth model with money. However, he has promised me that he will hold math and graphs to a minimum. I am curious how he will accomplish this. I think it should be illuminating. I am coming tomorrow night and plan to enjoy it. Good night and thank you for coming."

CHAPTER 5

CONTINUATION OF EDWARD'S SPEECH

The following night the Economics Club once again convened, with the only agenda item being the continuation of Edward's vision of how an economy's capital stock would be a preferred medium of exchange when compared to the island's antiquated fiat currency. Edward anticipated reinforcing his remarks from the previous night by using a mathematical handout titled <u>Capital as Money: Extensions of the Solow Model</u>, a paper which he prepared specifically for his presentation to the club membership (Edward's paper in its entirety is shown in chapter 7). He knew some of the club membership had formal training in mathematical economics, and his paper was primarily directed at them. However, he hoped that he would be able to explain the paper's most important points to the audience relying on economic intuition and using a minimal amount of graphs and equations. As the group assembled he was pleasantly surprised to see that most club members were present, even those with scanty mathematics skills. Most unexpected to Edward was that Tompkins ("Tooth") was in attendance, evidently undeterred by the rough treatment he had received from some of the club's members the night before.

Upon taking the podium Edward saw to it that everyone at the meeting had a copy of the paper that had been distributed and referred to the previous evening. Edward informed his audience that the material he was going to present was mathematical in nature, and to be as clear as possible he planned to use a chalkboard that was provided for his seminar to sketch and discuss a few graphs and key equations. He was aware that current electronic presentation technology had gone far beyond but he still had a preference for old-fashioned chalk and boards. He went on to remind the club membership of his intention to use the Solow model to argue in a formal manner that the island's saving and investment behavior has been suboptimal. Particularly, he would use the neoclassical growth model to show that the level of sustainable per-capita consumption is less than what it might be if individuals' savings were more efficiently targeted towards capital accumulation. He also planned on using the neoclassical framework to demonstrate that government-printed fiat currency is becoming irrelevant in the face of new technologies that remove any and all physical constraints on money's velocity. Edward told the audience that at times he might find it necessary to read directly from his paper, but the audience should feel free to interrupt and ask questions at any time. Following these preliminaries he began his presentation of the mathematical arguments.

"As economists, most of you have studied the neoclassical growth model of Nobel-prize winning economist Robert Solow. While the Solow model is necessarily an abstraction of the economy, it captures the essence of how capital, labor, production and consumption interact and evolve over time. As with any theory, the model is based upon certain simplifying assumptions. Those assumptions are carefully spelled out in the mathematical paper that you have been provided. Tonight I will use the Solow framework to describe the island's economy, and to bolster my argument that government printed fiat currency, as well as the banking and lending system that goes with it, has outlived its usefulness."

"There isn't enough!" an all too familiar member of the audience interjected.

"What was that?" Ted queried, peering intently at the membership.

"If you're going to subject us to another harangue as to why we should use capital for money then you can stop right now. There simply are not enough capital index shares to be used for the required volume of trade," Tompkins repeated in a triumphant tone. "That's the problem with you guys that live in the world of theoretical models and equations—you're not very good with the actual numbers that really matter. You told me last night, Ted, to remember my questions about using capital as money so I'm not going to be deflected by any more of your balderdash."

"I hate to disappoint you Tompkins, but I do occasionally check the numbers. Of course there is a sufficient volume of capital. The total value of the Islet 400 index, comprised of our 400 largest publicly traded companies is roughly equal to the value of our annual Gross Domestic product. This compares favorably in scale with the transactions money supply, fiat currency held by the public plus checking accounts, which is currently approximately 17 percent of our annual GDP." (These proportions are consistent with corresponding ones for the U.S. economy. The largest 500 U.S. publicly-traded companies have a total capitalization value of approximately $15.6 trillion and the current M1 money supply of the U.S. is about $2.5 trillion—or about 17 percent of GDP.)

"You're being particularly dense today, Ted," a beaming Tooth replied, glancing up from his portable notepad computer. "You're just not getting it. You suggest using capital index shares as money. I assume by that you mean the relatively new Islet 400 exchange-traded index shares, or index ETFs. Currently these index shares are a relatively new feature in our economy, and their total value is not equal to 17 percent of our annual GDP— it is much less than that."

"That is a problem of supply and demand to be solved by a well-functioning market," Ted wearily replied. "First of all, I did suggest using Islet 400 exchange-traded index shares as money, but I don't believe that is the only alternative. If you check the numbers carefully, Tompkins, you will see that approximately 40 percent of the total capital market value of our Islet 400 companies is already held in the form of index shares—either as shares that can be traded on the exchange, just like any other individual shares of stock, or as shares of mutual funds designed to replicate the index. Thus, the proportion of our capital market that is already indexed stands at approximately 40 percent of our GDP, or at about two and one half times the size of our transactions money supply. Yes, Tompkins, I know the mutual fund shares are not as liquid or as easily tradable as the exchange-traded fund shares, but that problem can be solved in the blink of an eye by their issuers and holders. They can be readily converted into ETFs if the demand is there.

"But, as it turns out, replacing the entire current transactions money supply probably isn't necessary anyway, as we move to capital-based money. You need to recognize that the velocity of a trading good, or the number of times it is exchanged during a given period is in the present day a notional variable—driven by trading intentions and desires rather than limited by some technological or physical constraint. With near instantaneous trading of money and settlement of accounts being possible, a much smaller money stock than what we currently use could easily accomplish all the trades required. Trust me Tompkins, I'll return to this topic in more detail toward the end of my presentation tonight."

"I'm not done yet," Tompkins replied firmly and triumphantly. "I want to return to my question from last night about how people could actually trade capital shares to accomplish their purchases and sales in any way resembling how we actually use money now. I will not be deflected. You haven't begun to seriously consider the problems of using capital as money, have you? First, as even you may know, Ted, it takes a minimum of three days for any exchange of capital shares to settle. Second, the charge for a share exchange at even the lowest cost brokerage firm is large and fixed. That would certainly seem to be enough to apply the brakes to any serious consideration to trading capital shares as a substitute for money—particularly in the case of small value trades. Finally, if capital actually did become money the amount of swindling and fraud that would occur can only be imagined. Based on these objections, alone, I think I can save us a lot of time tonight."

"Oh Tompkins," Edward shook his head sadly. "I bet no one has ever accused you of being visionary, of having great imagination, have they? None of the problems you raise are uniquely attached to using index shares of capital as money. Any monetary good would and does face the same issues. The basic problem is

170

accurately recording the ownership of shares of a fixed supply of money as trading occurs over time and doing so cheaply and rapidly. Of course, the problem is much worse in our current system of fiat-money and fractional-reserve banking. In our present economy, we cannot even say with certainty what the actual size of the money supply actually is! I'll remind you it used to take three days or longer to accomplish and record a trade and resultant funds transfer in our old banking system—before the recent development of instantaneous electronic transfer of funds. The computer mavens in our group would be quick to tell you that, in a world in which information can travel at the speed of light, three seconds or three days is an eternity.

"Secondly, Tooth, I know you distrust them, but you have probably heard of the workings of free, competitive markets. Once capital is money there will be a profitable business opportunity for agents to serve as custodians and record keepers documenting the transfer of capital index shares. Those agents will quickly become aware of the magnitude of the market, and the more astute among them will realize that the reward for this simple record-keeping function can be a microscopic sliver of any single transaction and they can still be hugely prosperous. It is likely they will perform this trading function for free for customers with whom they have other business relationships. I visualize consumers using some sort of electronic debit card on their accounts that will immediately transfer ownership of the appropriate quantity of capital index shares when they make purchases. Heaven help me for suggesting this, but even some of the old fractional-reserve banking institutions could probably save their hides by moving into this new index share exchange and custody role.

"Alas, Tooth, your last criticism has some accuracy. No free market system or monetary system is one hundred percent safe against fraud, swindles, and crime. Stealing is a potential threat as long as human nature remains unchanged. This is just as true for an economy using capital as money as it would be for an economy using any other good as money. Horrors, we might even suggest that protecting the public from this sort of problem actually is a 'public' good and would be an appropriate role for an otherwise unemployed central bank, no longer issuing fiat money. It could busy itself with auditing, facilitating, and recording the exchanges of capital index shares to accomplish trades. I'm amazed at myself for just saying that! Actually, I believe that the private marketplace could evolve institutions that would accomplish the same function. As always, astute, vigilant consumers and traders remain the ultimate and best protection for themselves—at all times and in all markets."

"But trading capital shares is exactly my point," protested Tompkins. "Ownership of capital represents an individual's precious retirement assets—the core of their arduously obtained lifetime wealth. People will tend to accumulate such shares, to hoard them. They will never trade them for some disposable consumption good like, for God's sake, a pizza. That is why capital will not work as money. Individuals will hoard it and save it, not trade it."

"Oh come on Tooth," Edward scornfully responded. "You're much too sophisticated to offer such a fallacious argument. Anytime we trade some of our output or accumulated wealth for a pizza, our true opportunity cost in making the exchange is the best and highest use we might have otherwise made of it as savings and investment. It makes no difference whether we are trading fiat money for it or the capital shares we could have owned instead. The opportunity cost of consuming the pizza is exactly the same in either case. If there is some sort of irrational 'casino-token' illusion at work here, which I doubt, and it takes trading with capital shares to bring home the true opportunity cost of eating your pizza then so be it. Your own argument, if correct, unwittingly illustrates the power and benefit of the increased transparency in using capital as money relative to our flawed current system of fiat money, banking, and exchange. Now let's get on with the model.

"Hold on! I'm not done yet Ted!" The wearily familiar voice again interjected. "I've thought about what you said last night and

I have a critical objection. What makes you think that something whose value is as volatile and uncertain as capital could ever be suitable as a preferred store of value and a medium of exchange?"

"Alright Tompkins, let's proceed with your objection. What do you suppose is the source of volatility in the value of capital?"

"The value of capital is derived from the stream of returns it is expected to produce in the future. Future returns to capital are uncertain because our economy is subject to a business cycle. Huge booms and busts that we cannot predict affect the demand for capital and labor in production and therefore make the future product of capital uncertain and its value volatile," triumphantly crowed Tompkins.

"Well said Tompkins. It might surprise you to learn that I largely agree with what you just said. However, I prefer to refer to the ups and downs as unanticipated shocks rather than a 'business cycle.' And what, Tompkins, do you think is the source of the ups and downs of economic growth relative to trend?"

Tompkins thought for a second before replying. "Why I suppose there is a list of causes. First, we might say the shocks of government fiscal and Central Bank monetary policies. Next, we could include real world shocks and natural catastrophes. Finally, and most importantly in my opinion, I would say the destabilizing effects of so called 'free-markets' and their participants left to their own devices. It's not surprising to me that uncontrolled markets are catastrophically volatile."

"Let's consider your points one-by-one, Tompkins. On your last point, we categorically disagree. I believe that uncontrolled free markets are typically efficient and stable. As to natural shocks, they exist but their effect on the aggregate performance of our economy is random and most often mercifully small. Fiscal policy, or the level of government spending, has a net real effect on the economy that is likely to be negligible in the short-run when the way in which the policy is financed, either by public debt or taxes, is taken into account. I say 'short-run' because obviously a particularly bone-headed fiscal policy can exert negative effects on our long-run growth. This leaves monetary policy.

"If we conclude that unexpected shocks that arise in our regrettable monetary system are the primary cause of short-run volatility in our economic growth rate, then they are the primary cause of volatility in the value of aggregate capital and its average marginal product. Where do these shocks originate? It's easy to see. Unexpected changes in the Central Bank's rate of fiat money growth result in unexpected changes in inflation and unexpected changes in the demand for all productive inputs, including capital. Further, unexpected holding or lending of reserves in our fractional-reserve banking system cause additional uncertainty in the size of the money stock as does changes in the public's preference for holding money as cash or checking accounts. To our recipe for disaster, add the further effect of bad, weak, or excessive lending by credit market intermediaries which can result in a credit market collapse, such as the one we are currently enduring. Finally, add the impact of unexpected manipulation of market interest rates, another Central Bank specialty.

"In short I agree, Tompkins, the market value of capital is the stream of its expected future products reduced to present value at an appropriate discount rate. Unexpected inflation, unanticipated fluctuations in the demand for capital as well as unanticipated changes in the discount rate will therefore all play havoc with the value of aggregate capital. Since it is our flawed, inept money, banking and credit system that is the author of these, it is therefore also the cause of the major short-run fluctuations in the value of capital. Replace the current monetary system with capital as money and I believe that volatility in the value of capital relative to other goods will largely disappear.

"This is my firm belief. However, what I do or do not believe is beside the point. Let's not mandate the change, but let's simply give capital as money a try! It is hard to imagine it being worse than our present system. Again, that is why I say that what the tractor can produce over the future is well known. However, the value of what it might produce over the future, subject to uncertain inflation, uncertain employment, and an uncertain interest rate—all products of our tragic, flawed monetary system—is not. Now without further distraction, let's get on with the Solow model.

"Now, I know that a few of you dislike abstraction, aggregation, and formal theoretical constructs. Rather, you view the macroeconomy as a hodge-podge of special cases, all in need of individual rules and attention by wise overseers who carefully direct outcomes in each and every instance." Resisting an urge to address only Tompkins, Edward continued. "And, for those of you who are more interested in minutiae than in broad ideas, well, you may not find this evening's seminar very satisfying. But, those of you who recognize the necessity of abstraction and modeling as a means of analyzing and capturing the essence of the macroeconomy are sure to appreciate the rich insights that flow from the Solow framework.

"The Solow model begins by recognizing that an economy's overall output of goods and services is a function of the amount of labor and capital employed in production. The model does not distinguish between different types of labor and capital—again it is an abstraction of the economy, not a detailed description of each and every part of it."

Edward had always enjoyed economic theory and abstraction, and was dismayed by those who did not. His puzzlement resulted in his tendency of sometimes wandering off topic and spending too much time arguing the importance and beauty of theory in macroeconomic analysis. Edward realized he was again heading too far in that direction and he caught himself, choosing instead to continue on with his description of the Solow framework. "In a leap of abstraction, the model assumes the economy produces a single 'composite output,' which is a type of good that can either be consumed or saved. As I mention in my paper, it may be useful for you to think of output in terms of a simple item such as corn, which can be eaten this year or saved and planted—invested—in

175

order to grow more corn next year. Output that is not consumed this year is saved, and thereby becomes capital that can be used to produce more output next year. The saving of this year's output to form capital for next year is the process of investment.

"Of course, workers are more productive when they have more capital, or tools, to work with. And, it is the ratio of capital to labor that is the primary focus of the Solow model. The model demonstrates that, starting from a wide range of different initial conditions, an economy will tend towards a given steady-state capital-labor ratio, where the amount of tools per worker remains constant over time. While the clock does not permit me to go through each and every equation of the Solow model this evening, I assure you that all the equations, derivations and conclusions that I will mention are fully demonstrated in the paper that you have been provided (for readers, chapter 7 of this book). Tonight I am going to spare you the mathematical manipulations and formal proofs, and only summarize the paper's most significant primary results. But, I encourage you to work through the paper on your own to further increase your understanding, and to verify that the conclusions I am presenting tonight do indeed hold.

"The fact that workers are more productive with tools than without can be expressed through a simple mathematical equation." With this Edward grabbed a piece of chalk and started to write on the board. As a result of his enthusiasm for mathematics he exerted too much pressure on the chalk, causing it to break in his hand and drawing chuckles from the crowd. Unabated, Edward picked up another piece and promptly wrote down the following equation:

$$y = f(k)$$

Looking at the board, Edward described the variables. "Now, the little k represents the ratio of capital to labor. You can think of it as the ratio of tools per worker. The amount of output per-worker is represented by the variable y. And, what this equation says is that per-worker output depends on, or is a function of, k. Of course, up to a point more tools per worker results in more output per worker, which means mathematically the function *f* has a positive first derivative." Edward ignored Tompkins, who rolled his eyes at the mention of a "first derivative." Continuing on, Edward discussed the law of diminishing returns. "As more and more tools are provided to each worker, each additional tool tends to increase the output per worker, but at a reduced rate. Mathematically, the second derivative of the function *f* is negative as a consequence of the law of diminishing returns. So output per worker increases with capital but at a diminishing rate, or *f* is an increasing and concave function." Edward quit talking and again returned to the chalkboard, writing down the following simple formula:

$$k = K/N$$

Edward continued, pointing to each variable on the board in turn. "The capital-labor ratio, *k*, is the ratio of total capital, *K*, to effective labor, *N*. The numerator of the capital-labor ratio, *K*, grows as a consequence of saving—only by foregoing present consumption are we able to obtain more tools for future use. The denominator, which I have called 'effective labor,' grows for two reasons." With this Edward wrote down another equation:

$$n = z + \alpha$$

"The variable *n* represents the growth in the effective labor force. Of course, the labor force grows as a consequence of growth in population, which is represented by the variable *z*. But, the effectiveness of labor also increases over time—each worker becomes more productive as a consequence of ever-improving technology. The variable, α, represents the growth that is attributed to improving technology. That is what we typically refer to as labor productivity. For our Island Confederation, the growth rate in population, *z*, has been about 1 or 2 percent per year, and labor's productivity, α, has increased about 2 percent each year. So, the effective labor force, which is the denominator of the capital-labor ratio, has been increasing at approximately 3.5 percent, which is the value of *n*.

177

"So, if the denominator of the capital-labor ratio is growing at 3.5 percent, then the numerator also needs to increase at 3.5 percent in order for tools per effective worker to remain constant. And, this is exactly what will happen, as was demonstrated formally by Solow—a proof which has been reproduced in the handout that you have been provided. The primary conclusion of the Solow model is that, given the ability to substitute capital and labor for one another in the production function and starting from wide range of different initial endowments of capital and labor, the capital-labor ratio will robustly tend towards a unique steady-state equilibrium, where the ratio of K to N remains constant through time. That unique equilibrium depends upon the particular savings rate, call it s, where s is between 0 and 1. It turns out that $sf(k)$ is the proportion of per capita output saved and, of course, the remainder not saved, $(1-s)f(k)$, is the proportion that is consumed. In accord with our intuition, the equilibrium capital-intensity is positively related to the choice of the savings rate, s. This is a very powerful central conclusion indeed. It suggests that the equilibrium growth of economies such as ours is a stable and robust outcome of normal market maximizing behavior by individuals. It is no accident and requires no direction."

Tompkins had listened intently to the presentation, not necessarily because he was fond of mathematical economics, but because he was hoping to poke holes in Edward's logic. And, now Tompkins thought he had found something. He raised his hand eagerly to get Edward's attention, which Edward at first tried to ignore. But, Tooth was not going to be denied, and he started swaying his raised hand from left to right, the motion was so annoying and disrupting that Edward decided it would be impossible to go on without first letting Tompkins speak his mind. After being acknowledged, Tompkins began. "Hold on just a minute. The capital-to-labor ratio remaining constant doesn't mean anything. Just because the ratio is constant still doesn't mean there are going to be sufficient tools per worker. I mean, suppose the number of workers is 1,000,000, and there is only one tool. Then, the ratio is 1/1,000,000. If the denominator grows by 3.5 percent, it is now

1,035,000. Even if the numerator grows at the same rate, so K is now 1.035, the ratio of tools per worker is still only 1/1,000,000! Just because you claim that K and N will be growing at the same rate, so what! You have told us absolutely nothing about what the ratio of capital to labor would or should actually be."

"Thank you bringing that up Tompkins, and very nicely said. In fact, you are exactly right—there are an infinite number of possible steady-state capital-labor ratios. And, as of yet we have said nothing about what the ratio of capital-to-labor should optimally be. As it turns out, if an economy has a very high saving rate then the equilibrium or steady-state capital-to-labor ratio will be high. An economy with a low saving rate will have a low capital-to-labor ratio.

"What capital-to-labor ratio is best? Is it better to have a high savings rate, s, and thus a lot of tools per worker? This might sound good, but remember, there is a downside to saving; saving means we get to consume less now. On the other hand, a low saving rate means we get to consume a higher percentage of our output in the year it is produced. But, the consequence of too much current consumption is that we won't have as many tools per worker going forward. So, what is the optimum? How do the tradeoffs get balanced best? When it comes to saving, is there some sort of 'golden-rule' the economy should follow? Or are we over-thinking this? Left to its natural individual optimizing behavior, might not an economy simply tend to move toward the level of savings and investment or the capital-intensity that actually maximizes sustained consumption and prosperity? I believe this is a reasonable conclusion. That in the effort of each individual striving to maximize his or her lifetime path of consumption lies our economy's attainment of a golden-rule or optimal capital-intensity.

"Let us start with that. The optimal or golden-rule capital-labor ratio is the one that would provide the highest growth path of sustainable per-capita consumption. And, it is this one that the economy would automatically tend towards were it not for our present system of fiat currency, fractional-reserve banking and criminally inept allocation of our scarce savings through an inefficient lending market. As I have previously argued, it is important to make a distinction between the pure monetary policy of changing the growth rate of a fiat currency and the sad, historical ponzi scheme of a fractional-reserve banking system with which we have been saddled. The current fractional-reserve banking system is an institutionally preserved inefficient relic. It is a vestige of the greed of bankers under a private commodity-based monetary system. Technology has made it an increasingly unnecessary adjunct to our money supply, if in fact it ever was needed. Since technology has allowed the exchange velocity, or use of money in trading, to occur at a rate limited only by the intentions of traders, the quantity of any monetary good to successfully accomplish required trades becomes increasingly unimportant. Yet the anachronism of a fractional banking system is still there—we are still saddled with it to our great and tragic opportunity cost. The recent credit bubble and collapse, one of many, that we have just suffered is sad testimony to that fact. Continuing economic volatility—booms and crashes—is a severe harm resulting from this ponderous and inefficient system. But perhaps a larger cost is the chronic underinvestment in the capital market because too much of our society's scarce savings and intended investment is allocated not to its "best and highest use" but instead to inefficient uses or even channeled back into consumption. The result is a capital-intensity for our economy which is well below that which would maximize our sustainable prosperity—that is the 'golden-rule' capital intensity.

"Why does this sad money, credit and banking relic continue to persist in an otherwise efficient market economy such as our Confederation? Tradition? The cold wind of technological change and competition has wiped out many traditional industries and activities in ruthlessly efficient free-market economies. The real reason fractional-reserve banking persists is that the power to make profits from leveraging the deposits of unwitting bank customers, by fraudulently violating their property rights, is a very profitable niche. To make profits from being the institutionally preferred

180

monopoly agents and intermediaries in the loan or credit markets—with responsibility for placement of our society's scarce saving—is a position that bankers and their bureaucratic regulators or overseers are loathe to surrender. It is a function that they have performed abominably because their compensation has typically been based upon the volume rather than the efficiency of their lending, as we have discussed at length elsewhere, but it is the 'raison d' etre' for the banking system. They probably would have been wiped out in a rational, efficient economy long ago except for one fact: There is no better way to protect and save an inefficient monopoly than to formally institutionalize it by placing it under government purview or central bank regulation. The trade-off is clear, it gains immortality and insulation from competition in return for government supervision, a government blessing, and a government barrier to new entrants or competition. In a competitive world, so-called 'natural' monopolies are very fragile and short-lived; they can only survive with government regulation and protection. It is an argument originally developed by the Nobel prize-winning economist, George Stigler. This they can maintain with generous contributions to the relevant legislators and regulators. It is high time for us to end the costly and unnecessary monopoly of the fractional-reserve banking system. Not by mandate, but by removing their protection and their preferred status in the money and lending markets. Viewed from the vantage point of exchange technology the irrelevance of a classical fractional-reserve banking and lending system is becoming increasingly clear.

"Let me get back to the Solow model, and use it to describe mathematically the characteristics of the 'golden-rule' capital-labor ratio. Then I can better explain why I believe our island's capital-to-labor ratio is less than optimal. Again, the 'golden-rule' capital-to-labor ratio is the one that would maximize per capita consumption over time. In any economy per-capita consumption actually grows at equilibrium at the rate of growth of labor productivity. In your copy of the paper (for readers, chapter 7 of this book) you will see a graph, Figure 2 shown in the handout, which is used to describe the optimum. Without going through all the mathematics, let me cut right to the conclusion. The golden-rule or consumption-maximizing capital-labor ratio occurs when the growth rate in effective labor, n, is just equal to the expected real rate of return to capital. I want to emphasize this point: If we have obtained the golden-rule capital-labor ratio it will be evidenced by equality between labor's effective growth rate and the long-term annual real rate of return associated with capital ownership. I will take this opportunity to mention a mathematical result proved more formally in my paper. The golden-rule capital intensity is the unique equilibrium that simultaneously maximizes consumption per unit of effective labor and per capita consumption at each point in time along the equilibrium growth path. Thus, it is clearly the unique and optimal consumption-maximizing equilibrium in every sense and there appears no reason that we should not expect it to be achieved as the sum result of the optimizing behavior of rational individuals acting in their self-interest.

"However a cursory look at the historical facts for our island suggests we have not achieved the golden-rule. The average annual growth rate in effective labor has been about 3.5 percent. But, the real rate of return to capital ownership has historically been about 7.0 percent. That is, over the long run those individuals who have owned a diversified portfolio of stocks have earned an annual rate of return of about 10.0 percent when measured in fiat currency. Of course, that is because there has been an average rate of price inflation of about 3.0 percent over the same time period, which means the real rate of return to capital ownership has averaged approximately 7.0 percent.

"Now, all of this is explained much more completely in the mathematical handout, and time does not permit me to reproduce all of the arguments in this meeting. But, the essence of my argument is that we have too little capital—we are operating at a capital-labor ratio that is below the golden-rule. Due to an inefficient system of allocating savings to investment, on net we have under-invested. Capital's marginal product, which is the same thing as the real rate of return to capital ownership, is high because we simply do not have enough of it! If the capital-labor ratio was increased it would lower capital's marginal product due to the law of diminishing returns. When we finally get to the golden-rule capital intensity we will know it—the real rate of return to capital would be equal to the 3.5 percent overall growth rate of effective labor and the economy. A lower rate of return to capital is not a bad thing—it is really something to be celebrated! It would mean we have finally got enough capital for each worker so that our economy's per capita consumption over the future—that is our prosperity—is maximized."

Edward was now determined to demonstrate his second major point. Namely, that the usefulness of fiat currency had run its course, and it was now time for the Island Confederation to move to the alternative of capital-based money. In his paper he had used the Solow model to illustrate that the Confederation economy was short on capital. And, Edward firmly believed that using shares of capital ownership as money rather than printed fiat currency would lead the economy towards the golden-rule outcome. Beyond that, however, his paper had another purpose, that being to demonstrate that advances in technology had made fiat currency and monetary policy increasingly irrelevant anyway. Recent attempts at stimulating the island's economy through new money creation had been less than effective, and Edward believed he knew why— changes in technology had removed any and all constraints on the velocity of money, which simply made the quantity of it no longer matter.

After a brief pause to collect his thoughts, Edward again began. "Kings, governments and central banks throughout history have limited the power of providing the medium of exchange and value, which is money, exclusively to themselves. First, through the crude mechanism of secretly debasing or diluting commodity currency and then through the more sophisticated technique of being the sole provider of a fiat currency ultimately backed by nothing except the faith and willingness of the public to use it— essentially legalized counterfeiting. How does the government actually extract revenue by printing money and what are the limits?"

Again moving to the blackboard, Edward wrote down the following equation:

$$G = dM / dt$$

He then began his explanation of the formula. "This equation characterizes a government that finances its entire spending, represented by G, with the printing of fresh, new currency, where the derivative dM/dt represents the change in the money supply. Besides printing money, another way for a government to finance its spending is with taxes. But, my purpose tonight is not to discuss fiscal policy, rather I am interested in monetary policy. Thus, I will focus on government spending financed by printing new money."

"The government doesn't print money for the Island Confederation," Tompkins blurted. "The Confederation Central Bank does. Again, your model is off the mark."

"As you know Tompkins, the government borrows money by selling bonds, most of which are purchased by the Central Bank. And where does the Central Bank get the money to buy these bonds? It creates it, of course. It is just as if the government got to print the money to finance its spending in the first place, and it is in this manner that the government gets to steal output from the rest of us. To understand why I refer to the 'stealing' of output, consider a government that covertly sneaks individuals into the marketplace to buy goods and services with currency indistinguishable from that already in circulation—except that it is brand new, clean and crisp. Through the overall impact on the price level, the government purchases of goods and services mean the rest of us, who are not associated with the government, can afford to purchase less with our fiat currency. Thus, the money financing of government expenditures is precisely equivalent to a tax: government is able to buy more, and individuals in the private sector can buy less. It is most useful to consider this equation in real terms per unit of effective labor to consider the burden of the inflation tax that the government or central bank extracts by printing money." Taking to the board, Edward now rearranges the equation using a minimal amount of algebra, resulting in the following:

$$G/PN \equiv g = (dM/dt/M)(M/PN) = \theta m$$

"All of the variables in this equation have been fully defined in the paper, but it might be useful to remind you of the definitions before continuing on with the discussion. The variable P is the overall price level, N is the effective labor force, and M is the supply of fiat currency. The variable g is the amount of real output per unit of effective labor that the government is able to expropriate through new money creation. The rate of growth in the money supply is the ratio $dM/dt/M$ which I have called θ. Finally, if you divide the amount of money M by the price level P you obtain the real money supply. Divide the real money supply by the effective labor force N and you have the real money supply per effective worker, which I define to be the letter m. Now, suppose the government gets greedy and decides to finance more government expenditure by printing more money. Will it work? Our first thought is that increased per-capita government spending can be accomplished by simply raising the rate at which it runs the printing presses. Alas for governments everywhere, it is not that simple.

"When government increases the rate of growth in the money supply, the sustained rate of inflation increases in step. As inflation increases, the opportunity cost of holding money balances increases and therefore rational individuals will seek to hold less of them over any given time and to accomplish their trades more efficiently and rapidly. This idea is developed more fully in my paper when we talk about what determines an individual's demand for holding money balances. For now, we simply recognize that holding fiat money is less desirable when the rate of inflation increases. Increases in the rate of money supply growth are known to cause higher inflation, and rational individuals increase the velocity of money when prices are rising rapidly—that is they try to hold less of it. Collectively, of course, they cannot all succeed. What they can do, however, is to cause the average price level to increase even higher than the cumulative effect of the inflation rate would suggest—in other words the price level actually overshoots the level we would expect simply by taking account of the sustained inflation rate. Thereby, individuals collectively cause the real purchasing power of money balances to fall and little m declines because of declining money demand. This is well known from past hyperinflations. History provides us with examples of severe inflation, when upon getting paid individuals promptly loaded all their cash into wheelbarrows and raced to the marketplace to exchange the fiat currency for real goods as quickly as physically possible. Now our current technology which allows rapid exchange and changes in custody of assets aids individuals in accomplishing this. What will happen when the government starts to increase the growth rate of the fiat money supply? As individuals collectively try to reduce their holdings of currency, the price level in the output market will rise, in addition to the sustained rate of inflation, thereby reducing real money balances to the lower level that individuals in the aggregate desire to hold. That is, the rate of growth in the money supply goes up, but m goes down as a result of a jump in the price level. Whether per capita government spending, g, goes up or down depends on which effect is dominant.

"It might be useful to enhance our understanding to refer to a graph, which is sort of a money-growth-rate 'Laffer' type curve. Consider a graph where the per-capita government spending is measured on the vertical axis, and the rate of money growth is measured on the horizontal scale." Edward took some time at the chalkboard and sketched the following graph:

Inflation Tax Proceeds versus Rate of Money Growth

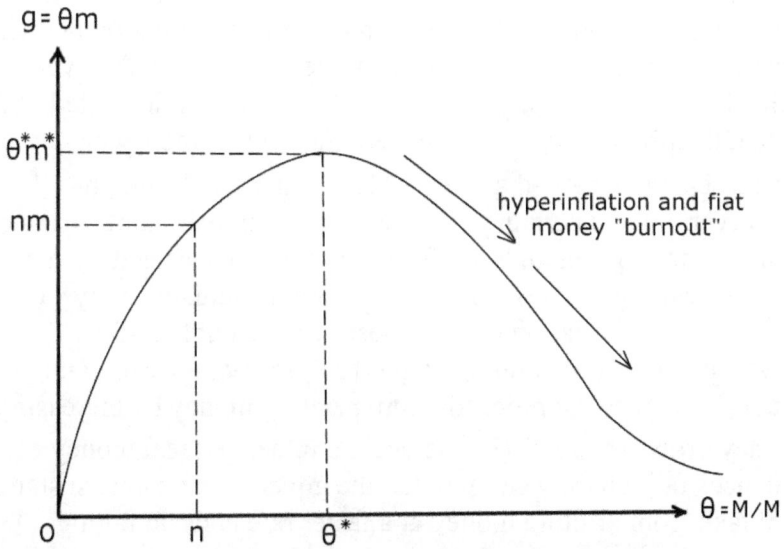

"This graph represents a lot of simple and, I hope, appealing intuition. The curve shows how per-capita government spending, on the vertical axis, is related to the growth rate in the money supply θ, which is measured on the horizontal axis. For starters, consider a responsible rate of increase in the supply of fiat money where the supply of fiat money is growing at the same rate as the equilibrium growth rate of the economy, n. As long as money is growing at the same rate as the real economy the result would be a stable price level, which is the zero target inflation rate advocated by responsible central bankers. As governments or central banks are tempted to accelerate fiat money growth above this—to 'monetize' previously issued government debt, for example—they may meet with some success as the real proceeds of the inflation tax rise to a maximum level shown as $\theta^* m^*$ in the graph. Note that the increased rate of fiat money growth increases per-capita government spending, but not by as much as might be expected. As the rate of fiat money growth increases from n to θ^* the rate of inflation increases, tending to raise the proceeds of the inflation tax. But, the public is not dumb, and the greater inflation tax will decrease their demand for holding money, driving up the average price level as individuals seek to rid themselves of unwanted cash. When the price level goes up the amount of real money balances decrease somewhat—that is m^* is less than m in the graph. However, up to a certain point the decrease in real money balances is not quite large enough to offset the effect of accelerating the fiat-money printing presses—so the government actually enjoys a real increase in the inflation tax it imposes on the public. If the government or its central bank gets too greedy, however, and attempts to raise the proceeds from printing money by increasing money growth beyond θ^*, the decline in desired real money balances falls sharply enough that the government's total sustained real take from printing money at a faster rate ends up falling. Desperate governments, that progressively ratchet the rate of fiat money growth, and inflation, in the hopes of supporting additional government spending will proceed along the disastrous trajectory on the right of the curve toward hyper-inflation and eventual monetary 'burn-out.' 'Burn-out' is the term used because at a high enough rate of inflation and money growth, the public's demand for currency goes to zero. Once this happens there is no hope for the government to capture any output through the inflation tax."[3]

One of the mathematically-talented club members sitting on the front row looked at Edward quizzically. When Edward paused she asked her question. "I understand your simple equation that says the level of real per-capita government spending that can be financed through new money creation hinges upon the product of θ and m. And, I see how an increase in money supply growth θ will cause the price level to jump further until the reduced demand

---

[3] An example of monetary burnout was provided by Germany in the 1920s.

for real money balances is restored, thereby increasing the denominator of m, which makes m smaller. But, if the government goes berserk and starts to increase θ without bound, how do we know that the product θm will go to zero?"

"That is an excellent question. A pure mathematical understanding of the quantity representing the proceeds of the inflation tax θm suggests it is unclear whether or not θm goes to zero or infinity, or some other value, as the rate of fiat money growth, θ, accelerates without bound. It seems to be a race, θ increases without bound and m decreases toward zero as θ increases. Who wins the race in a mathematical sense? Do we need to apply L'Hopital's rule?

"It is important to realize that descriptive math equations in an economic model are helpful in explaining and summarizing dynamic behavior. That is why we use them. However, they do not replace our economic intuition or behavioral common sense. A brief reflection upon economic behavior provides our answer. If any government or central bank increases the rate at which it prints fiat money without bound in order to increase its 'take' from the private sector, it will not get very far. Long before the rate of money growth becomes infinite, the individuals who comprise the economy will simply no longer accept fiat money for trades and will cease to employ it as a store of value for any period, no matter how short. In practical terms the abused fiat money will cease to be 'money,' because the opportunity cost of holding or using it becomes too high. It is at this point where we can assert that θm, the proceeds of the inflation tax, will be zero. Recall that, in the same way, the mathematical equations alone do not tell us that a market equilibrium will necessarily be a 'golden-rule' capital intensity. However, the neoclassical equations, taken with reasonable individual optimizing behavior, will achieve the equilibrium capital intensity that is consistent with maximizing sustained consumption. In short, a good mathematical economist uses mathematical modeling to augment and make succinct and clear the implications of economic intuition—not to replace economic intuition.

"Again, let's turn our attention to the graph, and talk a little bit more about a responsible government that prints money at the real growth rate in the economy, n. Even in this zero inflation case the government sector would still be extracting a real tax from the private sector in return for printing currency and providing the exchange good. The government, or more precisely those individuals who receive their goods and services from the government, are still stealing some of our real output. Compared to the debacle of our present monetary system, I suppose there is little enough harm in such an outcome. However, even the extraction of this low level of rent for providing the traditional trading good is unnecessary.

"Some of you appear puzzled at my contention that the power of the central bank to manipulate the inflation tax it can extract from the public through changing the rate at which it prints currency is limited and is shrinking as technology increases the speed and efficiency of exchange. To explain this, I will present one final graph this evening. Don't groan—I will be quick and I think this last graph will be useful in illustrating the impact of how improving technology is neutralizing the government's ability to steal output through the printing of new money." Edward then drew the following graph:

Inflation Tax Proceeds
Effect of Improved Exchange Technology

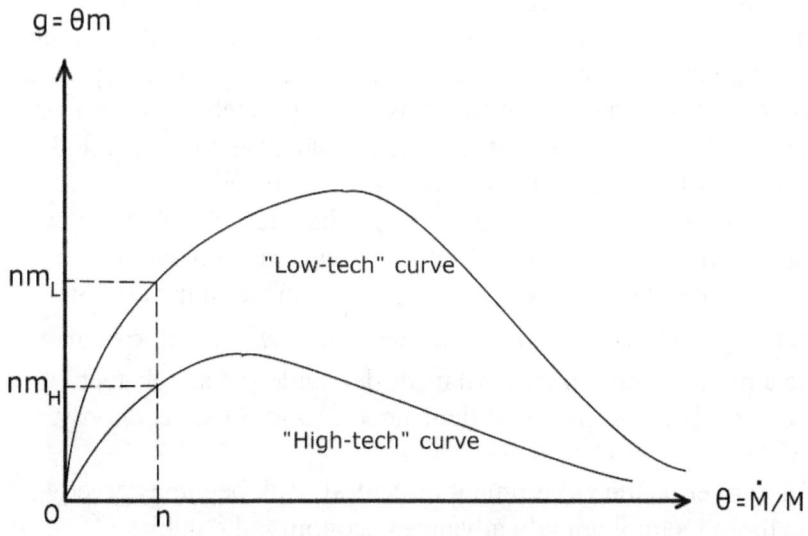

"This figure is my favorite and captures the gist of my argument as to why there is a limited future in fiat money and central bank fiat monetary policy. The figure represents what I believe to be the effect of ongoing technological improvements increasing the speed and efficiency of monetary transactions. Monetary exchange technology is allowing us to enter a world where the velocity of money becomes a truly notional or endogenous variable driven by the sum of individuals' desires and preferences rather than some sort of physical constraint representing the speed with which an archaic 'bricks and mortar' banking system can actually track and record ownership changes related to trades—instantaneous funds transfer and change in custody appears to be the current technological limit.

191

"Consider the impact of the technological improvement in exchange efficiency upon the revenue curve from printing fiat money. The graph shows two government revenue curves, one for a low-tech economy and another for a high-tech economy. Note that the level of real per-capita government spending that can be financed through monetization has shifted down, even when the government is increasing currency at the economy's real growth rate n. This is because individuals in a high-tech world can get along with a lower level of real money balances to accommodate a specific volume of exchange given our enhanced exchange technology. However, holding money balances is still a drag when compared to the real rates of return people can achieve on other assets, for instance capital. Therefore, even when the rate of money growth is low, m_H is still less than m_L or, ceteris paribus, the amount of real money balances demanded in a high-tech economy is lower than that demanded in a low-tech economy.

"Moreover, if the government or central bank becomes greedy in the more technologically advanced economy, the public collectively will tend to thwart it. As technology allows a given amount of money balances to accomplish more exchange without difficulty, individuals will have less patience with fiat money as a store of value over any time period, no matter how brief, and therefore will have less patience with any attempted inflation tax increase associated with the holding of it. As a result, their behavior and demand for money balances will tend to totally neutralize attempts to change sustained real revenue proceeds from the inflation tax on the part of a government or central bank. What happens is that technology aids in the achievement of the 'super-neutrality' of fiat money policy. The tolerance of people for any increase in the opportunity cost of holding money balances is slim and becoming slimmer. Central banks have to be careful because the trigger point that could lead to a monetary 'burn-out' or the point at which the public ceases to tolerate the cost of holding and using a fiat money at all is becoming more sensitive. Thus, the frequent lament of central banks that their monetary policy is becoming less effective and that their degrees of freedom in imposing it are becoming more constrained.

"When we say that technology is enabling the super-neutrality of monetary policy, what we mean is that, over the long-run, the rate of growth of fiat money will not affect the long-run capital intensity of the economy. It will not even significantly affect the level of real sustainable proceeds that the government can achieve from printing money. Since efficient and rapid exchange technology permits a wide variation in the stock of money which may be used to accomplish a given volume of real exchange, it really is true that fiat money's marginal product is approximately zero. Of course, this does not mean that having a single trading unit of exchange and valuation, a money, is not valuable in making production and trading more efficient. It simply implies that the ability of any single issuer of a fiat money to exploit the public by manipulating the speed of its printing presses has been sharply curtailed. The value of having an agreed upon monetary unit in enhancing production is not zero, although at the margin rapid increases in the stock of fiat currency adds no real value.

"It is important to realize that the arguments I have just made about the emasculation of fiat money policy on the part of central banks are distinct from the issue of the inefficient and destabilizing banking system that we are institutionally encumbered with. Unexpected fluctuations in the rate of money growth and inflation, the fractional-reserve banking system, the encouragement of successive layers of poorly motivated and poorly underwritten lending, and an opaque, over-intermediated credit market do exert harm on any economy, high-tech or low-tech. Therefore they can and should be eliminated. We think this result would probably happen naturally through market forces if the support, regulation, and insulation from competition provided by an over-seeing government and central bank was withdrawn. Technology has made the current monetary structure based upon a fiat-money-issuing central bank and a fractional-reserve private banking system a sad and costly anachronism. Since it is an institutionally mandated monopoly it still imposes severe efficiency costs upon an economy that, increasingly, no longer needs it. We should accept nothing less than its end.

"The solution is staring us in the face. In my paper I observe that past attempts to motivate the introduction of 'money' into the simple neoclassical growth model seem contrived, it is 'a station wagon in space.' This is because the model operates under transparency, certainty and is aggregated to the point that a unit of capital is the obvious numeraire and logical unit of valuation. No other is required. Is it possible that the example of the model is trying to tell us something?

"Imagine that we live in a world where the ownership of our diverse productive capital can be aggregated into a single composite good. Further suppose that units of the ownership of this capital can be traded instantly and efficiently to accomplish trades of all other goods and services. Finally suppose that valuation of all other goods and services in such 'composite' capital units evolved so that shares of the index performed all the traditional functions of a 'money.' Even the individual, disaggregated capital goods comprising the index would be valued in terms of the index. Where is such a world? In fact, we could be living in it. We have the electronic technology at present to compose index shares that broadly reflect units of ownership of our weighted capital market. Further the same technology allows these shares to be exchanged in custody or ownership at nearly instant speed.

"If using capital as our monetary or trading good were to evolve, a number of benevolent outcomes would occur. First, there would be a market-determined monetary system using a trading good of real value and expected return to accomplish trades—there would ultimately be no need for the present relic of our banking system and a fiat currency. Without a fiat currency, broad inflation would more than disappear, it would be a logical impossibility. Transparency and direct lending of available savings would prevail in the loan and investment markets. The resulting efficiency in the allocation of output between consumption and investment would make the attainment of a 'golden-rule' capital-intensity a real likelihood. There would be a real possibility of a monetary and financial sector that was so simple, logical, and transparent that it would be understood by our average citizen—one in which the risk and return to every loan would be weighed against the true opportunity cost of the real return to capital.

"Would we have reached Nirvana? Of course not. There would still be real world shocks and tragedies, ponzi schemes and bubbles, weather and earthquakes, scandals and frauds, and always the possibility of mistaken investment decisions and allocations, but, at least they would not be permanently institutionalized. Ironically in evolving toward such a system we are simply following impeccable logic in the robust tradition of the simple neoclassical model and finally wandering out of the woods of our present monetary debacle. I look forward to seeing all of you at the golden-rule. Not a magical point in some esoteric economic model, but a prosperity and consumption maximizing real world capital-intensity that the enlightened self-interest of individuals in unshackled and transparent markets will lead us to."

CHAPTER 6

EPILOGUE—TEN YEARS LATER

(At least 10 years later…)

The Economics Club is having its year-end meeting highlighted by a discussion between two of its leading lights over the past decade, Roberta and Edward. Edward is now the new president of the Club. They are both sitting at a table in front of the other members.

A more mature and confident Edward beams at the audience. "Tonight's guest—a longstanding member and former president of the Economics Club—needs no introduction. It pleases me to present our current Confederation Central Bank Chairman, Roberta. Nobody has seen more and done more in the last decade of change in our Confederation economy than she has. Members will recall that a number of years ago, we made a strong push as a club to move our economy toward the adoption of capital as money and the abolition of a fractional-reserve banking system— with the goal of a more simple, transparent and logical system of money, exchange and credit. To our surprise, the transition we advocated was actually allowed to occur. Again, no person has played a greater role in its actual application and evolution than Roberta. With no exaggeration, we might call you the 'midwife' of our new monetary system." There were groans and some laughter from the audience at this.

Edward continued on with the introduction. "As the current Club president, I suppose that my role this evening will generally be that of the preliminary questioner or 'griller,' if you will. This is not as autocratic as it may appear, since all of you have been asked to submit most of the questions I will be asking. So let me begin." Turning towards Roberta, Edward mischievously began with a blunt question. "How did the person I previously knew as a vociferous proponent of the abolition of the Central Bank instead become its current chairman? Have you been co-opted or corrupted?"

Roberta responded. "Midwife, indeed! What a loaded introduction you gave me, Ted. Thank you. As most of you know my father, Bob Jr., served as the previous chair of the Confederation Central Bank. In that capacity he surprised many of you by allowing and, in fact, facilitating the transition to a monetary exchange system based on using shares of a broad capital index as the main means of valuation and exchange. This was not a surprise to me because I knew of his rock-bottom intellectual honesty when he was finally convinced of the merit of an idea—even one which, at first, he had strongly opposed. He successfully advocated my appointment to the Board of Governors of the Confederation Central Bank and allowed us to begin to sail into the uncharted waters of a dual system of monetary exchange and then finally into the current system in which capital and the value of capital dominates valuation and exchange and the money-issuing function of the Central Bank has withered away, but not yet entirely disappeared.

"Those here will recall the exciting days when specific sectors and individuals in the private economy began the process of using broad capital shares as trading goods. We all had front row seats to a monumental experiment in macroeconomics, observing first-hand as individuals prudently weighed how many shares of a capital index should be traded for any particular consumption good or service and how the first exchanges should actually be accomplished. At the Central Bank we mandated nothing, but simply allowed the market to work. We saw our role more simply as supporting and facilitating the transition to a capital-based monetary system. From a small beginning, capital-based exchange and valuation spread as fast as did the newly introduced cell phones. My father would have been here to see all of it, were it not for his tragic accident of sliding off one of grandpa's fishing boats. It is a terrible memory. I was there with dad and gramps, and was looking forward to spending time with dad on one of the only vacations I can remember him taking. I still can't forget the image of him being devoured by sharks before he could be rescued. The horror of being eaten by sharks—always the bane of living on our island!"

Big Tuna's voice boomed mournfully from the back of the room. "I should never have let him go. That poor kid was always an accident waiting to happen when he got on the water. It was his clumsiness at sea that caused him to leave fishing and led to his successful career in banking in the first place."

After a somewhat awkward but respectful silence, Edward again addressed Roberta. "So we both thought that the printed currency or fiat money would disappear once capital became money. Why hasn't that happened yet?"

"You will recall," Roberta responded, "as the new monetary and exchange system evolved the Central Bank's position was that we would accommodate and not mandate. The only mandate the Central Bank made was in getting rid of the unjustifiable and destabilizing evil of the fractional-reserve banking system. We could not and would not be in the position of supporting an institutionally subsidized pyramid scheme that fraudulently violated the property rights of unsuspecting depositors. Interestingly, the elimination of fractional-reserve banking was not as difficult to accomplish as we had expected, although not surprisingly we met with stiff resistance from the traditional banking community. They had become used to making profits by loaning out the balances of depositors for a hefty interest rate while passing little or none on to those who were the actual source of the deposits. Outside the banking community, few had a significant problem with eliminating fractional-reserve banking once the property rights issues were carefully explained. This even came to include my dad after he realized that the Central Bank's job of managing the money supply could be much simpler without the severe contortions in the money supply produced by on-again, off-again bank lending during the last credit crisis.

"Once the shift to capital-as-money started to occur, the Central Bank was left in the position of accommodating the public's desire for continued printed currency, if that demand still existed. The approach of the Central Bank was to set a fixed exchange rate between the printed currency and shares of the capital index. As with any pegged exchange rate system, the official fixed rate can only be maintained as long as the Central Bank freely allows individuals to exchange either direction at the official rate. That is, an individual with a share of the capital index must be allowed to exchange it for the printed currency at the pegged rate if he wishes to do so. Likewise, a person with the printed currency is allowed to exchange it for shares of the capital index at the official rate if she wants to. Early in the transition to capital as money, the Central Bank issued a small amount of benchmark capital index shares itself. To create our index shares we simply used fiat currency to purchase the shares of stock that underlay the index. Then, we issued index shares, allowing individuals to buy or sell our newly-created index shares at a fixed exchange rate. Even after our index shares began to be widely used as money, to our surprise some demand for the old printed currency continued to persist. I say this surprised us because we expected that as the transition to capital as money matured, the vestigial need for the old paper currency would totally disappear. But, it didn't. So the Central Bank continues to maintain a supply of printed currency. It is not a fiat money however, because its supply is not independent. Rather the supply of currency is raised or lowered as necessary in order to maintain a constant exchange rate between it and index shares of capital. Currently, the old form of currency enters circulation through an open market purchase of capital index shares, or when the Central Bank uses it to buy the component shares needed to assemble and issue a new benchmark index share. Printed currency exits circulation through an open market sale of capital shares. The printed currency is still around only because, in our economy, a few people seem to prefer to have some currency about for pocket money and a security blanket connecting them back to the previous fiat currency with which they were familiar.

"Honestly, issuing the old Central Bank currency makes us all a little uncomfortable as something that still could be potentially abused by the Central Bank. However, if we did print too much of it, its exchange value in terms of capital shares would soon fall sharply and a disgusted public would and should soon retire it from even the most minor use in trade. Indeed, there is some evidence this is happening. As the public has become increasingly comfortable with using shares of capital as money and plastic transaction cards, interest in holding the old printed currency has continued to decline. The growing preference for capital as money has been made clear to us at the Central Bank, as increasingly individuals choose to exchange the old printed currency for capital shares. Of course, the goal of the Central Bank is to eventually retire all the paper currency when and if that is consistent with the public preference.

"I should emphasize that there are many possible paths on the road to a capital-as-money economy. The one we followed is just one of them. Had the Central Bank not embarked on the path to capital as money, it is almost certain that the market would have found another way. Without any government intervention or bureaucratic inertia to prevent it, I believe the evolution to a capital-as-money economy was inevitable. The violent contortions in the money supply and the extended failure of the bank lending market during the last credit crisis were hand-writing on the wall, even to my reluctant father."

Edward commented, "Actually Roberta, I was a little amused at how long markets—even the capital market—continued to maintain the convention of quoting prices in terms of the old printed currency units. This is predictable. People, after all, are creatures of habit who by preference change only slowly. But now, with few exceptions, prices are expressed only in terms of index shares. The other day I came across a barber shop that is still quoting the price of a haircut in terms of index shares as well as the printed currency. Hoping I might choose the type of payment that gave me the best deal, I did the math to see whether the haircut price was the same at the current fixed exchange rate. It was."

With this Edward continued to ask questions of Roberta. "Given the Central Bank's diminished role, going forward what do you see as the main functions and justification for the Central Bank in our economy in addition to providing small amounts of the old printed currency?"

"Well Ted, you will recall that in our old economy, there was a three day settlement or clearing period between the selling of equity or capital assets before the cash or currency became available. This kind of delay is, of course, unacceptable and unnecessary in a technologically-advanced economy which uses shares of capital as its medium of exchange. Now, index shares are not 'cashed out' but rather the record of ownership of them simply changes electronically as they are traded in appropriate market-determined amounts for other goods or services. The Central Bank is ultimately responsible for monitoring and making a record of these exchanges and changes in ownership quickly and accurately when they occur. The actual exchanges are facilitated by member custody and trading institutions, which in some cases, but not all, were the banks that previously performed this function. The exchanges are reported to the Central Bank. With electronic reporting and computer technology, this process and its verification now requires only seconds to accomplish. In addition, an end-of-day summary report is transmitted as well to verify and summarize trading activity. Individuals can and do check their accounts of share ownership electronically any time they desire.

"Discrepancies or disagreements cause us to investigate possible fraudulent exchanges or honest errors in recording index share ownership. There is no reason that this role must be performed by the Central Bank but, again, at this time the public seems more comfortable having us do so. I think that they even like the term 'Central Bank' because it symbolizes to them that some trusted auditing institution is monitoring and recording their exchanges. And, yes, one of our most important forecasts has been validated. We islanders do our job of exchange efficiently enough that technological limitations upon velocity or imposed by the volume of money are not a problem. Exchange proceeds at a velocity driven by and limited only by the intentions and desires of the individual traders."

After a brief pause, Roberta continued explaining the ongoing role of the Central Bank in the Confederation's economy. "Once the Central Bank began issuing the index shares it created, we opened the door for other issuers as well. Our intention at the Central Bank was never to be the only, or even the major, issuer of index shares. Rather, we initially issued shares only to get the ball rolling; providing a supply of index shares to the market at a fixed exchange rate as an alternative to the old printed currency. As you all know, index funds became extremely popular years ago as they provided a simple way for islanders to invest in a diversified portfolio of stocks without having to buy individual shares in each of the 400 companies comprising the popular Islet 400 index. There are now several issuers of index shares that are indistinguishable from one another, and are all being readily accepted as a medium of exchange. Now the final primary function for the Central Bank is making sure that all issuers of broad index shares of equity follow the same methodology in originating them and adjusting their weightings in response to relative valuations—so they may be exchanged for each other in a constant ratio. In other words, we enforce uniform standards for 'qualified' issuers of index shares.

"In the interest of uniformity and simplicity, some have suggested that the Central Bank itself should be the sole originator of capital index shares to insure the shares are originated according to a fully transparent paradigm. We have strongly resisted this because we believe it consolidates too much power in the hands of the Central Bank—a return to the 'bad old days'. We prefer instead to monitor the market process. In the future this function may be performed by private auditors in the absence of a Central Bank. In the final analysis, index share originators, who perform their function accurately and well, will be rewarded by the market by their shares being bought, preferred, and used as savings and readily acceptable as money. Right now, we reward issuers who conform to our benchmark index shares with the label 'qualified' shares—letting the market know that they are indistinguishable from the Central Bank's index shares in composition. Ultimately, those who do this job poorly will issue shares shunned by investors and by the marketplace.

"Actually, related to the index shares, I should mention another technical point that the Central Bank got involved in. One important characteristic of a valuation or trading good is, of course, divisibility. So it was important as we moved toward capital-based money that the capital index shares could be broken down and traded in small enough fractions to accomplish trades of even the smallest value. What we ended up doing was allowing trades to be specified in units down to one thousandth of the previous standard single Islet 400 Index share. Now since each index share represents a constant proportion of the total capital stock of the 400 largest publicly-traded companies, it will tend to grow steadily in value relative to the average consumer good or service as time passes. This means that periodically the index units of capital must be allowed to be even more finely divisible. What we are following right now is something we at the Central Bank like to refer to as the 'bubble gum rule.' That is, our smallest tradable unit of capital money should be sufficiently small to purchase a single piece of bubble gum.

"Currently there is a group that has suggested that concern with this arbitrary minimum tradable unit is silly. That is, with our current technology, the easiest solution is simply to allow capital trades in portions of a share down to whatever decimal point market pricing requires. Since most trades are electronic anyway, the problem of a smallest currency unit is moot, in my opinion. Both groups have their points and both are represented within the Central Bank, so it is an interesting debate."

"Well," Edward observed, "it doesn't appear to be a problem that the market cannot easily solve. Put my vote down for the argument favoring prices specified down to whatever decimal point causes supply and demand to efficiently equilibrate. When coins and paper were circulating, the smallest currency unit required was of some importance to the mint. However, when nearly all trades are electronic, the question of the smallest unit is, as you say, moot. Moreover, the beauty of market determination of the decimal point required is that the Central Bank will not have to worry itself, as the value of capital index shares increases relative to other goods, about defining smaller arbitrary minimum share divisions.

"Well, Roberta, it's time to get down to brass tacks. I next have a series of specific short questions for you to explain to us how the capital-as-money system actually works, what the structure is, and how it actually came to be. It's an interesting and elegant process, and one that even some Club members here may not be fully aware of. Are you ready for them?" Edward stared at her with a sort of frowning intensity.

Humorously mirroring his expression back at him, Roberta replied, "I'm ready. Are you ready for some detailed answers?"

"I was afraid you'd say that. In sympathy to me, try to keep your answers as simple as you can. First, suppose I buy a table from you. How does that trade actually happen?"

"Every good or service, or individual asset or equity, for that matter, has a market value expressed in terms of capital index shares. When you buy the table from me at an agreed upon price or trading ratio, most likely you would use your transaction card. I swipe it across my cell phone, you swipe it across yours, and the mutually agreed upon quantity of index shares are instantaneously transferred from your account to my account. I, in turn, give you the table. Each of us may check this transaction record at any time. If you are more old-fashioned, you might instead use the old Central Bank currency which has an exchange value in terms of index shares."

"Okay. You previously mentioned currency, Roberta. In more detail, how does Central Bank currency come into existence and how is it withdrawn and how is this related to the Central Bank's issuance of index shares?"

"Initially, early in the transition to capital as money, we purchased shares of the individual companies underlying the Islet 400 index at their going market prices in terms of the fiat currency then in circulation. We then began selling our own Central Bank exchange traded fund of index shares to buyers who found them desirable to own. Our own index shares were largely identical to the index shares of the one or two largest private issuers who were already selling index shares in the market. During the transition to capital as money, the composition, adjustment, and weightings of our shares became the benchmark for exchangeable index shares to be used as money. In fact, we gave a stamp of approval to 'qualified' private issuers of index shares whose composition and weightings conformed to our own.

"For the Central Bank, the process of creating of a new index share is quite simple. The process begins when we use some of the old printed currency to purchase the constituent individual equities necessary to create a new index share. Then, this newly-created index share is sold to the private market at the specified fixed exchange rate. When the index share is sold to the buyer, the payment for the share is made to the Central Bank in units of the old printed currency. If the public wants more index shares at the fixed exchange rate, we can repeat the process and create new ones at will. But, the index shares we create are backed by shares of the individual companies that underlie the index. The important distinction here is that every unit of capital money we issue has a real value based upon shares of ownership of real productive capital in our economy."

"That is an important distinction, Roberta. Continuing, how do private issuers of qualified shares respond to the supply and demand for tradable index shares? How important are they? Is the Central Bank the major issuer of index shares at this time?"

"At first we were afraid that we would become the dominant issuer of tradable index shares. It was not a business or a long-term role that we wanted. However, what happened with private issuers was a dramatic and beautiful illustration of the workings of market competition and the laws of supply and demand. The quest for profit insures there are always an adequate number of private providers of index shares. Their profit is kept in check, not by government edict, but by the workings of supply and demand. Excess profits are fleeting and profit to issuers trends toward a reasonable normal rate of return, as one would expect in a competitive free-market economy. Most interesting of all is how the supply of money is itself now entirely market determined. It is the market that insures there is always an adequate quantity of index-share money to meet market demand. If you think about it, this is natural and how it should be.

"To understand how and why new money is now created, start by visualizing a qualified issuer of tradable index shares with a few such shares in its inventory. In any economy there are times when demand for money is growing, including an economy utilizing index shares for money. When demand for index shares is strong the value of an index share, which by definition is one, might be greater than the value of the individual shares of stock that comprise the index. When this happens it presents the issuer of index shares with an arbitrage opportunity: A qualified issuer can use a single index share to purchase the underlying securities in the weights necessary to create another index share, and there will be a small arbitrage profit leftover. The issuer of index shares will be able to use one single index share to purchase the properly-weighted components that will allow them to issue $(1+x)$ new index shares, where x is the profit. Competitive forces are at work, and the profit is quickly competed away as issuers exploit the arbitrage opportunity. The profit opportunity is eliminated when x, once again, equals zero. On the other hand, suppose that there are too many index shares in circulation, as evidenced by market prices. When the supply of index shares is too large, the value of a single share will be less than the weighted value of the individual securities underlying the index. Now a qualified share issuer can sell the individual securities underlying a single index share and receive a payment of $(1+x)$. They can then buy and retire one outstanding index share, whose price is one. Again, a small profit of x is realized. As more arbitrageurs pursue the opportunity the arbitrage opportunity vanishes.

"The extraordinary thing that has happened here is that we now have a real-valued money whose supply is driven by the needs and demand of the marketplace, not by the whims or greed of a fiat-money issuer as in the past. It's a beautiful thing! In the face of such an efficient process, the Central Bank has become a very minor, token issuer of tradable index shares. We still continue our benchmark function to determine 'qualified' issuers, but we are hopeful that, in time, the private market can even replace this audit role."

"It is a beautiful thing indeed, Roberta! I think you may have just answered the next question in your previous response, but I'll ask it anyway. Is there a risk that the entire stock of shares of companies that make up the Islet 400 might become indexed?"

"Of course not. There is a distribution of rates of return across individual equities from highest to lowest, while an index share provides an average return to capital that appears to have converged relatively closely to the growth rate of our economy. As long as that is the case equity managers and individual stock pickers abound and they perform the very important task of valuing individual equities relative to each other, and to the index. And yes, Ted, as long as there are individual stock pickers and a variety of different opinions about which companies represent the greatest future value, index shares do get decomposed and retired."

Edward commented, "Presently, as you have stated, the Central Bank issues its own index shares designed to mirror the Islet 400, where the Central Bank's shares most importantly serve as the benchmark for private issuers to emulate. Only those firms that do a good job mirroring the benchmark are qualified as money issuers by the Central Bank. Can we expect the Central Bank to continue in this role forever?"

"I certainly hope not, Ted. It can be profitable to be a private issuer of index shares that the public trusts and prefers to use. Ultimately the public and private auditors can best determine who is qualified in much the same way they can determine the preferred wine or coffee. In this I see hope that the Central Bank and I may soon exit, stage left."

"I'm sorry to say it, Roberta, but on this point I must disagree with you. I see a wizened old spinster, all alone, in the solitary room that is all that remains of the once mighty Confederation Central Bank—creaking in her chair and still faithfully computing the composition of tomorrow's Central Bank benchmark index share. It is almost poetic, you, the famous midwife of the capital-as-money exchange system, will still be steadfastly establishing the weights and attributes of the official, trusted 'Mother of All Index Shares'. The public will expect nothing less and will gain comfort from that continuity."

Refusing to rise to this obvious barb aimed at her with other than a dry glance, Roberta remained calm and quiet.

After a pause, Edward continued, "Market economies don't do anything for free, Roberta, so what about fees?"

"Fees associated with indexing and with using capital as money fall into two main categories. First, there are the qualified issuers of the shares—the new money. We already talked about them. Qualified issuers are able to make a small profit as a result of the arbitrage opportunities that are created whenever there is a change in the demand for money. As long as they can make a profit by meeting the demand of the marketplace for tradable index shares they will continue to pursue this business without additional motivation."

"Secondly, there are the financial institutions that are traders and custodians of index shares. In some cases these institutions are the issuers of qualified index shares, but in most instances they are not. The primary purpose of these firms is to correctly record account balances, trades and transfers. The fees they receive from a client have not typically been based upon the number of trades, but rather upon the average account balances of index shares they custody. Recently, the trend has been toward this fee disappearing entirely as these institutions have grown more adept at capturing other business from their clients—for instance the trade and custody of individual equities. Thus, the volume of the business and bundling of services is creating a world in which the fees associated with the custody of index shares and their trading is imperceptible. I believe this compares favorably with the costs of inflation and foregone investment return that the fiat money and the fractional-reserve banking system previously imposed upon us."

Edward questioned, "I am still sometimes asked, Roberta, what happened to the rate of return to capital or to capital index shares?"

"Well, Ted, it sort of disappeared didn't it? At least, as it used to be expressed in terms of fiat money. After all, when aggregate capital is money it becomes the numeraire good and one index share is always worth just one index share. However, as our economy grows one index share steadily buys more consumption goods and services. This is where the real return to capital resides and it is, indeed, observable and hefty—it is measured in how much we can consume and the forward progress of our standard of living, not in the value of some fictitious, imaginary fiat currency. In terms of consumption goods and services, the value of one index share is steadily increasing. That is where you can measure the real rate of return to capital."

"Ouch, Roberta, after that last series of questions, now it's you who's making my head spin! I know I had it coming because I asked them. Attention to every last detail and moving part is one of the beauties of how free markets work at the micro level and if anyone is the acknowledged master of complexity it's you. The

Confederation can be forever thankful that, at this juncture, it was you and not me who was Chairman of the Central Bank. But still, you're giving me a headache and overloading me with detail. As you know, I'm just a big picture, theory kind of guy who thrives on simplicity."

Edward continued, "Let me try to put it in a nutshell and summarize what I think you just said, Roberta. By way of summary, the value of index shares is now well-established, the divisibility of capital shares allows trades to be accomplished on any scale from tiny to large, the speed of executing and recording trades is virtually instantaneous, and the market cost per trade is inconsequential. This has all happened because you—and I mean the Central Bank—started the process towards capital as money, and then you let the free market take over.

"Roberta, at the risk of getting mired down in more details, I do have another question. If you can answer me simply, what happened to credit cards? That's how I used to buy everything."

Roberta smiled and replied, "Going back to our transaction example, plastic is still how everyone buys almost everything nowadays and, again, we hope that our Central Bank printed fiat currency finally disappears. Most plastic cards are now just transaction, previously called debit, cards that instantaneously record a flow of capital from one account to another to electronically accomplish a purchase. Of course, credit cards have always had the same appearance as debit cards, but they differ in one important respect: Use of a credit card involves financing a purchase by borrowing from someone else. Credit cards can still be had, but they are starting to disappear. The real lending rate required in a capital-as-money world is a high enough opportunity cost that most users have come to prefer the instantaneous transaction cards. Is that simple enough for you, Ted?"

"Yes, thank you Roberta. See, you *can* do it when you try!"

"Well, I can't recall you ever having a problem with eye-glazing detail in your own harangues, Ted. However, to summarize, I suppose that you could say that the best role for a central bank in an economy evolving toward a capital-as-money exchange system is aptly described as a sort of a helpful 'midwife' to a process that will ultimately diminish its own importance—although I still don't like that word. However, in practice, helping make the economy simpler certainly has made my life more complicated!" Roberta concluded.

Edward responded philosophically. "You could have made your life much less complicated and more fulfilling if you had simply responded positively to my marriage proposal, years ago."

As seen several times during the past, Edward had made no secret of his romantic feelings towards Roberta. Edward's infatuation with her had not diminished. While the years had certainly matured Edward in most respects, it was still evident that he belonged to that benighted, peculiar, and socially-challenged minority who somehow thought that the more public a romantic proposal the better. Unfortunately, this trait of his had resulted in some accidental and intentional awkward moments and, at times, great amusement at his expense on the part of the club membership. Members were well aware that Edward and Roberta were both intellectually strong economists who were good friends. The somewhat edgy, competitive banter between them had always been a trademark of their relationship.

"Frankly dear, it was the thought of being married to you that made the alternative of a full time career with the Central Bank so attractive," Roberta acidly replied, but with a slight smile so as to indicate that she was having some fun at Edward's expense. There was scattered tittering about the audience at this.

Edward decided he should guide the conversation back to the evolution of capital as money. "I should have learned by now. Trading jibes with you has always ended badly for me. Moving on, let's compare how our actual economy has performed relative to the road map we thought it would follow when we originally introduced the idea of capital as our monetary good. What happened to price change? Did valuation in terms of capital cause broad inflation to disappear?"

"Inflation, when prices are measured in terms of shares of the Islet 400 index, has disappeared. Again, since a share of the capital index itself is now the numeraire, its value by definition is always one. All other prices are expressed relative to the shares of the Islet 400 index fund and, of course, individual price fluctuations do occur. Some prices go up while others go down, but there is no trend of prolonged increases in the overall price level as used to occur when the government was in control of printing fiat currency. Focusing on any particular consumption good, it is possible that there can be a jump in price due to a change in individuals' preferences, or any other factor that affects demand and/or supply.

"You may recall last year that there was a significant minority of our Confederation economy who thought the world was going to end—and as a result felt that they should consume their wealth before the end date. Sad to say, a transition to a more logical exchange and valuation system does not preclude such crazies. They bid up the price of parties and, particularly, alcohol as their hypothetical end date approached. It is still the case, even within a capital-based economy, that the relative prices of particular goods can and will fluctuate in response to such antics. You may remember at the time that the price of a fifth of rum went up from 1/100 of an Islet 400 index share to 1/50 of a share."

"Yes," Edward replied. "And I was gratified by how efficiently the financial marketplace rolled over them like a steamroller. Ironically those very risk-averse and prudent individuals to whom you referred earlier who value their holdings of the exchange good—capital—so highly were more than ready to accommodate the doomsayers by selling them liquor at a very high exchange rate in terms of capital. I think the 'world-is-ending' minority was swamped because the simple truth is that most of us instinctively behave in our saving and accumulation of wealth as if we expect to live forever more than we fear the end of the world. Or, we may just care a great deal about what we pass on to our children. For whatever reason, there were not enough squanderers to have any significant impact on the overall relative price of a representative bundle of consumption goods.

Gaining momentum, Edward said "In any market economy, at any time, there is always the theoretical possibility that some or many individuals may decide to sell their wealth on the cheap, set their houses aflame, and roast hot dogs and marshmallows over the resultant fires. Freedom means we cannot prevent such individuals from doing what most of us would consider stupid, short-sighted or crazy. Unfortunately, those amongst us who think they know better use such examples to question the very idea of free markets and individual freedom. They would argue that intelligent oversight of the fools that actually make up free markets— oversight by them, of course—is somehow a better system. Would be kings are always waiting in the wings to tell us sagely that the great unwashed masses of us cannot actually handle freedom—or even responsibly handle our own affairs. What happened of course, in our actual free market economy was that prudent, wealth-accumulating individuals recognized the fleeting opportunity and rushed to provide liquor to the crazies at a very high price and accumulate capital shares. The result reaffirmed the old adage that wealth will tend to migrate during such circumstances from weaker hands to stronger hands or, if you like, from weaker minds to stronger ones. Level headed individuals, steadily trading for their own advantage, are such a useful stabilizing tool for a marketplace. As always, a market economy efficiently responds to and sternly corrects such episodes—in a way that cannot be matched by the actions of our would-be overseers."

Roberta continued smoothly and with a wry smile. "I will finish my response to your original inflation question, if you will allow me. Despite periodic relative price fluctuations amongst the individual goods that comprise it, a broad bundle of consumption goods has, as we would expect, steadily declined in terms of Islet 400 index shares during the period that we have moved to a capital-as-money economy. With positive investment in capital occurring all the time, the value of a given percentage or share of our economy's broad capital stock would, of course, be expected to steadily increase in terms of average units of consumption goods—and it has. That is, a given percentage of the economy's capital stock of, say, one billionth, will tend to purchase more consumption goods over time as the economy's capital stock steadily grows. In fact the average price of a typical bundle of consumption goods has been falling at the same rate our population and productivity have been increasing. People seem to be quite happy with this outcome, and will remain so as long as the trend deflation is predictable and gradual. The gradual deflation is visible proof of our growing standard of living and prosperity. More interesting and perhaps an even more important long-term benefit than the trend deflation in the price of consumption goods on average is the drop in broad price volatility. This suggests that a more transparent and logical valuation and exchange system can reduce at least some of the uncertainty associated with pricing and exchange of consumption goods.

"Speaking of the Islet 400 index, the index itself is worth mentioning as a rather extraordinary thing in facilitating the transition to and operation of a capital-as-money economy. Think of it, Ted. Companies, representing an accumulation of capital and investment, can be born, grow and prosper, and wither and die due to technological innovation, changes in demand, competition, and/or management efficiency—being appropriately added or withdrawn in value from the index without a conscious decision or effort on the part of the typical holder and user of the shares. At the same time, of course, 'experts' are always welcome to try to discern and hold the companies or subsets of the index most likely to outperform in their opinions—and by doing so they perform the valuable consensus function of actually keeping the components that comprise the index, and therefore the index itself, efficiently valued. A smoother, better, market determined system could scarcely be imagined."

"I agree Roberta," Edward eagerly interjected. "The market capital index shares are indeed an extraordinary concept and people should be happily able to adjust to low, benign, and predictable deflation in the price of consumption goods. It makes a nice change from the historically more typical case of volatile inflation. More importantly what has happened to my golden-rule capital-intensity? Are we getting there?"

"Well. I hate to be the first to break it to you," Roberta coolly responded, "but we do not and never have lived in an economy described by your much beloved single-sector neoclassical model. We exist in a real world of disaggregated capital that wears out and/or becomes obsolete. We certainly must make our decisions without your neoclassical model benefit of perfect foresight. Indeed, it is the misfortune of a generally risk-averse humanity to always make decisions under the cloud of uncertainty and risk. I must admit that I never totally drank your kool-aid on the golden-rule equilibrium capital-intensity. Why must it be that one particular capital-intensity that the economy tends to, and not some other one? Even within the framework of the simple neoclassical model, of which you are so fond, there are an infinite number of possible stable equilibriums. Why should the one that occurs be the so-called golden-rule intensity? Furthermore, what happens if the rate of technological change or effective labor force growth or even the rate of population growth itself is not as nicely stable as you apparently think?"

"Alas, always the old skeptical Roberta. Your tired criticisms are not substantive and do not dilute or deflect the strength of the model's primary insights and conclusions," Edward replied with confidence. "As you well know, good models simplify and clarify fundamental reality. That is, they abstract from what is less important in order to more clearly illustrate what really is. I am firmly convinced that, as one of those, the Solow model captures 90 percent of reality in describing the behavior and trajectory of an aggregate economy. In particular, my argument which predicts the attainment of a golden-rule capital-intensity is not kool-aid, but rather a reasonable and robust expectation based upon simple human maximizing behavior. I would ask you why it is reasonable, under any assumptions, to expect that people either individually or collectively would not track toward the level of aggregate, cumulative capital investment that maximizes their expected long-term sustained consumption?"

Edward's voice grew slightly louder as he continued. "You mention that in the real-world there are risk-averse investors operating under conditions of uncertainty, and I totally agree with you. But please realize that when capital is money the risk-free or minimal benchmark rate of return actually does become the average or broad index real marginal product of capital. It is this rate that I believe will eventually converge to 'n', the sustained growth rate of the economy. The convergence occurs through the maximizing behavior of individuals, risk-averse or not, attempting to achieve the trajectory of maximum sustained real consumption. This is the reasonable base or risk-free rate of return investors should expect in order to defer consumption to the future. In our new capital-based monetary system, they achieve this rate of return simply by holding money—or capital. As we disaggregate the capital market and other financial markets investors may reasonably expect higher rates of return than 'n' for more risky investments. Ironically, it is the very risk-aversion characteristic of individuals that you refer to, Roberta, that most likely insures the attainment of a golden-rule capital intensity. Remember, when viewing economic behavior, we must learn to use the reference of our economy as it now is, not as it was.

"Upon further reflection, it is astounding that finance professionals used to refer to a government bond as the risk-free investment. How can an investment that promises to return a given number of units of a fiat currency possibly be seen as risk-free? I suppose that, since government ultimately controlled the printing presses, there was no risk to the investor surrounding the number of pieces of paper he or she would receive upon a government bond's maturity. However, there was enormous risk as to what goods and services those pieces of fiat currency would command in the marketplace. Those old government bonds promised a nominal return, but that was all. There was no guarantee that the printed currency returned to the investor would be able to purchase anything real. On the other hand, ownership of productive capital promises a tangible reward.

Edward continued on with a building enthusiasm. "A capital-based monetary system is more logical, more transparent and simpler, but nonetheless it represents a significant change in the structure of our economy. Risk-averse individuals will tend to accumulate and hold their wealth in terms of whatever asset they use as money—which in a capital-as-money economy means as broad index capital shares. As they collectively attempt to do this, investment in capital will increase and the marginal product of capital will fall. Thus, the very behavior of risk aversion to which you refer and which makes you skeptical of my golden-rule argument I believe will actually tend to drive the marginal product of capital toward its consumption-maximizing value. Put simply Roberta, from the perspective of one of your typical risk-averse investors, what better way is there in our economy than to hold their wealth in terms of a medium of exchange with a steadily increasing and low volatility value in terms of other goods and services—that is, capital? And further, an asset of index shares enables people to diversify away the event risk associated with capital ownership of any single company.

"Actually, I think the more intriguing question to ask is this: Will risk-aversion, plus the attractiveness of holding real wealth as capital actually cause us to overshoot the golden-rule capital intensity? Will we accumulate too much capital? I think the answer is no, because I cannot conceive of an economic behavioral motivation that could cause us individually or collectively to exceed the level of capital ownership that maximizes our sustained consumption. The purpose of accumulating capital is to increase sustainable consumption through time. If accumulating capital fails to add to long-term consumption, then its accumulation will cease.

"Roberta, in your attempt to discredit the neoclassical theory, you observe that in the real world the rate of population growth and technological change may not be constant as is assumed in the model. However, if the growth rates do change, it is typically very slowly relative to everything else. The expected real rate of return to capital and the expected real rate of growth of the economy should logically equal the expected reward for deferring present consumption to the future. If population growth went to zero or even negative, it doesn't change the gist of this argument—all it would mean is that those few of us eventually left to turn out the lights would be very wealthy indeed in terms of real asset ownership."

Under the amused stare of Roberta, it finally dawned even upon Edward that he had ceased asking questions, and instead had strayed too far down the path in delivering a lecture on one of his favorite subjects—the neoclassical growth model. "Trust you Roberta to reverse positions on me and get me to answer questions. In any case, our arguments about what might happen theoretically are, of course, now being trumped by what is actually happening in our economy as we have transitioned to capital as money. So I repeat my question, what is the empirical evidence so far? Can we say that our collective behavior is at least consistent with convergence toward a consumption-maximizing capital-intensity?"

"Oh my!" Roberta said with amusement, "it isn't hard to do, but I didn't mean to set you off on a path of academic ruminations. I'm sorry, but was the entire body of what you just said somehow a question? I should have known, give you an inch and you produce a lecture. I just never could stand to see you gloat. However, the fact is, as I'm sure you are well aware, the volatility of average stock prices as measured in terms of the number of consumption goods and services a share can command in the marketplace has decreased dramatically since we've transitioned to capital as money. At the same time, the trend marginal return to capital also appears to have steadily declined. I do not know if this is simply because making capital the numeraire for exchange and valuation has increased the demand and transparency of the capital market or if it is due to the convergence to some sort of consumption-maximizing capital-intensity as you seem to think. I hesitate to conclude that it is the latter in order to avoid the spectacle of you cart-wheeling about the room in glee. There appears no doubt, however, that because a capital-as-money economy has increased the efficiency, transparency and attractiveness of capital investment and capital ownership, it has exerted positive and beneficial effects upon economic growth."

"Come Roberta," Edward replied with his eyes twinkling. "It has always been nearly impossible to wring any kind of an admission from you. You've admitted that the marginal product of capital has gradually declined during recent years—meaning capital returns have fallen as the capital intensity has increased. But tell me, what happened to the value of capital, as reflected by the index shares, during the first years of adopting capital as money?"

Roberta responded, "As I discussed earlier this evening, now that capital is money we need to think differently about the value of capital, as well as the return to capital. Those of us who used to measure capital's returns in terms of fiat currency have had to adjust our thinking to the new reality. The way we now measure the return to capital is by examining how many index shares are required to purchase a representative bundle of consumption goods. To understand how this works, suppose at the beginning of a year a bundle of consumption goods can be purchased for a single index share. At year's end, suppose the exact same bundle of consumption goods can be purchased for only 0.94 shares. This outcome implies the return to capital was 6 percent. In this manner it is possible to get a numerical estimate of the return to capital.

"Now, back to your question about what has happened to the value of index shares. Relative to consumption goods there was an initial increase of over 40 percent in the trading value of Islet 400 index shares when capital was first adopted as the new medium of exchange. Most experts put that down to an initial beneficial impact on our stock market due to the additional demand for using capital as money. Since then capital's return has stabilized at a lower annual rate. But Ted, I'm not sure why you are asking this question, since you are certainly aware of this historical track record. What's your point?"

"Just this, Roberta. A sharp initial increase in the value of capital coupled with a gradual movement toward a lower trend rate of return to capital strongly suggests that individuals temporarily reduced their consumption and increased their demand for capital. In so doing, the aggregate rate of savings and investment in new capital was increased as we collectively sought to attain an optimal or maximum level of sustainable lifetime consumption. We decreased consumption temporarily in order to achieve a higher level of consumption over our lifetimes. The empirical results you've described are completely consistent with the movement of our economy toward a golden-rule capital-intensity!"

"Yes," replied Roberta. "They are either evidence of that or something else. You're so in love with the neoclassical growth model that you can't see that a given set of real-world empirical outcomes is consistent with many alternative theoretical constructions or explanations. Why can't you just relax for a moment and enjoy the good things that have happened to us since we've moved to a capital-as-money economy?"

"It really does pain you to admit that there might be any merit to my arguments doesn't it," Edward responded smugly. "I will simply note for the scientists amongst us that I made my neoclassical model forecast of what would likely happen before we transitioned to a capital-as-money economy and, after the fact, the observed results have been consistent with my forecast. This is the strongest test of a prior theory or hypothesis that we can make. I rest my case. However, continuing with our questions. What has happened to the lending market, the banking industry and agents?"

"Interestingly the lending market is still there and is still large. As you will remember, following our last terrible credit market collapse, the banking sector, which could have been accused of being lax in its underwriting, became the opposite. It displayed a frozen 'deer-in-headlights' mentality, would loan almost nothing, and was slavishly focused on accumulating more reserves—eventually, in the aggregate, its reserves even exceeded its demand deposits. This mood was exacerbated by increased stringent regulation by the Central Bank and government, which occurred after the horse was already out of the barn. Of course, lenders and borrowers were still there and they found ways to go around the frozen gatekeepers. The subsequent rise of the direct lending market was a healthy outcome and the trend since then has been an increase in direct lending's share of the total loan market. This has been accomplished by a sharply reduced number of intermediaries—thereby increasing transparency in the credit market.

"However, what faces the lending market is a mixture of bad news and good news from the vantage point of individual borrowers. In a capital-money based economy, the opportunity cost of lending has become a great deal more obvious to all. That means the loan to 'Uncle Bert' must now clear the hurdle of meeting at least the expected return to simply holding capital or money—a very good return, indeed. Of course, loans can be made to be repaid in fewer index shares than were initially lent—or at rates of return below that of simply holding capital. In fact, few, if any, are. That is the bad news for borrowers intending to put the proceeds of their loans to frivolous uses, or unlikely or unable to meet their debt payments. In our old system, they used to obtain these loans through an opaque and inefficient agent-driven banking and credit market. For these borrowers, the increased transparency, directness, and simplicity of the lending market is bad news. The good news for borrowers is that, as we have just observed, the hurdle rate of the expected return to capital has fallen substantially as both capital prices and investment in capital have increased. As a result, the lending market is still active, but is a good deal more transparent, sober, and understandable to both sides than it was. Alas silver-tongued, desperate borrowers are never absent from the marketplace and neither are gullible lenders willing to accommodate them. So loan defaults still occur. At least, however, we have no longer encumbered ourselves with money, credit, and banking structures that encourage, facilitate, and ultimately validate questionable loans by making all of us responsible for them.

"I don't want to leave you with the impression that it was all 'wine and roses' however. There was, as you might expect, a good deal of squawking, resistance and push-back from those activities or sectors of our economy, traditional banking in particular, whose rewards were dependent upon our complex and opaque previous system of money, banking and credit. Under the increased illumination of a simpler more logical system of value and exchange their artificial subsidies, windfalls and the resultant inefficient and distorted allocation of investment and savings flows became clear and was reduced or eliminated. This process still continues."

"I'll bet 'squawking and resistance' is putting it mildly!" interjected Edward sympathetically. "Untold tonight is an epic tale about the fight you fought with the entrenched bureaucracy of the old money, banking and lending system—the Central Bank, the banks, and the armies of lending intermediaries, agents and other gatekeepers all wanting their piece of the proceeds. The last refuge of the threatened institutionalist is to complain that their critics are unfair and naïve because they really don't comprehend the complexity and nuance of all the things they do and the myriad of regulations necessarily to govern them. They can't see that what is being questioned is the basic logic, or lack of it, to justify their existence itself. To the last, they see their critics as benighted and the job of their institution as unappreciated and indispensable."

"Well my dad actually helped more than you might imagine once he opened his mind," said Roberta. "There remains, however, a stronger market for agents than we might have expected in our naive predictions. This is fine as long as this market is transparent to buyers in two respects, what you pay and what you get. Apparently, most individuals still prefer to defer specific investment decisions to agents or 'experts' rather than being directly responsible for them. This may arise from the fact that agents perform at least two functions of value to individual investors. First, they are presented and marketed as experts allowing individuals to defer this function and get on with their lives and their own occupations. Second, some of the risk and uncertainty of performance of individual investments may be placed upon them because they can conveniently be hired or fired. They still perform a useful function in our economy because, while the volatility and risk of returns to the aggregate capital market has diminished, the risk associated with the return to individual investments in capital or other assets is still there. Moreover, investment experts play the critical role of keeping the individual companies comprising the index shares efficiently valued relative to one another.

"It is not surprising, I suppose, that many of those who used to populate the banking sector have adroitly moved to become these agents or institutions of custody and exchange. The best, brightest and most agile of banks and bankers have repositioned themselves—oh, stop your sniggering Ted, it is not an oxymoron—and are still profitably providing services. The good news for our economy is that all these functions are more direct and more transparent than they were before under our previous flawed money, banking, and credit system. At least now people know that they are making a conscious decision to hire an agent and what they are paying them—an improvement over our previous system. Put simply, there is nothing wrong with an agent or intermediary as long as it is clear to both sides what they have been hired to accomplish and what they are being paid. Transparency, simplicity, logic, and responsibility in financial asset markets have reduced the likelihood of irrational credit market and financial market bubbles and have led to an increased understanding of our economy by most citizens. Banks in their traditional bricks-and-mortar sense have, of course, largely disappeared."

Edward said, "So we have entered an era of continuous stability, growth and prosperity with steady convergence of the economy toward a consumption-maximizing equilibrium. Is it possible that the market has finally solved the riddle of an efficient free market economy?"

"Not by a long shot, Ted! Risk and uncertainty are unfortunate facts of nature. Economic shocks, wealth destruction and recessions can still originate within our economy and outside our economy. Weather, wars, and last year's earthquake have taught us that. For individuals in any economy scams, theft, and fraudulent exchange are still risks as they always have been—as is excessive speculation. In any economy, not all investments are good ones and not all loans should be made. Unscrupulous individuals and managements can still defraud and cheat others. What is within our power to achieve is the design and implementation of structures of voluntary exchange, saving and investment amongst individuals and enterprises that are as simple, transparent, logical, and efficient as we can make them. Furthermore, our institutions should be able to evolve and adapt as economic conditions, the marketplace and technology changes. What is inexcusable for any economy is to be saddled with impenetrable, obsolete, self perpetuating and self-serving institutions and bureaucracies that add to our risk and economic volatility rather than reducing them. There is enough natural risk and uncertainty in our lives and in our economy without our designing and tolerating institutions that add to it."

Edward interjected, "Speaking of instability and risk, how do you now respond to those critics who blanched at the thought of capital as the valuation good in our economy simply because of the historic volatility of the capital market?"

"That is the heart of the matter isn't it," Roberta responded. "However, you must remember that the historic volatility of the capital market occurred not in a cocoon but against the backdrop of our old system in which the money supply was determined partly by the rate at which the Central Bank injected fiat currency and partly by the pace of banks in making good or bad loans with the funds of unwitting depositors. This monetary system itself produced wide and unpredictable swings in production, market

225

interest rates, inflation and the employment of productive inputs, namely labor and capital. This made predicting the future real marginal product of capital difficult to say the least. In addition, remember that the stream of capitals' real marginal products was then valued in terms of an uncertain fiat money driven price level of output and discounted to a present value at a nominal interest rate embodying volatile inflationary expectations—again driven by the erratic and unpredictable trajectory of fiat money. Is it at all surprising in such a nonsensical world, that the nominal or fiat money value of capital was volatile? Instead ask yourself, is the marginal product of a tractor, for example, and therefore its value, so difficult to predict in real terms in a world of much steadier production, more stable pricing, and employment? Of course it isn't. That is what we have proven in practice with the increased stability and prices in an economy with value of all things based upon their exchange ratios with capital. It turns out our old system was using the wrong yardstick to value capital and everything else—and generating a great deal of unnecessary market volatility and smoke as a result. We found the reduced volatility of the average exchange value of capital a gratifying result of our movement to capital as money."

"It's not surprising, Roberta, you could have counted on it."

"But honestly now, Ted, doesn't the much lower volatility of the capital market since we transitioned to capital as money surprise even you a little bit?"

"Really no, Roberta, it does not. That is the real benefit of using broad capital as money. One more time, when the default option for an individual's savings is no longer fictitious fiat money accumulating in her bank account, but, rather, is ownership shares of our economy's productive aggregate capital, the comparison between current consumption and investment or future consumption becomes stark. The beauty of our new system is exactly the elegance of the central insight of the Solow model, made clear in real-world practice. The decision of accumulation of capital or consumption, at the margin, depends upon each

226

individual comparing the current opportunity cost of one to the other. The exchange ratio between capital and consumption means each one is priced in terms of the other. If speculators momentarily caused capital to be priced too high, then at the margin individuals would prefer current consumption to future consumption, investment would fall, and the price of capital, or if you prefer the trading ratio of capital for consumption goods, would fall and capital's marginal product would rise. If the trading ratio of capital for consumption goods should fall too low, individuals, in the aggregate, would tend to prefer saving or capital accumulation over consumption at the margin, and the price of capital would rise and capital's marginal product would decline. Equivalently the price of consumption goods on average would fall. This is such a natural, intuitive equilibrating process, when there is no intermediary between capital goods and consumption goods, it should almost go without saying. And, Roberta, please note that I expressed this argument without once referring to the golden-rule capital intensity that seems to irritate you so much."

"Thank you."

Edward continued with his questioning. "Pushing this stability argument a little further, what is your response to those who observed that using broad capital market index shares as the basis for value, was a tautological fallacy? Their argument was that the individual equities that comprised our broad stock index were valued in terms of the index itself, thereby creating a potential destabilizing feedback cycle for the value of the index and, by extension, for the economy."

Roberta answered, "We watched that carefully and with great interest, although, if you think about it, this is not a new argument. Almost any market in any economy at any time can be described as 'a potentially destabilizing feed-back cycle.' In its simplest form this objection can always be used by those who distrust the results and behavior of free-market economies—those who believe that markets are fundamentally unstable and could be managed better by intelligent overseers, themselves for instance. Any good can theoretically increase in speculative value relative to the other goods for which it may be exchanged. What limits this is that when a good's trading value increases sufficiently and without real reason, cooler heads tend to prefer to hold the other goods for which it may be traded—and its exchange value falls to a reasonable, market-determined level once again. Gratifyingly, the same has been true of our capital index shares, at least during the period in which we have used capital as money. That is why the value of an index of consumption goods and services has shown lower volatility, as I observed previously, since our economy moved to a capital standard of value. The same behavior occurs within the index, itself. If a single capital component of the index were to become 'speculatively overvalued,' cooler heads would again begin to prefer the other components and its relative valuation in capital index shares would decline. There is no tautological paradox here."

Edward thought for a moment and then spoke. "On another front, apparently unrelated, were you surprised to see the legislature actually vote for and institute a very flat and simple income tax and scrap everything else? I could say it almost restores my faith in politicians, if I ever had any. Can our transition to a capital-valued economy take any credit for this amazing result? What's next? Politicians voluntarily voting for term limits upon themselves, I suppose?"

A guffaw burst from Big Tuna, causing giggling throughout the room. When the laughter subsided Roberta answered. "Yes, I was surprised. When representative politicians give up their ability to steal output from those that vote against them in order to reward those who vote for them, it is a surprising change in sadly predictable political behavior. After all, the ability to steal real wealth and output legally and to appropriate it for one's own political gain, in an economy otherwise based on free and voluntary exchange, is what makes becoming a politician and retaining incumbency worthwhile. No, our transition to a capital-valued economy cannot take direct credit for this development. That belongs collectively to the voters in the last election.

However, we inadvertently might have helped to set the stage. First, what the government is taking from the private sector and its real value is now more obvious in an economy that uses capital as money. Secondly, government borrowing meeting a hurdle rate determined by the real return to capital becomes more problematic and thus a more difficult sale to voters. The shell game in which the indeterminate fiat money value of government assets is paid mysteriously by someone else in the future is less likely to be palatable to voters under our current monetary system than it was under the previous one. As for term limits, at this point we don't appear to need them. Desirability of incumbency is a good litmus test of the smorgasbord of economic spoils available for politicians to dip in to. Limit or eliminate the ability to steal and the only politicians who will try to remain incumbents will be those who wish, perhaps for selfless patriotic reasons, to use their wisdom and experience to actually serve the public."

"Speaking of serving the public," Edward responded, "why do we need you—and by 'you' I mean the central bank? If markets can perform their functions and everything is going so well, why do we need a bunch of bureaucrats to record and monitor capital exchanges, produce a benchmark share and 'qualify' the originators of capital index shares, and provide a vestigial paper currency? Can you be accused of making a comfortable bureaucratic featherbed for yourself at public expense?"

Roberta laughed. "If I responded to this question with vehement denial, you would already have your answer. However, you of all people Ted know that I harbor no great belief in or love of public goods and institutions in an economy that should be as free as possible. Central Bank chairman is not a job that I was looking for or seeking to retain. I ask myself everyday how the basic functions we perform could be privatized and market-driven with perhaps even better and more efficient results. However, it is still true that people love tradition and habit and generally abhor rapid change. The Central Bank will be here as long as the consensus or the market, if you wish, feels more comfortable with us being here and performing the functions that we do. When or if our functions become less important or redundant, in the eyes of the marketplace, we can disappear."

"So you're saying, Roberta, the capital-as-money world seems, on balance, a more natural place then?"

"Oh yes! To see why, simply consider the how strange the argument sounds for going back to where we were from where we now are."

"I see what you mean," Edward replied after a few moments of reflection. "It would seem awfully peculiar now, from our present frame of reference, to try to convince people that the most fundamental risk free-rate of return is not the average product of capital—the return to ownership of the productive tools of our economy, a rate of return, at an optimal equilibrium, that should be equal to the sustained real growth rate of our economy. What is more natural than that the risk-free reward to foregone consumption should be the growth rate of the economy itself?"

"There you go again, Ted, with your golden-rule argument. However, in broad terms I tend to agree. Especially if you were to argue that the risk-free rate of return should instead be the short-term lending rate on arbitrary and intrinsically worthless pieces of paper issued by the Central Bank, a fiat money whose supply was only limited by their whims in meeting the changeable and typically growing needs of government expenditure and deficit financing. An artificial short-term lending rate, not determined by the market, but one that could be, and was, typically manipulated by the Central Bank. What is natural or risk-free about that?"

"But couched in terms of our old monetary system, Roberta, the argument grows even more strained. Try convincing people now that instead of using the economy's most fundamental and primary measure of value, broad index shares of ownership of its productive capital as the foundation for trade and valuation, we would be better off using worthless scraps of paper whose only value is derived from the trust misplaced in them and the faith that

230

their supply will not be abused by the government or Central Bank that fires up the printing press and decides how many of them to issue.

"Further, if your audience is credulous enough to buy that, then argue that this fictitiously valued money supply should be multiplied by a banking system empowered to loan out most of the deposits made through an almost unlimited pyramid scheme to further balloon the total money stock and the supply of credit. Finally argue that these loans should be made by aggressive lending agents rewarded for the volume of loans they originate rather than the quality of those loans. Moreover, argue that banks should be rewarded with most of the fees and interest on the loans they create in this fashion, rather than the depositors whose deposits are, in fact, the source of the loans."

"It's sort of amazing," Roberta replied after reflection. "It really is hard to imagine a more contrived and less appealing scheme. It's an accident of history that we became saddled with such a monstrosity, although given the understandable motives of kings, governments, and banks, it's not too surprisingly that it evolved and got institutionalized. I just glad we've moved beyond it and I don't have to sell it. If we tried, we should be laughed out of this room."

"Speaking of the room," Edward mused looking about, "I would be remiss if I didn't acknowledge an old friend and member of our club, here tonight, who has so far been uncharacteristically quiet. Tooth, I just read that your firm for the custody and exchange of capital index shares has just become one of the Confederation's largest. Congratulations."

A grinning but slightly discomfited Tompkins acknowledged Edward and the audience with a nod and a wave. "In truth, Ted, I couldn't let your crack, years ago, about my lack of vision and imagination go unanswered, now could I?"

"Here's a last softball question for you, Roberta. Is there a lesson in all of this for us or others? Put simply, what have we done?"

"Only the usual one I suppose. Whenever the combination of our minds or ideas coupled with our tools or technology allows us the opportunity to restructure our market economy so that it is freer, simpler, and more logical, we should move ahead promptly— overcoming our fears and the inertia of embedded, intransigent institutions. You were wrong in your previous comment about me, Ted, when you called me a master of complexity. I also prefer to see things simply. What we have done is to observe the previous burden to our economy of the inefficient, unworkable, and costly structure of fiat money, fractional-reserve banking, and an indirect credit market. We suggested instead an alternative reference frame for trading and valuation—that of capital. Then the marketplace evolved to this alternative in our economy, not through edict but through voluntarily evolution. We simply allowed the Central Bank and other bureaucratic institutions to permit and aid this transition rather than block it. The result has been an economy that is simpler, more logical and transparent, an economy that is more stable and efficient, and an economy that is freer and more prosperous. In a nutshell we had a system of money and lending that seemed biased toward allocating society's scarce savings to consumption rather than investment. Now we have one in which the individual's default position of accumulating or holding savings as capital money balances tends to favor investment rather than consumption. The result seems healthy for our economy."

"That was the answer I wanted to hear, Roberta. The handwriting is on the wall. Since life has become simpler, more stable and more prosperous and since the Central Bank will no doubt continue to trend to minor relevance, I would like to renew in this public place my proposal to you. What do you say now to marrying me?"

"No."

CHAPTER 7

MATHEMATICAL APPENDIX—EDWARD'S PAPER

Capital as Money: Extensions of the Solow Model

Introduction and Preliminaries

When I make an assertion about how our current money, credit and banking system leads to an under-allocation to investment and a less than prosperity-maximizing capital intensity for our economy, respect for the more incisive minds of the Economics Club requires that I provide an illustration within the confines of a sound dynamic economic growth model. I will make my point in a framework which is already familiar to most of us in the Economics Club, which is the simple neoclassical growth model of Nobel-prize winning economist Robert Solow. Solow's single-sector, neoclassical growth framework provides a sublimely illustrative model of great simplicity and elegance. The simple assumptions of the model have led to criticisms leveled against it and, unfortunately, to its summary rejection as an illustrative tool by many of the more "sophisticated" economic thinkers amongst us. This is a shame, because this simple model is, in fact, a very powerful intuitive and instructive tool, whose so-called shortcomings may actually be benefits rather than drawbacks to correct economic understanding. As a robust teaching device, the basic truths and intuition of this model shine bright. The genius assumptions that differentiate this model are just two— substitutability of capital and labor in production of a given quantity of output is possible and each factor is assumed to have a declining marginal product in production as its quantity is increased while the other is held fixed.   As an economist, I have a strong belief that the most correct and instructive models and arguments are simple and cut to the heart of a logical proposition

233

or understanding. When a model is made more complex, it should call for sharp skeptical questioning as to why. Did the complexity make the model better or more realistic in trying to explain its central intuition, or did it simply obscure it and send us all off in pursuit of trivial rather than important results?

As most of you will recall from your formal economics training, the Solow model assumes one type of composite output that can either be consumed or invested to create future capital goods. (It might be helpful for you to visualize an item such as corn, which can be either eaten this year or can be saved and planted to produce even more corn next period.) The economy's production of output in each time period depends upon the amount of capital (K) and effective labor (N) that are combined in production. Also, within the Solow framework the economy is characterized by constant returns to scale, which is the logical condition that a doubling of the capital and labor used in production will result in a doubling of output. In this variation of the model, I will distinguish between the size of the labor force (L) and what will be called the "effective" labor force (N). The effective labor force grows at some constant rate (n) which comes about as a result of two factors: growth in the stock of labor (z) and growth in labor productivity α. At this initial stage there is no monetary good— the introduction of fiat money will occur later after first working through some of the model's preliminaries.

To begin, consider the stock of labor, L. The stock of labor is growing at some rate, z, which is a given rate that is exogenously determined. (By saying the rate is "exogenously" determined what I mean is that the rate of growth in the labor force reflects the overall growth in population, and how that rate is determined is not explained by the model.) It is also assumed that there is an exogenous rate of growth of labor-augmenting technological change which enhances the productivity of labor, resulting in a disparity between what will be referred to as effective labor (N) and the stock of labor (L). It is a fact that technology has been improving, and will likely continue to do so over time. As a result of improvements in technology, the average worker is more productive now than he was several years ago and will be yet more productive several years hence. Thus, letting n represent the growth in effective labor, the growth rate is explained by the sum

(7-1) $$n = z + \alpha$$

As was stated above, our economy's total output (Y) is produced by employing the two inputs in the production process, namely effective labor $N(t)$ and capital $K(t)$. Labor and capital both change over time, which explains the functional dependency on the variable "t" which is used to represent time. For ease of exposition, the "t" variable will normally be suppressed in what follows, but it is important to remember that the variables are all functions of time. Since output is a function of labor and capital, the production function is written as

(7-2) $$Y = F(N, K)$$

As was mentioned above, if both factors are increased by the same proportion, constant returns to scale implies output will also increase by that proportion. That is, if 10 workers and 2 machines can produce 15 units of output, then it stands to reason that 20 workers and 4 machines could be expected to produce 30 units of output. Mathematically, this property—that a doubling of inputs will cause a doubling of output—is expressed as follows:

(7-3) $$2Y = F(2N, 2K)$$

Or, more generally for any value of λ, constant returns to scale in production means that

(7-4) $$\lambda Y = F(\lambda N, \lambda K)$$

So, for example, if effective labor and capital are both tripled, then $\lambda = 3$, and the result is that output will triple as well.

In the Solow model the factors of production are substitutable one for another and they have the reasonable economic property of

235

declining marginal productivity; if we hold one factor constant and increase the other by small fixed increments, output increases, but by smaller successive amounts. That is, adding more workers to a given stock of capital will allow the economy to produce more output. But every worker added will increase output by fewer units than did the previous worker. Of course, as economists we are all very familiar with this property, and refer to it as "the law of diminishing returns." Mathematically, the idea that increasing either labor or capital will result in increased output means that the first partial derivatives of the production function $Y=F(N,K)$ are positive in sign,

$$\frac{\partial Y}{\partial N} \equiv F_N > 0$$

$$\frac{\partial Y}{\partial K} \equiv F_K > 0$$

The partial derivatives shown above are the marginal products of labor and capital, respectively. The law of diminishing returns implies the second derivatives are negative in sign. In the case of labor the law of diminishing marginal returns means that the marginal product of labor will decline as more workers are added to a fixed amount of capital. This is written mathematically as

$$\frac{\partial^2 Y}{\partial N^2} \equiv F_{NN} < 0$$

Likewise, capital's marginal product declines as more capital is added to a given stock of labor,

$$\frac{\partial^2 Y}{\partial K^2} \equiv F_{KK} < 0$$

Finally, within the Solow model it is assumed that adding more capital will make labor more productive (i.e., a worker will be more productive when he has more tools to work with). Returning to calculus, the idea that an increase in capital will increase labor's marginal product means the cross-partial derivative is positive:

$$\frac{\partial^2 Y}{\partial N \partial K} \equiv F_{NK} > 0$$

An economy's output can be either consumed or saved. Output that is saved in a particular period is invested, thereby becoming capital to be used in future production. I will represent the saving rate, or the "marginal propensity to save," by the variable "s", which is taken to be constant and exogenous for now. Clearly s is bounded by 1 and 0. Then, the marginal propensity to consume is given by $(1\text{-}s)$. The output produced in any given year can be consumed or saved, depending upon the saving rate. For example, if the saving rate is $s = 0.05$ and 20 units of output are produced ($Y = 20$), then 1 unit of output is saved and 19 units are consumed.

Total consumption in any period will be represented by the variable C, and is given by $C=(1\text{-}s)Y$. And, since output Y depends on how much effective labor and capital are used in production,

(7-5) $$C = (1-s) \cdot F(N, K)$$

Likewise, total saving, S, is given by

(7-6) $$S = s \cdot F(N, K)$$

All output is either consumed or saved, so

$$C + S = Y = F(N, K)$$

The act of investing refers to producing output and not using it for current consumption, but rather saving the output in order to increase production and the standard of living in the future. Take for example the fishing nets that were produced on our island last year. The production of those fishing nets required using some of the island's workers and machinery, where the workers and machinery could have been employed in the production of other consumption goods such as, say, volleyball nets. By producing fishing nets rather than volleyball nets, the island was able to accumulate capital which will enable us to catch more fish in the future—the island "invested" in capital. The immediate opportunity cost of the island's investment in new fishing nets was the lost volleyball nets. The act of foregoing current consumption, which is saving, is necessary if we are going to invest in new capital. That is, saving (S) is the same thing as investment (I), and results in the accumulation of new capital.

Growth in Labor, Capital and Output over Time

Returning to the formal mathematics of the Solow model, the rate of change in capital with respect to time is the derivative dK/dt. Throughout this paper a dot (•) over a variable is used to represent the time derivative in a more convenient, short-hand notation. The rate of capital accumulation ($dK/dt \equiv \dot{K}$) is determined by the amount of investment and the following equation must hold:

(7-7)
$$S = I = \dot{K} = sF(N,K)$$

The focus of the Solow model is on understanding the determinants of equilibrium levels of per-capita output and consumption in an economy. At the individual level, there is always a decision that needs to be made whether to consume or to save. The overall economy reflects the aggregation of the individual choices of the economy's agents. Ultimately, the economy's per-capita consumption and output will depend upon the savings rate (s) and the exogenously determined growth rate in effective labor (n). At first, I will simply assume that the savings rate is exogenous, but later it will be more reasonable to assume that it arises from the collective optimization of individual choices.

In order to focus on the output per unit of effective labor I will utilize the constant returns to scale property of the production function that was described previously. Referring to equation (7-4) shown above, let $\lambda = 1/N$. Then, the following holds:

(7-8) $(1/N) \cdot Y = (1/N) \cdot F(N,K) = F(1,K/N)$

Now, let output per unit of effective labor be represented by $y=Y/N$ and capital per unit of effective labor be $k=K/N$. Throughout this appendix the variable k will be referred to as the island's capital intensity or as the capital-labor ratio. For ease of exposition, the variable "y" will be referred to as per-worker output, although technically speaking the denominator of $y=Y/N$ is effective labor, N, which is not exactly the same thing as the island's stock of labor (L) (Per-capita output is given by the ratio Y/L.) These definitions allow equation (7-8) to be written as

(7-9) $$y = Y/N = F(1,k) \equiv f(k)$$

In words, equation (7-9) simply says that per-worker output y depends on the amount of tools available per worker, (k). Note that equation (7-9) can be rearranged as

$$Y = NF(1,K/N) = Nf(k)$$

Then, by differentiating and applying the chain rule one obtains

(7-10) $$dY/dK = N \cdot F_K \cdot (1/N) = f'(k)$$

Equation (7-10) implies $f'(k)$ is equal to F_K, which is the marginal product of capital and is greater than zero. Further,

(7-11) $$d^2Y/dK^2 = f''(k) \cdot (1/N)$$

Thus, $d^2Y/dK^2 = F_{KK} = f''(k) \cdot (1/N)$, and since F_{KK} is negative (due to the law of diminishing returns or declining marginal productivity), one can conclude

$$f''(k) < 0$$

239

As was discussed above, the rate of capital accumulation $\dot{K}$ is equal to saving (S), so

(7-12)

$$\dot{K} = S = s \cdot F(N,K) = s \cdot N \cdot F(1, K/N) = s \cdot N \cdot f(k)$$

Proceeding along the familiar road as it was originally paved by Solow, now divide both sides of equation (7-12) by N,

(7-13)
$$\dot{K}/N = sf(k)$$

In a growing economy the capital stock tends to increase over time, expressed mathematically as $\dot{K} > 0$, as does the effective labor force, $\dot{N} > 0$. The Solow model is focused on how the capital-labor ratio (k) evolves over time, as determined by the economy's marginal propensity to save and the growth rate in effective labor.

Recalling the quotient rule from calculus,

(7-14)
$$\dot{k} = d(K/N)/dt = \frac{\dot{K}N - \dot{N}K}{N^2} = \frac{\dot{K}}{N} - \frac{\dot{N}}{N}k$$

Substituting equation (7-13) and $n = \dot{N}/N$ into equation (7-14) gives the central conclusion and road map of the Solow growth model,

(7-15)
$$\dot{k} = sf(k) - nk$$

When the right-hand side of equation (7-15) is positive it implies $\dot{k} > 0$, and the capital-labor ratio is growing over time.

240

Conversely, if the right-hand side of equation (7-15) is negative it means $\dot{k} < 0$, and the capital-labor ratio is in decline. An equilibrium occurs when the economy's total capital stock (K) is growing at the same rate as its effective labor force (N), so that the capital-labor ratio k remains constant—that is, the rate of change of the capital-intensity is zero. From equation (7-15) we note that an equilibrium capital-labor ratio occurs (i.e. $\dot{k} = 0$) when k achieves the value, call it, k^e, such that

$$(7\text{-}16) \qquad\qquad s \cdot f(k^e) = n \cdot k^e$$

Equation (7-16) gives the precise condition for an economy to be in equilibrium. In an economy characterized by a growing population there is a need for savings. Without savings, a growing population will find itself with fewer and fewer tools per worker, and a declining capital-labor ratio. (Remember, a declining capital-labor ratio over time is mathematically expressed as $\dot{k} < 0$). Only when per-capita savings is sufficiently high will the economy be able to accumulate capital equipment rapidly enough to match the growth in its population, thereby keeping the capital-labor ratio constant. As indicated by equation (7-16), an equilibrium occurs when per capita savings $s \cdot f(k^e)$ is equal to the product of the growth rate in effective labor and the capital-labor ratio $n \cdot k^e$.

An interesting question is whether such an equilibrium capital-labor ratio k^e exists and whether it is, in fact, stable. If the economy is disturbed or pushed away from equilibrium some distance in either direction, will it tend to return to that equilibrium? The answer can be illustrated with an economist's favorite tool—a graph.

241

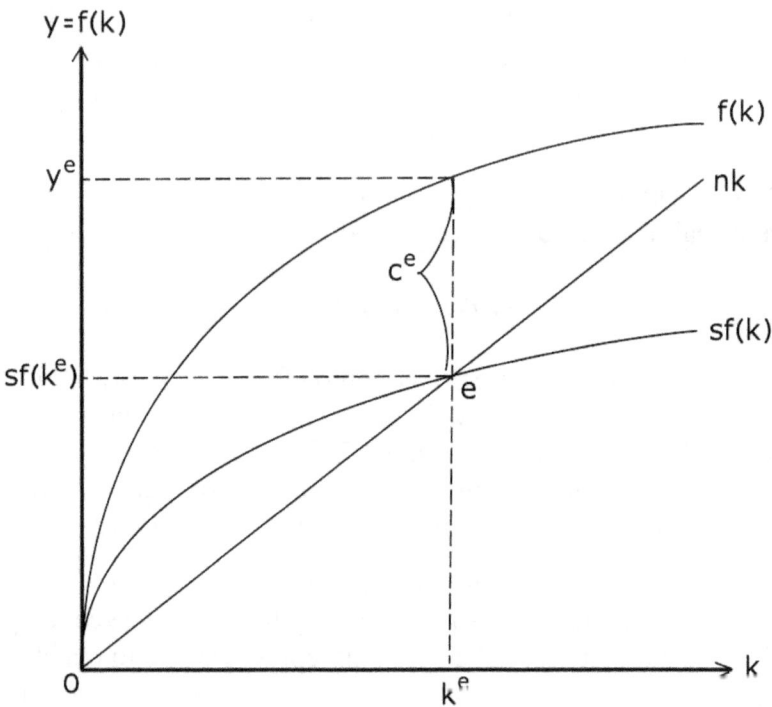

fig. 1   The Solow Growth Equilibrium

Figure 1 sketches out the shape of the per-worker production function, represented by the curve labeled *f(k)*. The curve has the properties that were described previously. Particularly, it is upward sloping, reflecting the fact that per-worker output is greater when tools-per-worker increases. However, capital's marginal product declines as k increases, as reflected by the concavity of the function *f(k)*. Per-worker savings is represented by the curve labeled *sf(k)*, which has the same basic shape as the *f(k)* curve, but lies below it. At low capital-labor ratios the curves *f(k)* and *sf(k)* have relatively steep slopes, as the marginal product of capital $f'(k)$ is very high when the first few tools are made available to labor. Finally, Figure 1 depicts the line whose equation is *nk*.

242

Obviously, the line extends from the origin and has a slope of n, which is the growth rate of effective labor.

Still referring to Figure 1 shown above, note that to the left of k^e the level of per-worker saving, as given by $sf(k)$, exceeds the value of nk, and equation (7-15) tells us that the time derivative $\dot{k}$ is positive. This means that savings is sufficiently high so that the capital-labor ratio will be increase over time towards k^e. On the other hand, for capital-labor ratios to the right of k^e the level of saving is inadequate to offset the growth in effective labor, or $sf(k) < nk$. Again referring to equation (7-15), the result will be a falling capital-labor ratio and movement towards k^e. Thus, the economy will automatically move towards k^e, and the equilibrium is therefore called a "stable" one.

So the Solow model shows that, under conditions of declining marginal productivity and factor substitutability, there is a stable capital-labor ratio, k^e. When the economy does finally converge to the equilibrium rate k^e, equation (7-15) implies the capital-labor ratio will no longer be changing over time, so $\dot{k} = 0$. At the stable equilibrium, the numerator of the capital-labor ratio (K) and the denominator (N) will both be growing over time at the same rate (n).

If our island's economy has built in tendencies to move to an equilibrium capital-labor ratio shown as k^e in the graph, what does that imply for islanders' overall standard of living? Given the level of technology, is per-capita consumption (C/L) going to be as large as possible, or can we do better? To address this question, define c to be the ratio formed by dividing total consumption C by effective labor N. Beginning with equation (7-5) from above, and again utilizing the property of constant returns to scale, one obtains

$$\frac{C}{N} = \frac{(1-s)F(N,K)}{N} = (1-s)\cdot F(1,K/N) = (1-s)\cdot f(k)$$

When the capital-labor ratio achieves its equilibrium, the ratio of C/N also is in equilibrium,

$$c^e = (1-s)f(k^e)$$

Since the equilibrium capital-labor ratio k^e is constant through time so is c^e, meaning that in equilibrium total consumption C is growing through time at a rate equal to the growth in effective labor N (both are growing at rate n). Likewise, $y = \frac{Y}{N} = f(k)$, so when k is constant at k^e it implies y is also constant; in equilibrium the economy's total output Y (the numerator of y) and effective labor N (the denominator of y) are growing at rate the same rate.

Per-capita consumption, which will be represented here by Φ, is determined by dividing total consumption by the stock of labor, $\Phi \equiv \frac{C}{L}$. To calculate the growth rate of per-capita consumption over time, note that

$$\ln(\Phi) = \ln(C) - \ln(L)$$

Differentiating with respect to time gives

$$\dot{\Phi}/\Phi = \dot{C}/C - \dot{L}/L$$

As has already been established, in equilibrium

$$\dot{C}\Big/C = n = z + \alpha$$

Then, since $\dot{L}\Big/L = z$,

$$\dot{\Phi}/\Phi = \alpha$$

Thus, in equilibrium the growth in per-capita consumption, that is to say the improvement in the "standard of living," is due to growth in labor's productivity—a reasonable and intuitively appealing conclusion is it not? Similarly, output per capita, which here will be represented by the symbol η, is growing at the rate of increase in labor productivity, as shown below. Begin with the per capita output, $\eta = Y/L$. Taking the natural logarithm gives

$$\ln(\eta) = \ln(Y) - \ln(L)$$

Differentiating with respect to time yields the following:

$$\frac{\dot{\eta}}{\eta} = \frac{\dot{Y}}{Y} - \frac{\dot{L}}{L} = n - z = \alpha$$

Then, to summarize, over time the economy tends towards a steady-state equilibrium where per-capita consumption and per-capita output are both growing at the rate of labor productivity growth, α.

The Optimal Capital-Labor Ratio for Long-Term Sustainable Consumption

One of the primary purposes of my presenting this particular paper is to bolster my argument that the island's economy has saved too little. Through the banks' and lending agents' misdirecting of individuals' cherished savings into current consumption, rather than into capital accumulation, the standard of living is lower through time than it could be. To see this in the context of the model requires a little more math along with some further graphical presentation.

By now the astute reader may have realized that the equilibrium capital-intensity ratio k^e is a function of the saving rate (s), which up until now has been assumed to be exogenously determined. Is there instead a preferred value of s? And, if there is an optimal

245

saving rate, how would an economy necessarily get there? To
address that issue, consider Figure 2 shown below:

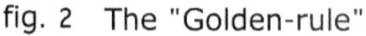

fig. 2   The "Golden-rule"

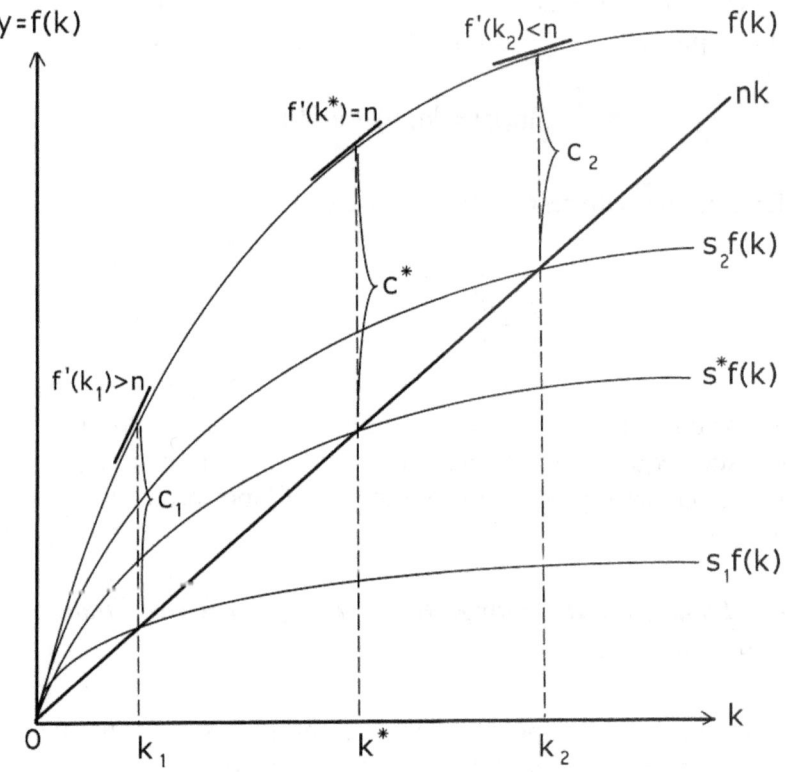

The intuition of Figure 2 describes what has been referred to in the
Solow growth model literature as the "golden-rule capital
intensity." The search for the golden-rule capital intensity is
simply the quest to determine the amount of capital per (effective)
worker that will maximize per-capita consumption. As has been
discussed throughout this appendix, saving facilitates the
accumulation of more tools per worker. But saving for the future
always involves a current opportunity cost—it means less
consumption now. How do we find the optimal saving rate? Of

course, most of us would like to find a saving level that provides us with a maximum consumption stream over time—which is the golden-rule capital intensity of the Solow model.

Refer to Figure 2, and note that the level of output per unit of effective labor is shown by the highest curve, which is the function $f(k)$. When capital per worker is nonexistent, $k=0$, and output is also zero as indicated by the function's initial value shown at the origin in the figure. If we start from this rather miserable circumstance, the addition of a small amount of capital leads to an enormous gain in per-worker production. This is reflected in Figure 2 by the steep slope of the $f(k)$ function occurring when the capital-labor ratio is small. More formally, the derivative $f'(k)$ is extremely large at low values of k. As k increases, the slope of the $f(k)$ function begins to decrease as a result of the law of diminishing returns.

Continuing to examine Figure 2, observe that the amount of saving per worker $sf(k)$ depends on the saving rate s. The saving per worker in the graph is sketched for three different savings rates: a very low rate s_1, a high rate s_2, and an intermediate rate s^*. Associated with each savings rate there is a unique stable capital-labor ratio, depicted as k_1, k_2, and k^* respectively.

Consumption per worker is determined by the difference between output and saving, which in the graph is the vertical distance $f(k)$ - $sf(k)$ and is shown for each of the three different savings rates. Note that when the saving rate is low, for example saving rate s_1, the economy is essentially saving and investing too little of its output with the result that sustainable consumption per unit of effective labor is less at the equilibrium than it could be. That is, the consumption per worker, shown in the graph by the vertical distance c_1, could be greater if the capital-labor ratio is increased towards k^*. When the savings rate is high, such as shown by the saving rate s_2 in the graph, then the economy is over-investing in capital. And, the result is that sustainable consumption per unit of effective labor is not as great as it could be (shown by the vertical distance c_2 in Figure 2). In the real world, this second result could probably only happen in some sort of weird command economy which invests too much under the decree of a totalitarian government that is obsessed with capital accumulation.

So, what is the best capital-labor ratio for maximum long-term consumption? Again referring to the figure, the vertical distance between output per unit of effective labor (y) and savings per unit of effective labor, $sf(k)$, is maximized where the slope of the production function, $f'(k)$ is just equal to the rate of growth of effective labor, n. To see this mathematically, start with output per effective worker, which is $f(k)$. Then, subtract saving, $sf(k)$, to arrive at consumption per effective worker, resulting in the equation shown below:

$$c = f(k) - sf(k)$$

When the economy is in an equilibrium steady-state, the saving per effective worker satisfies the condition $sf(k)=nk$. Substituting this into the above equation gives an alternative expression for consumption per effective worker for an economy in equilibrium,

$$c = f(k) - nk$$

What capital-labor ratio maximizes c? The maximum occurs when the derivative dc/dk is zero. Differentiation of c with respect to k and then setting the derivative equal to zero gives the following:

$$dc/dk = f'(k) - n = 0$$

Thus, the capital-labor ratio that maximizes consumption per effective worker (and therefore also maximizes per-capita consumption) occurs when the marginal product of capital is equal to the growth rate of effective labor.

Of course individuals or individual households and businesses in a real-world economy can hardly be expected to know and apply the Solow growth model and its graphs to their individual saving and consumption decisions—much less to apply calculus in order to find the optimal saving rate. However, it is not hard to suppose that in a simple and transparent economy, individual actors would tend to gravitate to the savings rate that they would reasonably expect to maximize their sustainable level of consumption—perhaps another sort of "invisible hand" associated with self-interest maximizing behavior. An economy would reach this savings rate not because people understand the neoclassical growth model and its assumptions and implications, but rather through simple optimizing behavior of economic agents seeking their highest possible sustainable consumption growth path. Moreover, if people tend to behave like this on average within the aggregate, it is not unreasonable to believe that the end result of such individual maximizing behavior could be the achievement of the economic equilibrium that results in something equal or very close to the golden-rule capital intensity—that is an economic equilibrium where the real marginal product of capital (or the real rate of return to capital) is, on average, just about equivalent to the rate of growth of the labor force plus labor productivity growth (which is the growth rate of real output).

Now let's step away from all the equations and graphs momentarily to apply the intuition we have derived from the Solow model to some empirical real world numbers from our own economy. This part of our argument is, of course, a conjecture, but it is still strong food for thought. In the case of our Island Confederation economy (with which you are all familiar) it happens that the annual growth rate of the effective labor force, n, has historically averaged in the range of 3 percent to 4 percent, which results from the combination of 1 to 2 percent population growth (z) plus 2 percent productivity growth (α). This has also been the approximate average rate of real output growth; together the combination of population growth and productivity growth have resulted in a 3 to 4 percent average rate of growth in our island's real GDP. These numbers are well known historical facts, and are not derived from the Solow model. But, it is useful to think of these real-world numbers in the context of intuition derived from the Solow framework. If our economy was at the golden-rule capital-labor ratio the real return to capital would be about the same; it should also be about 3.5 percent. Of course, our island economy is characterized by a fiat currency and thus we have experienced a long-term average inflation rate of roughly 3 percent. So, if our economy was at the golden-rule capital-labor ratio you should expect to obtain a nominal long-term market return to the ownership of capital, or an annual average return to a diversified portfolio of stocks, somewhere in the range of 6.5 percent. A nominal rate of return of 6.5 percent is the combination of a real return of 3.5 percent (consistent with the golden-rule path) and an inflation premium of 3.0 percent.

However, as you well know, the nominal long-term historical annual average rate of return to equity ownership in our economy is in fact close to 10 percent, not the 6.5 percent that we would expect as the optimal golden-rule rate of return. This suggests that we are operating at an actual capital intensity that is well *below* the one that would maximize our long-term prosperity and economic welfare. In the language of the Solow model, and referring again to Figure 2 above, we are at an equilibrium capital-labor ratio such as $k_1 (< k^*)$. For our island economy, the historical nominal return to capital has been 10 percent, implying capital's real rate of return has, in fact, been a lofty 7 percent—well in excess of the 3.5 percent that is the consumption maximizing long-term rate of return. This high rate of return to capital suggests our workers are short on machinery; we could benefit greatly from more saving, investment, and capital accumulation.

The reader might believe that I am caught in a contradiction here; it appears that I am saying the island's savings rate is less than adequate to achieve the prosperity-maximizing capital intensity, while previously I have argued that there is a good reason to believe that individual decisions makers could be reasonably expected to save at the rate that will maximize their sustainable level of consumption. What is the cause of this apparent contradiction?

Returning to the arguments I have made to the Economics Club and elsewhere on the under-allocation to investment and capital, consider the following explanation. Suppose we have intermediaries or agents in the credit or loan market who behave as if they overestimate the supply of loanable funds actually available because of the illusion of a fiat money backed, fractional-reserve banking system. Suppose further that these agents are compensated, as they typically are, based upon the volume of loans they originate rather than upon the quality of these loans. It is then easy to suspect that a sizable portion of scarce savings would be steered inefficiently to ne'er-do-well consumers and loan agents rather than to the best and highest investment use of capital accumulation (proper steering of funds would increase k toward k^*). Thus, I believe underinvestment is due to the endemic sub-optimality of the money, lending and banking institutions that we find ourselves saddled with—rather than irrational or inefficient behavior on the part of individuals. As I've stated previously, the net effect of such efficiency-draining intermediaries and agents (bankers) is to effectively cause a less than optimal aggregate saving rate ($s < s^*$), too low of capital intensity ($k < k^*$), and therefore high real returns to the all-too-scarce capital ($f'(k)>n$). This, then, is the central tragedy of our money, credit and banking system, and why it needs to be replaced with a simpler more transparent exchange good alternative. The market fails to drive us to an optimal capital-intensity not because it is irrational or inefficient, but rather because of an inherently flawed institutional money and banking system that has ironically been made permanent through government and central bank regulation, control, and oversight. Worse, this argument is compounded if you happen to believe that a significant portion of our scarce pool of savings is taxed away or borrowed by the government rather than being allocated to its best and highest use, which is capital formation.

Common Criticisms of the Solow Model

I realize that those who find it insufferable to attempt to draw such conclusions from a framework as simple in its assumptions as the Solow neoclassical growth model are now squirming in frustration in their chairs, so in this section of my paper I will discuss some of the major criticisms that have been directed at the Solow model.

As a first criticism, it is based on a heroic level of aggregation— the model assumes just two inputs into production and one type of output. In fact, a real world economy consists of many types of capital, labor, and other inputs into the production function and many different types of output as well. However, I have found that attempts at extension of the Solow model to more complexity through disaggregation appear to result in considerably more complexity, but not necessarily to more meaningful or different conclusions. Indeed, too much added complexity makes it impossible to draw useful conclusions from any model. It is the nature of economic analysis to abstract from overwhelming real-world detail and complexity in order to focus on those variables and results most relevant to obtaining a clear understanding.

Secondly, the model is based on an implicit assumption of perfect foresight—that is, there is no explicit consideration of uncertainty or risk. This can be joined together with the first point on aggregation. Disaggregating into many products and outputs, and many trades broken up over time and space may make the Solow model richer and, in fact, would lead to the uncertainty that would make a monetary good tend to arise. Moreover, real world shocks that we are familiar with such as weather, disease, war, etc. could make us survey the future from a world considerably more complex and uncertain than that assumed in the Solow model, but it doesn't change the fundamental intuition of the model nor provide a convincing argument that individuals should not (or would not) follow a path that maximizes their sustainable individual consumption. The only plausible counter case would be an "eat all your corn immediately" one, in which we were certain of a near-term, world-ending event. Some would suggest that the

252

difference between the 6.5 percent "golden-rule" return to capital and the real world historical 10 percent average simply reflects the risk-premium required to own risky capital with the observed volatile valuation in capital prices. This argument appears to have some validity, but we would hasten to indict our money, banking, and credit system for capital's apparently volatile value. When the value of a tractor fluctuates wildly, we would ask: Is this uncertainty or volatility in the value of a tractor based upon uncertainty in the value of the real output it can produce, or is this volatility in the value of the tractor due to uncertainty in the value of the fiat money, inflation, and the market rate of interest in which the value of the tractor's production is to be measured? The value of the tractor in what it can do or produce is pretty concrete. The problem is uncertainty in the measuring stick, fiat money. Put another way, if, as I and others propose, we made an index of capital, K, the numeraire or monetary good through which the value of consumption goods or services were determined, wouldn't much of the uncertainly or volatility of the capital market subsequently disappear?

The third criticism of the Solow model is the absence of any need for money. In a single-sector Solow growth model, there is no logical reason for a monetary good—in an economy with only one composite good there is no need for money to relate prices across items. As was discussed above, the introduction of a fiat money into the model results in the possibility of inflation, and a divergence between the nominal interest rate and the real interest rate. Obviously, at the heart of economists' past attempts at introducing money into the Solow model has been the goal of making a very simple model more closely resemble the real world. I believe this effort has been wrong-headed. The question that should instead be posed is: How can the real world and its institutions be made simpler and more transparent so that it more closely resembles the neoclassical model? The money, credit and banking institutions that have arisen appear to be more an accident of history and greed, facilitated and made permanent by the regulation and oversight of regulators and governments—rather than being optimal for individuals who wish to produce, trade, consume and save/invest as efficiently as possible. Clearly the real world is characterized by many inputs and many types of output, and the separation of a multitude individual consumption and production decisions makes the need for an exchange and valuation good obvious. It is a misfortune and a tragedy of history that this has led to the current millstone of a fiat money, a central bank, and a fractional-reserve banking system as well as an intermediated credit and investment market.

The result has been well-demonstrated with historic cycles of instability and financial market over-valuation and collapse. We are caught in a repetitive loop of misplaced euphoria and crash—a manic-depressive world. Why would or should we expect anything else from such a complex, convoluted system? The sad thing is that the call for correction has always been in the direction of yet more complexity, regulation and oversight, rather than in the direction of more transparency, logic, and simplicity. Again I ask, why not make a fiat currency and the central bank irrelevant, why not do the same with the bricks and mortar fractional-reserve banking system, why not start trading and valuing goods in the obvious alternative of shares of a broad index in capital? Why not stop worrying about the volume of money when we now have a technologically advanced system that allows for instantaneous funds transfer? Why not return more closely to the simple intuition and transparency of the neoclassical growth model? Accomplish this not by mandate or regulation—there has been too much of that already, but by competition—by simply practicing trade and valuation in the new capital-index based monetary good. Let a superior alternative evolve and win.

A final criticism of the original Solow model is that it assumes no government. This is a criticism?

Entering Money into the Solow Model

Money creeps in everywhere. The careful reader of our golden-rule commentary above, as it relates to our island economy, will have noted that we began the discussion of inflation and the difference between the nominal and the real return to capital. Any such discussion makes an implicit nod to the existence of money—particularly fiat money. The remainder of this paper explicitly introduces a fiat money into the simple neoclassical model. The reason to add money to the framework is because the simplicity of the model makes some important money and growth conclusions and properties crystal clear. Nonetheless, the careful reader will be troubled by the fact that there is little reason for money to be needed for exchange in an economy with only one good and an assumption of perfect certainty. I concur. In fact, we all may be forgiven for believing that a fiat money in the context of the Solow model may be almost as contrived and senseless as it is in our current economy. But I digress. First, I ask the reader to be patient and to journey with me a little further for enhanced understanding, before we reach the conclusion that fiat money has passed the point of its usefulness in our current technologically advanced economy and should be discarded.

A way to start this process is to follow Solow in examining the theoretical relationship between the interest rate, the marginal product of capital, and the real rate of return to capital. Of course, prices in an economy with a fiat currency, such as our island's silver certificates (not really backed by silver, of course), are expressed in terms of the fiat currency, otherwise it makes no sense to talk of them or of inflation. Measured in terms of Confederation silver certificates, the price of one unit of real output is a function of time, expressed here by $p(t)$. Likewise, the money wage rate is a function of time, denoted by $w(t)$. Also, for a producer to rent a unit of capital stock it is necessary to pay a rental rate, represented by $q(t)$.

In a competitive economy the real wage rate and the real rental rate on capital will be equal to labor' and capital's marginal products respectively:

$$\frac{\partial F}{\partial N} = \frac{w}{p}$$

255

$$\frac{\partial F}{\partial K} = f'(k) = \frac{q}{p}$$

Following Solow's original presentation, to see the relationship between $f'(k)$ and the nominal interest rate consider an individual who owns exactly one unit of the fiat money, which is a silver certificate. If he loans out the silver certificate at a nominal interest rate $i(t)$ for some time Δt he will earn $i(t) \cdot \Delta t$ in interest and at the end of the period he will have his certificate plus interest, $1 + i(t) \cdot \Delta t$.

Recall again that in Solow's model the type of output being produced and the capital good used in the production of that output are one and the same—there is only one "composite" commodity in Solow's world. Thus, rather than extending a loan, the owner of one silver certificate has another option: he can purchase $1/p$ units of output which then can be rented out for price q over some time period (Δt). At the conclusion of the rental period the owner of the capital can sell his $1/p$ units for the end-of-period price $p(t + \Delta t)$. Measured in terms of silver certificates, the end-of-period wealth from this course of action will be the sum of the rental income, $\left(\frac{q}{p}\right) \cdot (\Delta t)$, and the proceeds derived from selling the one unit of capital, $(1/p(t)) \cdot p(t + \Delta t)$.

In equilibrium the operation of efficient markets should result in the outcome from the two courses of action being equated:

$$1 + i(t) \cdot \Delta t = \left(\frac{q(t)}{p(t)}\right) \cdot \Delta t + \left(\frac{1}{p(t)}\right) \cdot (p(t + \Delta t))$$

Subtracting 1 from both sides of the above equation, dividing both sides by Δt, and doing a bit of rearranging gives

$$i(t) = \left(\frac{q(t)}{p(t)} \right) + \left(\frac{p(t + \Delta t) - p(t)}{\Delta t} \right) \left(\frac{1}{p(t)} \right)$$

Then, take the limit as $\Delta t \to 0$ to obtain the following:

$$i(t) = \frac{q(t)}{p(t)} + \frac{\dot{p}(t)}{p(t)}$$

If prices are constant (so $\dot{p} = 0$), the real rental rate of capital $(q(t)/p(t))$ is equal to capital's marginal product $f'(k)$, which also equals the nominal (or real) interest rate. However, in general there is not a constant price level in a fiat money economy. When there is inflation it is the case that capital's real rental rate (and also the marginal product of capital) will be equal to the difference between the nominal or market interest rate $i(t)$ and the rate of inflation $\dot{p}/p$. That is, the real interest rate will also be identical to the real marginal product of capital. Of course assuming a "money" in the Solow model begs an explanation of how it comes to be there and what possible purpose it might serve. That is, Solow's demonstration implicitly assumes the existence of a fiat money and thereby a possible non-zero inflation rate that is not otherwise motivated in the model. Why, we could ask, would there even be a price level or inflation in a world that did not include or assume the existence of money? These are not trivial questions to brush over in a very simple model of perfect foresight. They are the reason we will carefully consider the implications of a fiat money in the context of the Solow model. Again, not because we believe money necessarily belongs there, but in order to obtain increased understanding of fiat money equilibrium conditions and dynamics in a growth model. Once again, the careful reader will note a contradiction, since an inherent requirement for the evolution and use of a monetary good in storing value and facilitating exchange is uncertainty.

Money Financing of Government Expenditure

In order to support my position that the standard of living among the island's citizens has been hampered by inadequate capital accumulation it was necessary to introduce a fiat currency and inflation into the discussion. In a more perfect world, where the economy's capital stock itself serves as money, of course there could be no inflation. There would most certainly be changes in the relative prices of items, but there could be no change in an overall, expenditure-weighted price index. The term "inflation" cannot even enter the discussion unless there is a price level of output in terms of a monetary good—a fiat money. By explicitly introducing fiat money into our analysis, I open a door to a discussion of inflation, and inevitably to a discussion of governmental attempts at wealth expropriation through the printing of new money.

In writing this mathematical paper, I initially wanted to avoid this excursion into the existing neoclassical money and growth literature. I thought it was unnecessary—a distraction. Now, upon careful reflection, I think that this side trip will prove a blessing— so illuminating that it may provide perhaps the best and simplest insight on why an economy, in particular the Confederation economy, is currently ready to move away from fiat money and toward a broad index of real capital as its logical unit of valuation and exchange. Capital-based money is the endgame, providing the most transparent and most logical monetary good.

We all know the old, familiar story as to why an economy finds a monetary good to be a valuable and useful tool for organizing exchange. Complex trades can be broken up into simpler ones, the number of possible exchanges is reduced and also simplified, and we get used to a common metric for valuation as well as a readily acceptable universal trading good. We go so far as to allow the central bank (or the government) the exclusive privilege of providing a fiat currency in order that we might more readily trade one with another (or perhaps it is the government who has recognized it can extract a rent from this exclusive privilege and seized it). We hope they will be rational in exercising their exclusive franchise to print our currency and in return we even allow them to pursue and prosecute monetary counterfeiters in our midst (without realizing that the government or central bank is, in fact, the greatest counterfeiter of all).

However, in the back of our minds where instinct and common sense abide, we are very uneasy with this exclusive charter or agreement. We actually would sleep easier at night if we knew our fiat money had some real value based in something other than our faith or trust that the central bank or the government will not abuse its supply—a trust that instinct and past experience tells us should be very thin indeed. Truth be told, most of us would probably prefer a monetary or exchange good that had a basis in real value of its own—as a scarce commodity or a good with an established real value in production or consumption. At the heart of our uneasiness with a fiat money is instinct, whether we are trained economists or not, that the printers of such a fiat currency can and will be sorely tempted to steal real output from us if we are not watchful. We know that counterfeiters can steal from us, and we are correctly unclear as to what precisely the real difference is that distinguishes them from a government-sanctioned central bank. In fact, our fears are well-placed; stealing real output is exactly what governments and central banks do and exactly why monopoly over the fiat money printing press is so valuable to them and so jealously protected. We have, of course, explored this topic at length in previous papers and Economics Club discussions and, so far, I am telling you nothing new here. What is important to realize is that a fiat money and inflation do not enter an economy by accident or fate. It is rather a matter of institutional evolution and design—and perhaps, at rock-bottom an additional attempt to covertly raise government revenue.

Inflation can be viewed either as a pervasive rate of increase in the prices of most goods and services or, equivalently, a pervasive rate of decrease in the purchasing power of a unit of money. From either vantage point, a sustained positive rate of inflation simply means that the central bank (with apologies to Roberta's dad) is printing its fiat currency faster than the rate of growth of the economy. In what follows, you will see that when we introduce money into an economy that inflation is, in fact, a tax rate which is imposed upon the private sector of an economy as a cost that comes from holding and trading with the government's fiat money. The higher is inflation, the higher is that tax rate. However, as you shall see in the neoclassical growth model with the addition of money, even if the inflation rate is zero, the printers and purveyors of the currency will still be enjoying a stream of real output for their efforts.

Without further delay, let's get into the revised neoclassical model (which broadly follows the history of the neoclassical money and growth models—see, for example, Stein, 1971) by introducing a government budget constraint and then using the historic rationalizations for holding and using a monetary good (although I repeat my warning that, by doing so, they will contradict the assumptions of the neoclassical model—which with perfect foresight and only a single output would seem to have no need of a "money").[4] Begin with the government budget constraint that would exist if printing money was the only way that the government had to raise funds for its own expenditure. This is such a simple government budget constraint that it employs only printing money as the source of government revenue, excluding the issuance of government debt and taxes as other possible funding sources.

Of course, debt can be readily ignored in the case of a government which issues debt that is promptly purchased by the central bank, as is typically the case in our Island Confederation. When the government issues debt to the central bank, and the central bank purchases the debt by new money creation, then it is effectively the same case as if the government printed the money to directly finance government spending itself.

---

[4] See Jerome Stein, *Money and Capacity Growth,* Columbia University Press, 1971.

Government spending financed entirely through new money creation gives the following budget constraint:

(7-17)
$$G = \dot{M}$$

where G represents the rate of government expenditure in terms of units of fiat currency, and the derivative $\dot{M} \equiv dM/dt$ is the rate of increase in newly printed units of fiat currency.

Equation (7-17) captures the return to legalized counterfeiting in currency units which may be used by the appropriate authorities for any means of expenditure—for example, they may directly fund Roberta's dad's famous turtle-soup dinners (apologies, again, Roberta). Since we are operating in a neoclassical model with money added through equation (7-17), let us convert all our currency units into units of real output per unit of effective labor. That is, divide the money supply M by the average price of a unit of output P to obtain the "real" money supply. Then, divide again by the size of the effective labor force N to obtain the real money supply per unit of effective labor, which we will define as m. Thus,

(7-18)
$$m \equiv M/PN$$

Now, with a bit of algebra the government budget constraint can be written as,

(7-19)
$$G/PN \equiv g = (\dot{M}/M)(M/PN)$$

where "g" is government expenditure in real output per unit of effective labor.

Equation (7-19) can be further simplified to

(7-20)
$$g = \theta \cdot m$$

261

where θ is the rate of growth of the money supply (that is $\theta = \dot{M}/M$).

Beginning with the definition of real money balances $(m=M/(PN))$, one can take the natural logarithm to obtain

(7-21) $$\ln m = \ln M - \ln N - \ln P$$

As each variable in equation (7-21) is a function of time, the equation can be differentiated with respect to "t" to obtain the following

(7-22) $$\frac{\dot{m}}{m} = \frac{\dot{M}}{M} - \frac{\dot{N}}{N} - \frac{\dot{P}}{P}$$

or

(7-23) $$\frac{\dot{m}}{m} = \theta - n - \pi$$

where $\pi \equiv \dfrac{\dot{P}}{P}$, which is the rate of inflation when prices are measured in terms of the fiat currency.

When the right-hand-side of equation (7-23) is equal to zero the stock of real money balances per unit of effective labor is constant, or $\dot{m} = 0$. Note that this yields a very logical condition consistent with the famous quantity equation (with which every economist is familiar). When the real money supply per unit of effective labor is constant the rate of inflation is equal to the difference between the growth rate in the money supply and the rate of growth in real output,

(7-24) $$\pi = \theta - n$$

262

There is now a money market inserted into the neoclassical model, and in order to have an equilibrium it must be the case that the supply of money balances per unit of effective labor is just equal to the demand per unit of money balances per unit of effective labor, or,

(7-25) $$m = l(?)$$

where,

l = demand for real money balances per unit of effective labor.

For the time being we have inserted a question mark in parenthesis, rather than indicating the variables that money demand might be dependent upon. The topic of what variables should be inserted in the parenthesis—that is, what variables determine money demand—will be taken up below.

In economics there is a simple idea, known as Say's principle, which asserts if there is excess demand in one market there must be excess supply in another. Similarly, Say's principle asserts that, in an economy with two markets, when one market is in equilibrium so is the other market. There is no reason to suppose the output market is in disequilibrium in the Solow model since the price P can be assumed to immediately adjust to restore equilibrium. Thus, by Say's principle, it must be true that the price adjustment will also restore equilibrium in the money market, which is the condition that $m=l$ shown in equation (7-25).

Now, let us return to what the arguments should be in the money demand function $l(?)$ shown above. We can briefly follow the somewhat peculiar literature of the neoclassical money and growth model in rationalizing possible arguments of the demand for real money balances per unit of effective labor.

Let us begin by considering the equilibrium condition in the money market, $m=l$. Further, let us follow the literature by supposing that the demand for real money balances per unit of effective labor increases with the level of real output per unit of effective labor, y. This, at first, appears a reasonable assumption as it is likely that as real output increases then the demand for trades or transactions would also increase, so people would want to hold more money. Thus, demand for money can be written as $l=l(y,?)$, and the partial derivative of money demand is positive, $\frac{\partial l}{\partial y} > 0$. However, in the Solow framework real output is a function of the capital-labor ratio, written as $y=f(k)$. Thus, money demand ultimately depends on k,

$$(7\text{-}26) \qquad\qquad l = l(f(k),?)$$

Are there any other arguments that should enter into the money demand function shown in equation (7-26) above? In perusing the literature we find that the other traditional argument in the money demand function is θ, which is the rate of growth of the fiat money supply (or alternatively, a measure of the tax rate of inflation). The logic is as follows: as θ (which is $\dot{M}/M$) increases, so does the equilibrium rate of inflation from equation (7-24) and so does the government's intended inflation tax in the real government budget constraint, equation (7-20) above. However, as the government raises the intended inflation tax rate, the typical holder of real money balances rationally responds by reducing their demand for real money balances (or increasing their demand for real output) so l drops. The price level of output instantly rises to equate supply and demand in the money market (and/or the output market), thereby reducing the real money supply $m=M/PN$. Thus, for stability in the model,

$$(7\text{-}27) \qquad\qquad m = l(f(k),\theta) \equiv l(k,\theta)$$

where $l(\theta,k)$ is the money demand function whose partial derivatives have the sign $\partial l/\partial k > 0$ and $\partial l/\partial \theta < 0$.

The astute reader who has some familiarity with macroeconomic models will note that θ, at equilibrium, has already become a proxy for the nominal rate of interest, i, in the money demand function with the expected sign on the partial derivative (more on that below).

Where else does money appear within the neoclassical money and growth model? We are going to follow the extant literature, which, as we have mentioned, is somewhat controversial in rationalizing how a fiat money comes to be relevant in the Solow neoclassical growth world. Later, we are going to more carefully examine how money's relevance has been affected by new technologies that eliminate any constraints on money velocity. But, for now, let us follow the traditional arguments as to why money might matter. First, go back to the traditional story that economists use to motivate why money is important—that is it simplifies trading, greatly reduces the number of trading posts required, and allows exchanges to be broken up from complex ones to simple ones in space and time. Money also allows a standard unit of exchange and valuation and allows for the storage of value over time (although if the inflation tax becomes excessive, some may wish to debate this last attribute). If all this is true, the argument goes, then by simplifying trade and making it more efficient, real money balances (per unit of effective labor) belong in the production function. That is,

(7-28) $$y = h(k, m)$$

and both k and m increase output (so the partial derivatives $\partial h / \partial k$ and $\partial h / \partial m$ are both positive in sign).

Further, the argument goes, if real money balances belong in the production function, because they enhance production, then real money balances—representing real output—have a real contribution to aggregate wealth (perhaps representing the capitalized value of their marginal products within the output production function). If real money balances constitute a positive part of aggregate real wealth, then they also belong as an argument

265

in real consumption. That is, since $c = (1-s) \cdot y = (1-s) \cdot h(k,m)$, we can recognize consumption's functional dependency on k and m and write

(7-29)
$$c = c(k,m)$$

where $c(k,m)$ is real consumption per unit of effective labor and increases in either k or m tend to increase c.

One final step completes the development of a traditional money and growth model (and would allow us to play hypothetical monetary policy games, if we wished). We note that equilibrium in the money market requires that the price level adjusts to equate supply and demand in the money market ($m=l$) as well as in the output market. Therefore, the money demand function, l, can be substituted for m in equations (7-28) and (7-29), above and they can be simplified to,

(7-30)
$$y = h(k, l(k, \theta)) = h(\underset{+}{k}, \underset{-}{\theta})$$

And

(7-31)
$$c = c(k, l(k, \theta)) = c(\underset{+}{k}, \underset{-}{\theta})$$

where the $+$ and $-$ signs under a variable indicate the derivatives with respect to each variable are positive and negative respectively.

The intuitive argument for the partial derivative of the rate of growth of the fiat money being negative in production and consumption is fairly simple. If the government or central bank was to raise θ in an attempt to impose a higher inflation tax on individuals, then the demand for real money balances per unit of effective labor would fall, the price level of output would rise to equate money demand with money supply, and therefore m would decline. As m declines both y and c would fall.

Now we have completed the expansion of the Solow model to include a simple government budget constraint (equation (7-20)), a

266

money market equilibrium (equation (7-27)), and described the way in which the monetary policy variable θ can possibly affect real production and consumption per unit of effective labor (equations (7-30) and (7-31)). We have also demonstrated the direct and intuitively appealing relationship between an economy's rate of fiat money growth, its output growth and the rate of inflation. My presentation followed along the lines of previous literature which was concerned with money's relevance to an economy's real activity. I must confess that, for reasons that I will develop below, I am not a believer in the relevance of changes in the growth rate of a fiat money to the long-term real level of economic activity. I believe that in our current economy, central bank monetary growth rate policy is largely neutral in the long run. (That theoretical conclusion is of course distinct from my argument that our cumbersome, embedded institutional monetary structure, itself, imposes a long-term efficiency cost upon our economy and its optimal use of resources and saving). I apologize in advance to the diligent reader who has carefully and painstakingly followed this exposition so far, because my ultimate purpose in exploring a fiat money in a very simple growth framework is not to bolster fiat money's relevance to the real economy, but rather in understanding it to ultimately doubt it and discard it.

Let us back up and summarize what we now have. We have followed the traditional neoclassical money and growth literature by injecting one more good, money, into the simple Solow growth model. Since, the simple Solow model has only one good, output, which may be either consumed or invested and assumes no explicit uncertainty, motivating the value of money to simplify exchange and valuation is strained. Nonetheless the Solow model with money has some appealing properties at equilibrium. First, by definition an equilibrium occurs when real money balances and capital per unit of effective labor are constant over time, or $\dot{m} = 0$ and $\dot{k} = 0$. Constant real money balances, in turn, requires that the equilibrium rate of inflation be equal to the rate of money growth minus the rate of growth of effective labor (which is also the equilibrium rate of growth of real output). This is a logical and intuitively appealing result, consistent with the lesson we first learned as macroeconomists that inflation is caused by "too much money chasing too few goods." Further, in the Solow model, without money, we obtained the result that the marginal product of capital is $f'(k)$ and it is the reasonable real required return for lending a piece of output (or capital) to another individual for future use for one period. Moreover, as we have shown above, if there is money in the economy and a market-determined nominal interest rate (i) and real interest rate (r) at which money balances are lent out over a period into the future, it must be the case that

$$f'(k) = r = i - \pi$$

Recall previously in our exposition of the Solow model that the equilibrium capital-intensity at which consumption per unit of effective labor could be maximized was called the "golden-rule" capital intensity. The logic by which a rational economy with foresight and transparency should converge to a "golden-rule capital-intensity" equilibrium is compelling. Since the equilibrium rate of growth of the economy is n, this is what a rational individual would reasonably expect to obtain as the reward for foregoing consumption for one period; that is for giving up (lending) 1 unit of output for one period they would reasonably expect to obtain ($1+n$) units of output at the end of the period. But, if k is less than the golden-rule capital-intensity, what actually happens is a person can lend 1 unit of output for a one-period return of ($1+f'(k)$) where,

$$(1 + f'(k)) > (1 + n)$$

Of course, at the margin, rational individuals will be lenders or investors whenever this condition obtains since they are receiving more compensation than they would normally expect for deferred consumption. Moreover, rational borrowers can only pay the rental rate of $f'(k)$ by promptly investing any output lent to them in creating a capital good. This natural process of preferring investment over consumption at the margin will continue, thereby raising the capital intensity and reducing the real marginal product of capital until

$$(1 + f'(k)) = (1 + n)$$

or

$$f'(k) = n$$

and the "golden-rule" equilibrium capital-intensity is thus achieved.

An opposite argument can be applied if it happens that the capital intensity k is greater than the "golden-rule capital-intensity." If k is greater than the golden-rule value it implies one unit of output can be lent for a return of $1 + f'(k)$ and

$$1 + f'(k) < 1 + n$$

Therefore, at the margin rational individuals would choose not to lend or invest because they would be realizing a return that was less than what should reasonably be expected as the reward for deferring consumption for one period in an economy with an equilibrium growth rate of n. In this case, the natural process of preferring consumption over investment at the margin would continue, causing k to decline and $f'(k)$ to rise until once again an equilibrium is reached where $f'(k) = n$.

Thus, a logical long-run rational equilibrium condition in a neoclassical model with money is

(7-32) $$f'(k) = n = i - \pi = r$$

And, more importantly, we can intuitively understand why plausible rational maximizing individual behavior will tend to drive us back to this condition whenever we deviate from it.

Further, at the equilibrium of the model all real variables are growing at the rate of growth of output—real output, real consumption, and real capital all are growing at rate n. Alternatively, in equilibrium the ratio of all of these variables to effective labor is constant.

Again, my ultimate purpose in this mathematical paper is to show that fiat money is irrelevant in a technologically advanced, exchange-efficient economy. In other words, I illustrated fiat money and its equilibrium properties in order to bury it, not to glorify it. In fact, I appreciate the patience of readers who have followed my review and definition of the model to this point—it can be a test of determination to lay out and consider the various assumptions and relationships of any mathematical description of the economy. However, at this point we are just about to reap the rewards of considering and critiquing the implications of a change in monetary policy in this framework.

Monetary Policy, Technology and Velocity, and the Neutrality of Money:
The Demise of Fiat Money

Kings, governments and central banks throughout history have limited the power of providing the medium of exchange and value, which is money, exclusively to themselves. First, through the crude mechanism of secretly debasing or diluting commodity currency and then through the more sophisticated technique of being the sole provider of a fiat currency ultimately backed by nothing except the faith and willingness of the public to use it—essentially legalized counterfeiting. How does the government actually extract revenue by printing money and what are the limits?

Recall the government budget constraint that was introduced into the money and growth model,

(7-33)
$$G = \dot{M}$$

This equation characterizes a government that finances its entire spending (G) with the printing of fresh, new currency, where the $\dot{M}$ represents the change in the money supply. To understand why I refer to the "stealing" of output, consider a government that covertly sneaks individuals into the marketplace to buy good and services with currency indistinguishable from that already in circulation—except that it is brand new, clean and crisp. Through the overall impact on the price level, the government purchases of goods and services mean the rest of us, who are not associated with the government, can afford to purchase less with our fiat currency. Thus, the money financing of government expenditures is precisely equivalent to a tax: government is able to buy more, and individuals in the private sector can only buy less. As we did above, it is useful to consider this equation in real terms or real terms per unit of effective labor to consider the burden of the inflation tax that the government or central bank extracts by printing money,

(7-34)
$$G/PN \equiv g = (\dot{M}/M)(M/PN) = \theta m$$

Now when the government gets greedy and decides to finance more government expenditure by printing money, equations (7-33) and (7-34) as well as our intuition would suggest that it is simply of matter of raising the rate at which it runs it printing presses. Alas for governments everywhere, it is not that simple. You have probably already surmised the answer. When the government raises the rate of growth of the money supply it also raises the equilibrium rate of inflation in the economy, since

$$\pi = \theta - n$$

As inflation increases, the opportunity cost of holding money balances increases and therefore rational individuals will seek to hold less of them over any given time and to accomplish their trades more efficiently and rapidly. Our current technology which allows rapid exchange and changes in custody of assets aids individuals in accomplishing this. Obviously, as velocity of money increases in the aggregate it is impossible to reduce the amount of nominal money in circulation. What will happen? As individuals collectively try to reduce their holdings of currency, the price level in the output market will rise, in addition to the sustained rate of inflation, thereby, reducing *real* money balances to a lower level that individuals in the aggregate desire to hold. This is best explained by the following graph (a sort of a money growth-rate "Laffer" curve) that is hopefully well understood by central banks and governments.

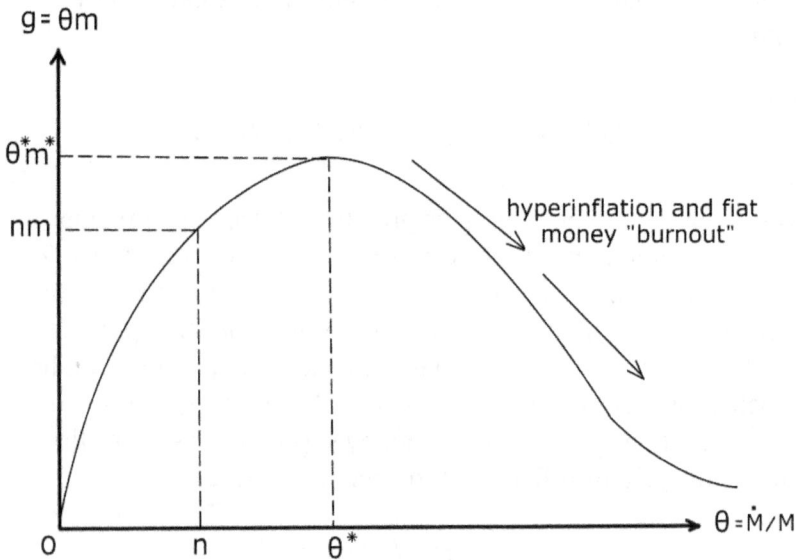

fig. 3   Inflation Tax Proceeds versus
Rate of Money Growth

Figure 3 represents a lot of simple and, I hope, appealing intuition. First, consider a central bank that is expanding the supply of fiat money at the same rate as the equilibrium growth rate of the economy, n. This is the stable price or zero target inflation rate solution advocated by responsible central bankers. As governments or central banks are tempted to accelerate fiat money growth above this—to "monetize" previously issued government debt, for example—they may meet with some success as the real proceeds of the inflation tax rise to a maximum level (that is, $\theta^* m^*$ in Figure 3). What is going on here is that as the rate of fiat money growth increases inflation increases, tending to raise the proceeds of the inflation tax, but, due to decreased demand on the part of the public for holding money, real money balances decrease somewhat—that is m^* is less than m in Figure 3. However, the decrease in real money balances is not quite large enough to offset the increase in revenue due to accelerating the printing presses—so the government actually enjoys an increase in the inflation tax it imposes on the public.

If the government or its central bank gets too greedy, however, and attempts to raise the proceeds from printing money by increasing money growth beyond θ^*, the decline in desired real money balances falls sharply enough that the government's total sustained real take from printing money at a faster rate actually falls. Desperate governments, that progressively ratchet the rate of fiat money growth (and inflation) in the hopes of supporting additional real expenditure in the short-run will proceed along the trajectory on the right of the curve toward hyper-inflation and eventual monetary "burn-out" (for example, Germany in the early 1920s). "Burn-out" is the term used because at a high enough rate of inflation and money growth, the public's demand for fiat currency logically falls to zero.

Now once, again, a pure mathematical understanding of the quantity representing the proceeds of the inflation tax θm suggests it is unclear whether or not θm goes to zero or infinity, or some other value, as the rate of fiat money growth, θ, accelerates without bound. It seems to be a race, θ increases without bound and m decreases toward zero as θ increases. Who wins the race in a mathematical sense? Do we need to apply L'Hopital's rule?

It is important to realize that descriptive math equations in an economic model are helpful in explaining and summarizing dynamic behavior. That is why we use them. However, they do not replace our economic intuition or common sense. A brief reflection upon economic behavior provides the answer. If any government or central bank increases the rate at which it prints fiat money without bound in order to increase its "take" from the private sector, it will not get very far. Long before θ becomes infinite, the individuals who comprise the economy will simply no longer accept fiat money for trades and will cease to employ it as a store of value for any period, no matter how short. In practical terms the "burnt out" fiat money will cease to be a "money," because the opportunity cost of using it has simply become too high. It is at this point where we can assert that θm, the proceeds of the inflation tax, will be zero. Recall that, in the same way, the mathematical equations alone do not tell us that a market equilibrium will necessarily be a golden-rule capital intensity. However, the neoclassical equations, taken with reasonable individual optimizing behavior, will achieve the equilibrium capital intensity that is consistent with maximizing sustained consumption. In short, a good mathematical economist uses mathematical modeling to augment and make succinct and clear the implications of economic intuition—not to replace economic intuition.

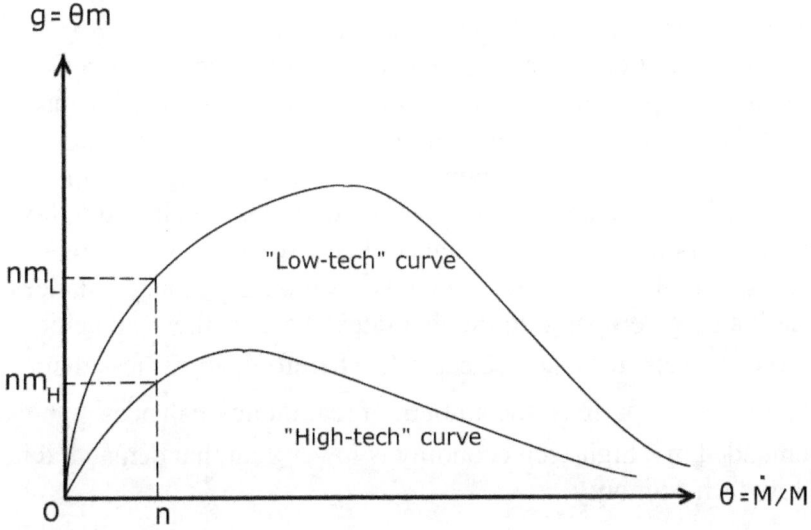

fig. 4   Inflation Tax Proceeds
Effect of Improved Exchange Technology

$g = \theta m$

nm_L

nm_H

"Low-tech" curve

"High-tech" curve

O n

$\theta = \dot{M}/M$

Figure 4, above, is my favorite and captures the gist of my argument as to why there is a limited future in fiat money and central bank fiat monetary policy. This figure represents what I believe to be the effect of ongoing technological improvements increasing the speed and efficiency of monetary transactions. Monetary exchange technology is allowing us to enter a world where the velocity of money becomes a truly notional or endogenous variable driven by the sum of individuals' desires and preferences. It is no longer some sort of physical constraint representing the speed with which an archaic bricks-and-mortar banking system can actually track and record ownership changes related to trades—instantaneous funds transfer and change in custody appears to be the current technological limit.

Consider the impact of this technological improvement in exchange efficiency upon the revenue curve from printing fiat money. Figure 4 shows two government revenue curves, one for a low-tech economy and another for a high-tech economy. Note that the intercept on the vertical axis—which is the level of real per-capita government spending that can be financed through printing money has shifted down, even when the government is increasing the money supply at the non-inflationary rate n. This is because individuals can get along with a lower level of real money balances to accommodate a given volume of required exchange, given enhanced exchange technology. They do not see an inflation tax imposed upon their money balances because broad prices are, on average, stable. What they do see is that holding money balances is still a drag compared to the real rates of return they can achieve on other assets, for instance capital. Therefore, m_H is less than m_L or, ceteris paribus, the amount of real money balances demanded in a high-tech economy is lower than that demanded in a low-tech economy.

Moreover, if the government or central bank becomes greedy in the more technologically advanced economy, the public collectively will tend to thwart it. As technology allows a given amount of money balances to accomplish more exchange without difficulty, individuals will have less patience with fiat money as a store of value over any time period, no matter how brief, and therefore will have less patience with any attempted inflation tax increase associated with the holding of it. As a result, their behavior and demand for money balances will tend to totally offset and neutralize attempts to change sustained real revenue proceeds from the inflation tax on the part of a government or central bank. What happens is that technology aids in the achievement of the "super-neutrality" of fiat money policy.

The tolerance of people for any increase in the opportunity cost of holding money balances is slim and becoming slimmer. Central banks have to be careful because the trigger point that could lead to a monetary "burn-out" or the point at which the public ceases to tolerate the cost of holding and using a fiat money at all is becoming increasingly more sensitive. Thus, the frequent lament of central banks that their monetary policy is becoming less effective and that their degrees of freedom in changing and imposing monetary policies are becoming more constrained.

When I say that technology is enabling the super-neutrality of monetary policy, what I mean is that, over the long-run, the rate of growth of fiat money which the central bank chooses will not affect the long-run capital intensity of the economy. It will not even significantly affect the level of real sustainable proceeds that the government can achieve from printing money. Since efficient and rapid exchange technology permits a wide variation in the stock of money or real money balances which may be used to accomplish a given volume of real exchange, it really is true that money's marginal product is approximately zero. Of course, this does not mean that having a single trading unit of exchange and valuation, a money, is not valuable in making production and trading more efficient in the overall economy. That is, the total value or product of a fiat money for trading and valuation may still be significant, but its product at the margin is not. Improving technology for the speed and efficiency of exchange implies that the ability of any single issuer of a fiat money to exploit the public by manipulating the speed of its printing presses has been sharply curtailed. The value of having an agreed upon monetary unit in enhancing production is not zero, although at the margin rapid increases in the stock of fiat currency add no real value.

The arguments I have just made about the emasculation of fiat money policy on the part of central banks is distinct from the issue of the inefficient and destabilizing banking system that we are institutionally encumbered with. The fractional-reserve banking system, the encouragement of successive layers of poorly motivated and poorly underwritten lending, and an opaque, over-intermediated credit market can and should disappear. The impotence and irrelevance of fiat monetary policy makes our technologically advanced economy currently ripe for change, if change is allowed. I think this result would probably happen naturally through market forces if the support, regulation, and insulation from competition provided by an over-seeing government and central bank was withdrawn. Technology has made the current monetary structure based upon a fiat money issuing central bank and a fractional-reserve private banking system a sad and costly anachronism. Since it is an institutionally mandated monopoly it still imposes severe efficiency costs upon an economy that, increasingly, no longer needs it. It should come to an end. A private, rational and efficient system of value and exchange should supplant it. The logical alternative is the ownership of capital, itself, used as money.

Practically all the arguments of the Solow model and this paper are discussions of long run economic results and equilibria. Of course, as we have previously remarked, money-financed government spending can still exert non-neutral effects upon the real economy in the short-run. The limited reason for these short-run effects is that when the government and central bank change the growth rate of the money supply (and hence the rate of inflation), and the changes are *unexpected* by the private sector, then short-term contracts for wages and the pricing of output will be based upon incorrect expectations. There will be winners and losers and resultant short-term disequilibrium in markets that will persist until contracts are either revised or replaced. Similarly, if no one but the government knows that θ has been increased, then for a very brief period, the government will be successful in stealing more output. However, over longer periods of time, the sustained inflation rate will rise and desired real money balances will fall. That is why capital adjustment models such as the Solow model are best viewed as a representation of the long-run adjustment of an economy's capital-intensity to an equilibrium level. Thus, in its horizon, we abstract from the very short-run effects of changes in money growth to confidently assert that the government will be ultimately unsuccessful in exploiting monetary policy as a sustained revenue-raising tool.

The careful reader will note that government or central bank monetary policy exerts real effects, even in the short run, only to the extent that it is *unanticipated* and therefore a surprise or a shock to markets and to the economy. Therefore, one is well-justified to ask, "Of what value are such destabilizing surprises or shocks if the stated goal of government/central bank monetary policy is to stabilize and support markets or the economy?" That question is one that is very difficult to answer for any government which resorts to unpredictable monetary policies. A government that abuses it exclusive power to run the monetary printing presses (by being too volatile or excessive in changing monetary growth) risks losing and should lose its fiat money privilege.

So where else does m, (real per-capita money balances) potentially affect an economy in the money and growth models, besides through the government budget constraint and the demand for money? As we have seen, in the money and growth models, money balances was assumed to appear within the production and consumption functions—equations (7-28) and (7-29) above. And, perhaps in our old economy, fiat money did have some impact on production and consumption. However, in a mature, technologically efficient monetary economy, we can reasonably argue "Why should it?" Given that monetary velocity can easily adjust as it must to facilitate exchange, it is also reasonable to argue that, in a technologically advanced monetary economy, the marginal product of real money balances over quite a wide range is approximately zero. Since money in an advanced exchange economy can essentially transfer at the speed of light, does it really matter how much of it there is? The time has arrived where further increases in the fiat money supply add nothing to our economy's real output or productivity. That is, the value to an economy of having an agreed upon 'money' is huge, but the value of additional units of it at the margin is negligible. Moreover, if the marginal product of m is zero in the production function (or the partial derivative of y with respect to m is zero) it is hard to argue that small changes in m affect real wealth within the aggregate consumption function (thus the partial derivative of c with respect to m is zero, as well). This logic restores the intuitively appealing long-run neutrality of money to an economy; or perhaps I should say that technology and market efficiency have pushed us toward the long-run neutrality of fiat money.

It is logical that the government or central bank in a mature, technically advanced, rational monetary exchange economy should not be able to exert real effects upon the equilibrium real inflation tax it can extract, the equilibrium level of output or consumption, or the equilibrium capital-intensity through its arbitrary manipulations in the sustained rate at which it prints arbitrary paper certificates backed by nothing. To assume the opposite seems contrived. Thus, the only thing the government or central bank can affect is the equilibrium rate of inflation via equation (7-24). Through fiat money policy the government or central bank may be able to do short-term harm, but they do not have the power through the printing press to do long-term harm or good. There is no tooth fairy (sorry Tompkins).

Consider the neutrality of money from the asset equilibrium discussion that began our foray into the neoclassical money and growth world. That is, any borrowing rate for a unit of money balances must necessarily equal the lending rate on a unit of real output, or capital ($(f'(k) = r = i - \pi$). Remember that the Solow model is best viewed as a long-run model of capital-intensity adjustment. We might ask, "Since a monetary policy changing the rate of growth in the money supply also changes the equilibrium rate of inflation and the nominal interest rate, i, why does it not also exert an effect on equilibrium capital intensity?" The answer is simple, there is no paradox here. At a neoclassical growth model equilibrium, the nominal interest rate consists of simply the real interest rate plus the rate of inflation. If the marginal product of money is zero in the production function in a mature, efficient monetary exchange economy as we would expect, simply changing the rate of money growth and inflation does not have any impact whatever upon the equilibrium marginal product of capital or, therefore, upon the real interest rate. Again, equation (7-15), above, prevails. Where does the nominal rate of interest, i, enter our long-term money and growth model? Well, since the real interest rate is constant and equal to the real marginal product of capital, $f'(k)$, the only thing that is variable in the nominal interest rate is the rate of inflation, or, through equation (7-24), above, θ. When θ is increased, inflation and the equilibrium nominal interest rate rise by equal amounts. When money growth is decreased, inflation and nominal interest rates fall by equal amounts. There is no effect upon the real interest rate or the real marginal product of capital in either case.

Central bankers have been lamenting for years that they are shackled, that monetary policy does not have the power that it used to in affecting the trajectory of the economy. Cynically, we at the Economics Club viewed such statements as self-serving—that central bankers were simply trying to "white wash" themselves by attempting to place the responsibility for their actions and, more importantly, their errors elsewhere. Now, I am tempted to concede that they may be right, that their protests of impotency may not just be simple evasions. As we have argued, in an economy such as ours, where the technological constraints on the speed at which monetary trades may be executed and changes in ownership booked, the velocity of money becomes endogenous, the velocity of money simply becomes whatever it needs to be. Since the exchange function of money can be successfully performed over a wide range of nominal and real stocks of money balances in our economy, advances in the technology and efficiency of exchange really do have the result of pushing central bank monetary growth policy closer to neutrality and irrelevance.

I predict that a fiat money printing central bank, overseeing a fractional-reserved banking and lending system will be viewed in the future as just an intermediate station on the way to a more rational, transparent and logical system of exchange and valuation—that is one using capital as money. The old destabilizing horror of a fiat money, fractional banking and an excessively intermediated inefficient lending system is a sad anachronism. Due to institutional and bureaucratic inertia, we are still saddled with it far beyond its useful economic life or relevance. Its endemic instability results in cycle after cycle of prosperity-destroying booms and busts inflicted upon us. It has been enough. We must allow the evolution toward capital as money. The requisites are a broad, recognizable and divisible composite index unit of capital and the technological ability to accomplish trades at a velocity only constrained by human desires and intentions. At this time we have both.

BIBLIOGRAPHY

Frederic Bastiat, *Economic Sophisms*, The Foundation for Economic Education, Inc., 1964.

Eugene Fama, "Short-term Interest Rates as Predictors of Inflation," *American Economic Review,* 1975.

Milton Friedman and Anna Schwartz, *A Monetary History of the United States,* Princeton University Press, 1963.

Milton Friedman, "A Theoretical Framework for Monetary Analysis," *Journal of Political Economy,* 1970.

Milton Friedman, *Capitalism and Freedom*, University of Chicago Press, 1962.

John Maynard Keynes, *The General Theory of Employment, Interest and Money*, London, Macmillan, 1936.

John Muth, "Rational Expectations and the Theory of Price Movements," *Econometrica*, 1961.

Lawrence S. Ritter and William L. Silber, *Principles of Money, Banking, and Financial Markets: 6th Edition,* Basic Books, 1989.

Thomas Sargent, *Rational Expectations and Inflation,* Harper and Row, 1992.

Robert Solow, "A Contribution to the Theory of Economic Growth." *The Quarterly Journal of Economics*, 1956.

George Stigler, *"The Citizen and the State: Essays on Regulation*, The University of Chicago Press, 1975.

Jerome Stein, *Money and Capacity Growth*, Columbia University Press, 1971.

Akira Takayama, *Mathematical Economics*, Dryden Press, 1974.

BIOGRAPHY OF BRIAN MCGRATH

Brian McGrath received his Ph.D. in economics in 1980 from Brown University. Areas of emphasis were monetary economics, macroeconomics and mathematical economics. He is currently a partner in D.B. Fitzpatrick & Company, a Boise investment management firm. He has previously taught undergraduate and graduate courses in economics at Boise State University and Indiana University. He has also been a consultant to private corporations, a bond portfolio manager with emphasis in mortgages and mortgage-backed securities, written numerous articles and made numerous professional presentations.

BIOGRAPHY OF L. DWAYNE BARNEY

Dwayne Barney received his Ph.D. in Economics from Texas A&M University in 1984. He is presently a professor of finance at Boise State University, where he is formerly the Chairman of the Department of Marketing and Finance. While at Boise State University he has taught courses in both the economics and finance areas. As a researcher he has published numerous articles in professional journals such as *The Journal of Risk and Insurance,* the *Journal of Applied Corporate Finance,* and the *Journal of Financial Research.*

www.ingramcontent.com/pod-product-compliance
Lightning Source LLC
Chambersburg PA
CBHW061503180526
45171CB00001B/21